GOODSPEED'S

HISTORY

OF

MONTGOMERY COUNTY,

TENNESSEE

Vertical Limits Publishing Co.
Broken Arrow, OK

Reprinted from Goodspeed's History of Tennessee
Originally Published 1886

Copyright © 2016.

All rights reserved. New material may not be reproduced, distributed or transmitted in any form or by any means, including photocopying, recording, or other electronic or mechanical methods, without the prior written permission of the publisher, except in the case of brief quotations embodied in critical reviews and certain other noncommercial uses permitted by copyright law.

Goodspeed's History of Montgomery County, Tennessee.
ISBN: 13: 978-1-942702-01-6
ISBN: 10: 1-942702-01-9

Contents

PART ONE

HISTORY OF

MONTGOMERY COUNTY

MONTGOMERY COUNTY is bounded on the north by Kentucky; on the east by Robertson and Cheatham Counties; on the south by Cheatham and Dickson Counties, and on the west by Stewart County. It comprises about 540 square miles, or 345,600 acres. It is divided into twenty civil magisterial districts. The elevation above the sea level varies from about 325 to 575 feet, and averages about 500 feet. The records of the survey of the Memphis, Clarksville & Louisville Railroad, now the Memphis Branch of the Louisville & Nashville Railroad, shows the height of the stations along the line to be as follows: Cumberland River bottom, at Clarksville, 326 feet; passenger depot at Clarksville, 454 feet; Stewart College, 496 feet; Red River bottom, one and fourtenths miles from Clarksville, 329 feet; Steele's Spring, 385 feet; Allen's Switch, 382 feet; Palmyra, 388 feet; Carbondale, 383 feet; Sailor's Rest, 385 feet; Cherry's Station, 557 feet; Hampton's, 533 feet, and State line, 563 feet. The Cumberland River affords the principal drainage. From the south its tributaries are as follows: Barton's Creek, (forming a part of the southeast boundary line), Hurricane Creek, Camp Creek, Channel's Branch, Buddie's Creek and Yellow Creek, the latter with its branches watering a considerable part of the southwestern part of the county, as Barton's Creek the southeastern. The tributaries of the Cumberland from the north are Horse Branch, Brush Creek, Muddy Branch, McAdoo Creek, Cooke's Branch, Red River, Brown's Spring Branch, Cummin's Branch, Hog Branch, Blooming Grove Creek, Sugar Creek and Howard Creek. Besides these there are smaller streams on both sides of the Cumberland. Red River is the principal tributary of the Cumberland in this county. The branches of the Red River from the south are Sulphur Fork and Parson's Creek, and from the north Cave Branch, running from Dunbar's Cave, and Big West Fork. Big West Fork has two tributaries, Spring Creek from the east and Little West Fork from the west. This is one of the counties of the Highland Rim, and is on the Subcarboniferous formation. This formation consists of two strata, the upper of which is recognized by the prevalence of a fossil coral known as the Lithostrotion Canadense. The lower stratum being destitute of lime, is much less fertile than the upper one. Both strata crop out in Montgomery County, but by far the larger portion has for its surface the upper or more fertile of the two strata mentioned. The Lithostrotion bed, sometimes known as the St. Louis limestone, affords valuable building material. Caves are numerous; one of these known as Dunbar's Cave is a favorite resort in summer. The southern portion of the county was originally for the most part covered with magnificent timber, consisting of oak principally, but there were large quantities of hickory, walnut and beech. Previous to the late civil war iron furnaces were numerous in this as well as other counties in Middle Tennessee, and by them large quantities of the timber were consumed in the manufacture of charcoal. North of Red and Cumberland Rivers is the great wheat and tobacco-growing region, producing three-fourths of all the tobacco grown in the county.

Montgomery County is also prolific in iron ore, and at one time led all the other counties in the State in the number of her furnaces and forges. In Districts Nos. 4, 8 and 9, north of the Cumberland, iron ore is quite abundant and of the best quality. In all the districts south of the Cumberland there is iron ore, and in all of them in times past have been either furnaces or forges or both. In District No. 16 are the Tennessee and LaFayette ore banks, the ore from which was used over seventy-five years ago, and continuously, until the civil war broke up all the iron works in the county. The rich bank known as Steele's, lying on Yellow Creek about one mile from Sailor's Rest Station, has been penetrated to a depth of twenty-three feet without reaching the bottom of the ore, which lies in horizontal strata eighteen inches thick, separated from each other by a layer of red clay half an inch thick, this thin layer of red clay being the entire amount of dead matter. The ore is entirely free from flint and yields about 57 per cent of pure metallic iron. Competent authority has pronounced this ore second only to the famous pipe ore used in the manufacture of the Sligo boiler-iron.

This county, together with Stewart and Robertson and the contiguous counties in Kentucky, constitute the Clarksville District, and supply the various markets of this country and Europe with the celebrated Clarksville tobacco. The best tobacco land is known by a native growth of blackjack and scrub hickory with an undergrowth of hazel and black gum. The average quantity of tobacco raised annually is about 3,500 hogsheads, or about 5,000,000 pounds, the average yield being about 850 pounds per acre. Since the war the quality of tobacco raised has deteriorated on account of the necessity of employing free labor.

The best uplands in this county are believed to be equal to any land in the State for the cultivation of wheat. The silicious soil impregnated with lime give plumpness to the berry and strength to the straw. The yield occasionally reaches forty bushels per acre, though the average is about ten bushels south of the Cumberland, and fifteen on farms in the northern part of the county. About 70,000 barrels of flour are annually manufactured for export, besides that made for home consumption. Indian corn yields from forty to fifty bushels per acre; potatoes, Irish and sweet, are raised all over the county, the former yielding about 100 bushels per acre and the latter from seventy-five to 100. Clover is a favorite crop, finds a congenial soil and is by the best farmers regularly rotated with other crops. German millet, Hungarian grass and timothy are raised in considerable quantites, the yield from timothy sometimes reaching three tons per acre.

The compact clay subsoil in certain parts of this county, render the apple and the peach tree short-lived, but south of the Red River, where the subsoil is mainly gravel, these trees grow vigorously, produce abundantly, and in some localities the peach tree never fails to produce a crop. Certain kinds of cherries produce satisfactory results, as do also dwarf and standard pears, and there are few if any portions of Tennessee better adapted to the cultivation of the grape, provided the right kind of grape be selected, which seem to be the Ives Seedling, Concord, the Diana and Rentz. There are numerous mineral springs in this county, the most important of which are the Idaho Springs, near Dunbar's Cave. The waters of these springs consist of red, white and black sulphur, alum and chalybeate.

Among the earliest hunters in this part of Tennessee was Capt. De Munbreun. He was a native of France and in the summer mouths his place of residence was at what has since been named Eaton's Station. He was here as early as 1775. Two years later than this, having made a trip to New Orleans, on his return he stopped at Deacon's Ford, near where Palmyra now stands and there he found a little company of six white men and one white woman. This party of pioneers had stopped where Rockcastle River enters the Cumberland, and descending the latter stream had occasionally hunted on its banks. They reported having seen no Indians but had seen immense herds of buffalos, and one of their number, William Bowen by name, had been run over by these animals and so severely trampled as to die from his injuries. The names of others of his party were James Ferguson and John Duncan. Soon afterward they all left the country and were cut of at Natchez in 1779.

The next party to arrive in what has since become Montgomery County, was the famous expedition of Col. John Donelson On the 22d of December, 1779, the "good boat 'Adventure' " and many others, left Fort Patrick Henry on the Holston River, "intended by God's permission for the French Salt Springs, on the Cumberland." Col. John Donelson, of the "Adventurer," was placed in command of the entire fleet, consisting of thirty or forty boats. The destination of the majority of the boats was the French Lick Springs, now Nashville. After a perilous journey of nearly four months down the Tennessee, up the Ohio and Cumberland, through a country inhabited by hostile Indians, during one of the severest winters on record, they reached the mouth of the Red River, just below the present site of Clarksville, April 12, 1780. This river was so named by Moses Renfroe and was the destination of himself and family. Here he and they took leave of their compagnons de voyage, and the "good boat 'Adventurer'" moved on up the river to join Robertson at the Bluff.

Albert V. Goodpasture, who is considered good authority by the people of Montgomery County, and to whom this sketch is largely indebted, says that those who disembarked near the mouth of Red River to settle on the banks of that stream were the following: Moses, Isaac, Joseph and James Renfroe, Nathan and Solomon Turpin, Isaac Mayfield, James Hollis, James Johns and a widow named Jones, with their respective families. These were the first to attempt a permanent settlement in Montgomery County. These families ascended Red River and made their settlement on the north side of that stream opposite the mouth of Parson's Creek. At this place they erected what has since been known as "Renfroe's Station." It was not long after the establishment of Renfroe's Station before the Indians killed a settler near Robertson's Station, and news of its occurrence soon reached the settlers at Renfroe's. They were thus brought to realize their own danger. In June or July two of their own number were killed and scalped near the station at the mouth of Parson's Creek, and with these evidences of Indian hostility they more and more felt their isolation and inadequate means of defense. All therefore made hasty preparations to abandon so unsafe a locality. Some proposed to go to Freeland's Station and others to Eaton's Station. Concealing such of their goods as they could not conveniently carry, they set out upon their journey, encamping about dusk. Here, after a short consultation, a part determined to return for more of their personal effects. By break of day next morning, having collected what they preferred not to leave behind, they were ready to resume their journey. By night of the second day they reached and encamped upon a small stream since known as Battle Creek, about two miles north of Sycamore Creek.* During the night or early next morning an attack was made upon their camp. The firing seems to have been unexpected and was certainly destructive, about twenty persons being killed, among them Joseph Renfroe and James Johns, with his wife and family. It is believed that some of those who did not return awaited the return of the party with the goods, and were thus included in the general massacre, while others proceeded on their journey to the upper settlements, reaching their destination in safety. Of those who were attacked only one escaped to tell the sad tale. This was Mrs. Jones, who, by following the trail of the first party of fugitives, was enabled to reach Eaton's in safety, after a perilous journey of about twenty miles through bushes and underbrush, through which she had hastened with all possible speed, and which, during her flight, had almost entirely denuded her of clothing. A relief party immediately started for the scene of the massacre, but found none who needed relief. This was the first massacre of any magnitude which oc-curred in the settlements near the Cumberland, and resulted in the tem-porary abandonment of Renfroe's Station.

The settlement at Renfroe's Station having been destroyed, the Indi-ans seemed determined to drive all the pioneers out of the country. The occupants of the feebler stations took refuge at the Bluff. Immediately after the Revolution the Legislature of North Carolina conferred rights of pre-emption upon settlers upon the Cumberland, and the result of these and other causes was a generous tide of immigration. In the year 1782 a company including Francis Roberts and William Prince left the Spartanburg District, S. C, and, arriving in this county, established Prince's Station, about 100 yards from the Cave Springs near the present site of Port Royal. Soon afterward the wife of William Prince died, and he returned to his native State, whence he conducted to Prince's Station a second company of immigrants, among whom were James Ford and William Mitcherson.

James Ford was one of the most remarkable men in the county in those early days. He was over six feet high, rather fleshy, and of com-manding appearance. In 1784 he was fourth captain in the Davidson County militia, and afterward became colonel in the militia of Tennes-see. In 1787 he had command in the Coldwater expedition and in the Nickajack expedition in 1794 He was the representative from Tennessee County in the Legislature of the "Territory of the United States south of the River Ohio," from 1793 to 1796; and was a member of the constitu-tional convention in the latter year. After Tennessee was admitted into the Union he was State senator from Montgomery and Robertson Counties in the first and second General Assemblies.* Moses and Evan Shelby came to this county in 1783 and settled here. Moses was a colonel and Evan a major in the militia of the county. In 1787 Moses participated in the expedition against the Indians at Coldwater. Maj. Evan was killed by the Indians near the mouth of Casey Creak, Trigg County, Ky.

In January, 1784, John Montgomery and Martin Armstrong entered the land upon which Clarksville is now located. This land they had surveyed in the fall, and upon it Martin Armstrong laid out a town. A fort was erected at the spring, a number of lots were sold, and in accordance with the desire of the purchasers, the General Assembly of North Carolina, in November, 1785, enacted "that 200 acres of land, lying in the fork of Cumberland River and Red River, on the east side thereof, belonging to John Montgomery and Martin Armstrong, who have signified their consent for this purpose, be established a town and a town common, agreeable to a plan laid off by said Martin Armstrong, Esq., by the name of Clarksville." About the same time Clarksville was established Nevill's Station was erected on Red River between the former place and Prince's Station. This was by George and Joseph B. Nevill, natives of South Carolina, who came to this county and built their fort about this time. The Legislature of North Carolina was very liberal toward soldiers who had served in the "Continental line."

The first entry upon the records of the public register of Montgomery County, is as follows:

April 27, 1789.

John Stewart, North Carolina, Tennessee County:

Know ye, that we, pursuant to act of General Assembly, entitled "Ah act for the relief of officers and soldiers of the Continental Line, and for other purposes," and in consideration of the signal bravery and persevering zeal of Isaac Titsworth, one of the guard of the commissioners for laying off the land allotted the officers and soldiers of the said line, have given and granted, and by these presents do give and grant unto John Stewart, assignee of said Isaac Titsworth, the tract of land containing 320 acres, lying and being in our county of Tennessee, on Red River, beginning at a stake in Robert Heaton's line, running north; thence 320 poles to a post oak; east across the said river at seventy-two poles, in all 160 poles to a stake; south 320 poles to said Heaton's line; west 160 poles crossing said river to the beginning; as to the plan annexed doth appear, together with all woods, waters, mines, minerals, hereditaments and appurtenances to the said land belonging or appertaining, to hold to the said John Stewart, his heirs and assigns forever," etc., which land was surveyed for the said "John Stewart, May 28, 1785, by James Sanders, deputy surveyor, by consequence of a military warrant No. 509, located July 5, 1784. This grant was signed Thomas Johnson, with the seal of the State affixed and dated the 10th of July, in the thirteenth year of our independence, in the year of our Lord 1788, and countersigned.

'Test, BENJAMIN HARDIN,
Public Register.

JAMES GLASGOW,
Secretary.

The next entry is the record of a deed dated May 6, 1789, between John Ford, of the county of Davidson, N. C, and John Baker, Esq., of the county of Gates, of the same State—John Ford selling to John Baker, for the consideration of £500, four tracts of land lying and being in the county of Tennessee, in said State, containing by survey. 2,560 acres of land.

One tract containing 640 acres, surveyed under a warrant numbered 927. One tract containing other 640 acres, surveyed by virtue of a military warrant numbered 953. One other tract containing 640 acres, surveyed by virtue of a military warrant numbered 2445 One other tract containing 640 acres, surveyed by virtue of a military warrant numbered 921. All of which tracts of land join each other and lie on Persons' Creek and Brush Creek adjoining the land of Persons and McKee.

[Signed] JOHN FORD.

Acknowledged before the Hon. John McNairy, I. S. C. L. E. Registered May 9, 1789

Witnesses: S. COX TATUM,
A. HART.

'Test, BENJAMIN HARDIN,
Public Register

The next is the record of a very large grant of land, and must indicate extraordinary "bravery and persevering zeal" on the part of the grantee, John Davis, Esq. The grant was for "3,840 acres, on the south side of the Cumberland River, at the mouth of Beaver Creek." This grant was surveyed February 10, 1786, in consequence of a military warrant numbered 295, and was located October 17, 1784. It was signed by Richard Caswell, and countersigned by James Glasgow. Rebecca Parkerson was granted 2,560 acres of land on account of the bravery and perserving zeal of James Parkerson, a lieutenant in the Continental line. This grant was made to her as the heiress of James Parkerson, and was located in the county of Tennessee, on the head of the First Big Creek below Harpeth, on the south side of the Cumberland. Charles Thompson's preemption of 200 acres was sold to Isaac Titsworth. It began at the south side of Sulphur Fork of Red River, about sixteen rods above the mouth of Conrad's Spring Branch, etc., the tract having been granted to Charles Thompson by the State of North Carolina April 17, 1786. One of the most interesting entries perhaps on the records, is that of a grant to William Washington, heir to Etheldred Washington, who had been a fifer in the Continental line, of "1,000 acres in our county of Davidson, now Tennessee, at Parson's Creek, a branch of Red River that empties in on the south side opposite Renfroe's old station." This grant was surveyed for William Washington, February 11, 1785, by Robert Nelson, deputy surveyor, by virtue of a military warrant numbered 560, located February 10, 1785, signed by Richard Caswell, and countersigned by James Glasgow. William Linton, a captain in the Continental line received a grant of 1,417 acres of land, which was surveyed for him by Robert Nelson February 10, 1785, located July 26, 1784, and signed March 14, 1786. He sold this grant to Thomas Persons December 26, 1786, for $100.

A partial list of early settlers is here inserted. James Wilson came from North Carolina and settled above Port Royal, near Mallory's Meeting-house; Willie Blount settled on Parson's Creek, about five miles from its mouth. He was afterward governor of Tennessee. David Slaughter came from North Carolina and settled in the same neighborhood, as also did Austin Hamlett, James Basford, James Blackwell, John Calvin, James Norfleet and James Hamlett. The latter came to this county in 1805, and is still living, in his ninety-first year. He was a soldier in the war of 1812, a member of Capt R. Benson's company, Tennessee militia, Col. Arthur Cheatham. Joseph Woolfork was also an early settler. All of the above, except James Hamlett, came before 1805. Samuel Wilcox was here many years before that time, as were Jonathan Stephenson and William Connell.

Trouble with the Indians, which really commenced with the massacre of Battle Creek in 1780, did not cease entirely until 1796, but from 1782 to 1786 comparatively few depredations were committed. In the latter year the Cherokees, who had been parties to the treaty of

Hopewell in 1785, killed Peter Barnet on the waters of Blooming Grove. They also killed David Steele and desperately wounded William Crutcher. Mr. Crutcher, however, recovered from his wounds and lived to a good old age. On the 3d of July, 1791, Thomas Fletcher and two other men by the name of Harry, were killed on the north side of the Cumberland near the mouth of Red River, and their heads entirely skinned, and on the 5th of November following a Mr. Granthram was killed near the same place. About this time, on account of the warlike demonstrations of the Cherokees, Gen. James Robertson called for volunteers, rangers and spies. Col. Valentine Sevier had then lately arrived with his family and settled on the hill between Clarksville and New Providence. His three grown sons asked and, notwithstanding the weakness of his own station, received his permission to join Gen. Robertson at the French Lick. On the 7th of January, 1792, they started up the river, together with John Curtis, John Rice and a few others. They had not proceeded far when they were discovered by a Cherokee chief, named Double Head, and his party. As they passed along near Seven-mile Ferry they were fired upon by Double Head and his band, who had rapidly crossed the country for the purpose of intercepting them. By the first volley the three Seviers, Curtis and Rice were killed. Those in the boats not killed rowed to the opposite side of the river and commenced its descent, and the Indians, seeing that all were not killed, reloaded their guns and crossed the isthmus, intending to intercept the boats on their return. The boats, however, were hastily abandoned, and the Indians boarded them, scalped the slain, and carried away provisions and goods. When a day or two afterward Col. Sevier learned the fate of his sons he strengthened his defenses, receiving the assistance of the settlers at Clarksville, and assisting them in return. On the 14th of the same month the same party of Indians killed a Mr. Boyd near Clarksville. In view of the murders which were thus frequent and which caused a general feeling of unsafety to prevail, a meeting of the committee for the county of Tennessee was held February 1 following. Capt. William Prince was chairman of the committee which adopted and forwarded to Gen. Robertson a petition, setting forth the dangers by which the settlers of that part of Tennessee County were continually beset, the distressed condition to which they were reduced, and the fatal consequences that must necessarily ensue unless some speedy means were adopted to secure them from further attacks of the savages. This address appears to have been productive of very little good. On March 25 an individual, whose name is now unknown, was killed near the mouth of Red River, and on the 15th of July, Isaac Pennington and a Mr. Milligan were killed and a Mr. McFarland wounded. Later in the same month two other murders were committed on the Cumberland near Clarksville. Not receiving from Gen. Robertson, as he was unable to grant it, nor from the governor, of Tennessee any substantial aid, the settlers were thrown entirely upon their own resources for protection. But depredations and murders could not be prevented. On the 16th of January, 1793, Col. Hugh Tinen, while clearing and fencing around his cabin which he had erected on Red River a few miles from Clarksville, was fired upon and wounded by a party of Indians, who immediately seized his horses and fled. Two days afterward Maj. Evan Shelby, James Harris and a colored man belonging to Moses Shelby, were killed in a salt-boat on the Cumberland, and a negro woman belonging to Maj. Shelby was taken prisoner. On the 19th of April two men were killed near Clarksville. On the 20th of August a party of Indians were discovered plundering an abandoned house; they were pursued by a party of seven men, overtaken about midnight, fired upon and one killed and two wounded. Next day the Indians retaliated by killing Mrs. Baker and all of her children but two, who effected their escape. About this time, also, Mrs. Robert Wells and her two children were killed, Mr. Wells being away from home. Probably the last persons killed by the Indians in 1793 were John Dier and Benjamin Lindsey. John Dier was quite a remarkable man, and was by profession a hunter. He would not clear or till the soil, and made his contracts payable in the products of his unerring marksmanship. The following appears on the records of the county court:

Estate of John Dier
To John Edmonson, Dr.

To your note of Hand for 85 Hundred weight of Buffalo Beef, dated October 4th, 1793, and payable the 1st of November Ensuing at Two Dollars per Hundred. 70 dollars.

He spoke fluently both the Creek and Chickasaw languages, and it is thought also the Choctaw. For this reason Gen. James Robertson offered him 100 bushels of corn per year to live with him in Nashville, and as much cleared land besides as he chose to cultivate; but the proposition was declined. Mr. Dier insisted on a money consideration. Gen. Robertson then tried to induce the Government to employ Dier, saying in a letter to Gov. Blount: Would it be reasonable that the United States paid such a person, as the Creeks will be much here as well as the Chickasaws and Choctaws, whenever they may be at peace? Sir, will you be so condescending as to write me on this subject? I would pay half myself sooner than be without him." His murder in the latter part of the year 1793 effectually prevented any such arrangement. On March 18, 1794, an attempt was made by the Indians to burn the house of Thomas Harris, who lived a short distance from Clarksville. They set lire to the wooden chimney, but Mr. Harris, after the fire was started, thrust something through the chimney to push away the burning brush outside, and seeing an Indian by the light of the fire instantly shot him down. Other Indians rushed up to drag him away and were also fired upon. They soon left the place.

The month of November, 1794, was a disastrous one to the settlers in Montgomery County. Isaac Titsworth remained in the settlement with his family from 1784 to 1794, and rose to the rank of colonel in the militia of the county. In the latter part of the latter year he determined to move to Kentucky. November 5 the family commenced their journey, and at nightfall had penetrated four miles beyond the outmost settlement. While thus encamped they were suddenly surprised, attacked and most horribly massacred. Seven persons were killed and scalped, and a white man, three children, a negro man and a daughter of Col. Titsworth taken prisoners. The next day the Indians were pursued by the militia, but although closely followed they succeeded in getting away with everything except the property and the three children, whom they tomahawked and scalped. One of the children died next day. In August, 1795, Col. Titsworth visited the Creek nation and recovered his daughter, who had been held a prisoner nearly ten months. Six days after this massacre a furious attack was made on Sevier's Station by a party of Creek Indians who lived in a town called Tuskege. The havoc was dreadful. Anthony Crutcher and John Easton wrote letters descriptive of the scene, but the most comprehensive account is probably that of Col. Valentine Sevier himself, written to his brother, Gov. John Sevier. It was as follows:

CLARKSVILLE, December 18, 1794.

Dear Brother:

The news from this place is desperate with me. On Tuesday, 11th of November last, about 12 o'clock, my station was attacked by about forty Indians. On so sudden a surprise they were in almost every house before they were discovered. All the men belonging to the station were out except Mr. Snyder and myself. Mr. Snyder, Betsy, his wife, his son John and my son Joseph were killed in Snyder's house. I saved Snyder, so the Indians did not get his scalp but shot and tomahawked him in a barbarous manner. They also killed Ann King and her son James, and scalped my daughter Rebecca. I hope she will still recover. The Indians have killed whole families about here this fall. You may hear the cries of some persons for their friends daily.

The engagement commenced by the Indians at my house, and continued about an hour, as the neighbors say. Such a scene no man ever witnessed before. Nothing but screams and roaring of guns, and no man to assist me for some time. The Indians have robbed all the goods out of every house, and have destroyed all my stock. You will write our ancient father this horrid news; also my son Johnny. My health is much impaired. The remainder of my family are in good health. I am so distressed in my mind that I can hardly write. Your affectionate brother till death,

VALENTINE SEVIER.

Valentine Sevier died about July, 1800. Col. John Montgomery was killed by the Indians November 27, 1794, and although not in the county named in his honor, yet his life for about fourteen years prior to his death was closely identified with the history of the county. He was born in Virginia, and as early as 1771 explored the Cumberland country, and was with Col. Donelson's expedition in 1780. He was one of the signers of the original compact of government entered into by the settlers on the Cumberland, and in 1783, upon the reorganization of their court, was elected sheriff of the district. While he was probably prospecting or locating lands beyond the stations, reports reached the governor of North Carolina causing him to issue his proclamation to the effect that Montgomery was an " aider and a better in treasonable and piratical proceedings carried on in the Mississippi against the Spaniards." On the 6th of January, 1784, he appeared before the court and gave bonds in the sum of £150 for his appearance at the next term, with Elijah Robertson and Stephen Ray as his securities. Gov. Martin, becoming satisfied that his first proclamation was issued upon misinformation, issued a second proclamation countermanding the first, and the county court, with reference to his bond, says that "inasmuch as the said proclamation was afterward countermanded, the court considered that the said recognizance had become void." In 1785 he became commissioner of the town of Clarksville. In 1789, upon the organization of Tennessee County, he became one of the justices of the peace, holding the office until his death. In 1794, having become a colonel of the militia of the county, he was in immediate command of troops in the famous Nickajack campaign. Upon his return from this campaign he went on a hunting excursion to Eddyville, Ky., and on the 27th of November, 1794, the party was attacked in camp by the Indians. Col. Montgomery might possibly have escaped, but while defending his wounded friend, Col. Hugh Timon, he was himself shot in the knee, and then rushed upon by the savages and stabbed to death with knives. John Rains went next day with a party, including Montgomery's son, and buried his remains where a tree had been torn up by the roots. The last victims of savage cruelty near Clarksville, and probably in the county, were Thomas Reasons and wife and Miss Betsy Roberts, in 1796.

Patton's still-house was situated on a small tributary of Red River, in District No. 6. It was owned by Joseph Patton, and was a place of public resort. Putnam's History of Middle Tennessee says in reference to it, that the frequent orders by the county court for "viewing, laying off and clearing out" roads "to it," "from it" and "by it," led one to infer that it was a "favorite watering place in its day." "Jacob Winemiller was appointed on the first jury to view and lay off a road from Clarksville, by Brantley's Ferry, to the still-house, and he had associated with him eleven worthy men, such as John Montgomery, Hugh F. Bell and Philip Hornberger. All the jurors were directed to select and take the nearest and best road to Patton's still-house.'" Men met there for the purpose of carousal and debauch; they spent their nights there as well as their days;

in consequence of which the women, in their righteous indignation, threatened Patton with lynching if he did not cease to entice their husbands from home and to their ruin. In 1801 Joseph Patton sold to John Edmonston, "two stills, one of 207 gallons and the other of eighty gallons, with iron shutters, and twenty hogsheads and cags for stilling, for the sum of $250."

A curious clause was inserted in the bonds of "ordinary" or tavernkeepers in those days. Samuel Stout obtained a license to keep an ordinary at his dwelling house in Clarksville in 1790, and gave bonds in the sum of £500; containing one among other conditions, that he "shall not suffer or permit any unlawful gaming in his house, nor on the Sabbath day suffer any person to tipple or drink more than is necessary." It will be observed that this restriction was limited to the Sabbath day.

Since that time the temperance sentiment has so increased that at the present there are but few places for public drinking in the county, and those few restricted to the incorporated towns of Clarksville and New Providence. In 1831 the State Legislature passed an act providing for the emancipation of slaves under certain conditions. Willie B. Johnson of Montgomery County, on the 21st of July, 1834, made a plea to the county court that his petition for the emancipation of his negro boy Sidney, had been granted, and the court being satisfied that Sidney was of good moral character, and, inasmuch as he had given bonds and security that he was not to become a county charge, ordered that he be emancipated and made free. On the same day P. H. and A. Caraway petitioned that their negro boy, Stewart, be emancipated for the reason of his meritorious conduct, and the further consideration that the boy Stewart had paid $600 for his freedom. An interesting case of emancipation occurred in 1842. It was that of the setting free of two negro women by Samuel W. Anderson. Their names were Martha and Indiana, and in giving them their freedom Mr. Anderson took into consideration their faithful services to him from infancy, and their good character, as well as higher motives of humanity. His petition was granted by the court and he gave bonds in the sum of $1,000, the obligation being void in case of the immediate removal of the two negro women from the State. At the December term of the court, 1844, Mr. Anderson emancipated another of his slaves, named Jane, giving bonds in the sum of $500, without the condition that Jane leave the State. An illustration of a different kind is here introduced: A negro woman named Maria died on the premises of N. B. Green, in May 1846. N. F. Trice, who was then coroner, submitted to the county court a report of the inquest held over the dead body, which was to the effect "that one N. B. Green, on the 25th of May, 1846, in the county of Montgomery, with force of arms, did then and there feloniously and in the heat of blood, lash, whip and so abuse said slave Maria as to cause her death, against the peace and dignity of the State." A few weeks after this event, Samuel W. Anderson having died, the remainder of his slaves were emancipated, and permitted to remain in the State upon giving bonds according to the provisions of an act of the Legislature passed in February, 1842.

The last decree in this county for the sale of slaves was made January 8, 1861, in the case of W. E. Thompson et al vs. Daniel W. Neblett et al. It was in words as follows:

It appearing to the court that there are only eight heirs and only four slaves, that it is impossible to divide the slaves, and that a sale is necessary for a division; it is there fore ordered, adjudged and decreed by the court that the clerk of this court advertise the same according to law and sell the slaves in the pleadings mentioned at the late residence of Mrs. Jane Barney, in Montgomery County, Tenn.

The last free bond given in this county was by Lucy Ann Booth, formerly Palmer, in the sum of $500 with John H. McFall and John F. Shelton as sureties, and having given bonds Lucy was permitted to remain in the county. The last division of slaves was in the case of W. C. Batson et al vs. John C. Batson et al, January 19, 1862. The slaves divided had been the property of Thomas H. Batson, who died intestate. They were divided among the heirs and distributors by commissioners appointed by the court as follows: Thomas Ramey, W. I. Holmes, L. D. Watkins, John P. Dailey and L. C. McCurdy, freeholders and slave-holders, any three being authorized to act.

In November, 1788, the Legislature of North Carolina passed an act organizing Tennessee County. The language of the act was as follows: Beginning on the Virginia line; thence south along Sumner County to the dividing ridge between Cumberland and Red River; thence westwardly along said ridge to the head of the main south branch of the Sycamore; thence down the said branch to the mouth thereof; thence due south across the Cumberland River to the Davidson County line; all that part of Davidson County west of this line was erected into a new County called Tennessee."

In pursuance of this act, the court of pleas and quarter sessions of the new county composed of Francis Prince, chairman; Brazel Boren, John Philips, Jacob Pennington, John Montgomery, Benjamin Hardin, George Bell and George Nevill, Esqrs., met at the house of Isaac Titsworth, about two and a half miles south of Port Royal, April 20, 1789, and completed the organization of the county. This was done by electing the following officers: Barkley W. Pollock, clerk; Joseph B. Nevill, sheriff; Benjamin Hardin, register; John Philips, ranger, and Joseph Martin, coroner. No tax collector was elected, but in June, 1790, Joseph B. Nevill was appointed collector of the taxes for 1789. With reference to the court it should be stated that the inferior court of pleas and quarter sessions had jurisdiction in all cases involving the property, liberty or life of the citizen, and was the only court held in Tennessee County. The Superior Court of Law and Equity of Davidson County was established in 1785, but it was considered doubtful whether its jurisdiction extended to the counties of Sumner and Tennessee until these three counties were erected into the district of Mero in 1788.

At the first session of the General Assembly of the State of Tennessee, an act for the division of the county of Tennessee into two distinct counties was passed April 9, 1796. A part of Sumner County was included.

On the 23d of October 1799, a portion of Montgomery County was annexed to Robertson County, by the following enactment:

Be it enacted, etc., That the bounds of Robertson County shall be as follows, viz.; Beginning at the upper end of the first bluff above James McFarland's "(McFarlins in former act)" on the Red River near Allen's (Allin's) cabins; running thence a direct course to the Sulphur Fork, one-fourth of a mile below Elias Fort's; thence a direct course, so as to leave the plantation whereon Col. James Ford lives, in Montgomery County, and that on which Maj. John Baker lives, in Robertson County, and to strike the road leading from Davidson's ferry to Robertson Court House, one-fourth of a mile east of Capt. James Hollis': thence a direct course to the mouth of Big Brush Creek, which empties into the Cumberland near Col. John Hogan's; thence continued the same course to the Indian boundary line; thence eastwardly with said Indian boundary line to Davidson County line; thence north with Davidson County line to the mouth of Sycamore, with Davidson County line to Sumner County line, thence with the extreme height of the ridge eastwardly to the Kentucky road, leading from Nashville; thence northwardly with said road to the Kentucky State line; thence west with said line to such place as a southeast line, leaving Joseph French in the lower county, will strike the beginning.

On the 29th of October, 1801, the boundaries were again changed, according to which the boundaries of Montgomery County were fixed as follows:

Beginning one hundred and fifty yards east of Joseph Woolfork's house on the Sulphur Fork; thence south to the latitude of Capt. James Hollis'; thence east to a point twelve and a half miles east of the meridian of the court house in Clarksville; thence south to a point twenty-five miles south of the Kentucky line; thence west to the Indian boundary line; thence with said boundary line to the Kentucky line; thence with said line to a point from which a due south course will strike the beginning.

Henry Johnson and Benjamin Weakley, or either of them, were appointed commissioners to run and mark the lines between Montgomery and Davidson Counties. An act was passed July 31, 1804, to alter the lines between Montgomery and Stewart Counties, so as to change the settlement at Guise's Creek into Stewart County. It was as follows:

Be it enacted, etc., That the line which divides the counties of Montgomery and Stewart shall be as follows: Beginning on the Kentucky line sixteen miles west of the meridian of Clarksville; thence south 15° east to intersect the line of Dickson County about three miles east of the line run heretofore for Stewart County; thence with the ridge which divides the waters of Yellow Creek from the waters of Guise's and Well's Creek to the Indian boundary line, and with said line westwardly to the line run for Stewart County.

On November 8, 1809, the following act was passed:

Beginning at a point twelve and a half miles due east of the meridian of Clarksville, which point is a corner of an offset on the present line near to Capt. James Blackwell's on Parson's Creek; thence a direct course to a point on the south bank of the Sulphur Fork of Red River, about midway between the dwelling houses of Maj. James Norfleet and Cordall Norfleet; thence down Sulphur Fork with its meanders to a point where the present line of the county now crosses the same; and thence with said line to the Kentucky line.

In 1860 a change was made so as to include Joseph Weems in Dickson County. On October 4, 1858, the boundary line between Montgomery and Cheatham Counties was ordered to be run anew or resurveyed in response to a request from Cheatham County, her agent, Samuel Watson, proposing to pay all necessary expenses. It was also ordered by the Montgomery County Court that there be a stay of proceedings in the case of Montgomery County vs. Cheatham in the chancery court at Clarksville until a report of the new survey should be made. This case was compromised and dismissed at the defendant's cost, and the county line remained unchanged. On the 6th of July, 1868, the county court resolved that the Hon. T. W. King be appointed a commissioner to file a bill for the recovery of the territory given to Cheatham County. Finally a commissioner was appointed by each county to settle the boundary line question, which committee made its report April 5, 1869, in which they said they had fixed upon a line running from the mouth of Barton's Creek north forty-six degrees east seven and a half miles to the corner designated in an act of the Legislature of March 20, 1869, as I. W. Moody's corner. In 1883 a change was made in this line so as to include Wiley B. Stewart in Cheatham County.

On July 17, 1810, the following persons were elected to office by the county court: Sheriff, John Cocke, who gave his bond to Willie Blount, Esq., Governor in and over the State of Tennessee, in the penal sum of $12,500. He also gave bonds in the penal sum of $5,000 that he would well and truly pay and account for all moneys, fines and forfeitures to be by him collected to the treasurer of Mero District. Henry Small was then appointed coroner for the county, bond $1,000; and James Huling, county trustee, bond $2,000. On the 28th of January, 1835, the following persons were appointed judges of election, to be held on the first Thursday and Friday in March, on the adoption of the new constitution: At Clarksville, Benjamin E. Orgain, Samuel McFall and Thomas W. Frazer; at Port Royal, Zachariah Grant, James Reasons and F. Northington; at Fredonia, James Williams, John C. Weakley and Pleasant Bagwell; at Cabin Row, Samuel Smith, John S. Mosely and Thomas H. Batson; at Yellow Creek, Henry McFall, James Nolen and Berry Rye; at Palmyra, John Neblett, William Moore and I. P. Bellamy; at Vincent Cooper's, Bird Hardy, Andrew Walker and Joel Bayless, and at Clidon Cooper's, L. C. Taylor, Armstead Rogers and Thomas Hester. Samuel McFall was elected clerk of the county court in 1836, and gave bonds in the sum of $5,000. In the same year one constable was elected for each of the fifteen districts into which the county had recently been divided. John Thomas was elected county surveyor; Nace F. Trice, coroner; James Hinton, ranger; Henry L. Bailey, register, and Gabriel A. Davie, county trustee. Fifteen revenue commissioners were then appointed, one for each civil district.

In March, 1840, Samuel McFall was elected clerk of the county court, bonds $12,000; George J. McCauley, sheriff, bonds $45,000; G. A. Davie, county trustee; Henry L. Bailey, register; William M Shelton, surveyor. On Tuesday, 3d, 1841, the enumeration of the free white persons who were citizens of the county on January 1, 1841, was submitted to the court by William M. Shelton, commissioner. The report was as follows: District No. 1, 164; No. 2, 98; No. 3, 101; No. 4, 134; No. 5, 141; No. 6, 304; No. 7, 126; No. 8, 113; No. 9, 110; No. 10, 128; No. 11, 111; No. 12, 128; No. 13, 126; No. 14, 92; No. 15, 156. Total number of voters, 2,033. On the 28th of January, 1854, the commissioners appointed for the purpose submitted their report of a redisricting of the county. Up to this time the number of districts had been fifteen. Now the number was increased to twenty, and each district was entitled to two magistrates, except the Twelfth and Thirteenth, each of which had three. In 1856 the following officers elect gave bonds as follows: Sheriff, Thomas Ramey, bonds $25,000; register, John D. Bradley, bonds $12,500; county trustee, Robert McMordie, bonds $5,000; collector of the State and county revenues for Montgomery County, Henry Lyle, bonds $20,000; clerk of the county court, William Rogers, bonds $46,000. The last county officers elected before the war were as follows: Sheriff, S. E. Ramey; circuit court clerk, Charles Bailey; county court clerk, William Rogers; county trustee, George Smith; register. J. D. Bradley; coroner, John A. Bailey; revenue collector, Henry Lyle; census taker, John" B. Martin.

But little information respecting elections in early times is obtainable. Records do not seem to contain them, and newspaper files previous to 1836 have not been preserved. At the presidential election of 1836 Montgomery County cast 745 votes for the Hon. Hugh L. White, for President, against 466 for Martin Van Buren.

In May, 1839, Col. W. B. Johnson and Henry Frey were candidates for the State Senate from this county, the latter favoring and the former opposing the "tippling act." Col. Johnson received 947 votes, Mr. Frey 801. At the same time Marcenas Jordan received 844 votes for representative, and W. K. Turner 864. For governor, James K. Polk received 824 votes, and Newton Cannon 963. For Congress, Gen. Cheatham received 914 votes, and the Hon. Cave Johnson 861. One of the, greatest events in the history of the Whig party of this county occurred October 7, 1839. It was called a "grand rally" of the Whigs. Eloquent speeches were made by Peter C. Buck, Gen. Patrick Henry, Gustavus A. Henry and James B. Reynolds. The speech of G. A. Henry was especially admired by his friends for its lofty eloquence and for its earnest denunciation of the administration then in power. In 1840 Bigger, the "Harrison candidate" for governor, received 165 majority over Howard, the "Van Buren candidate," and the Whig vote for President was 1,101. while the "Locofoco" vote was 794. In 1841 James C. Jones received 925 votes for governor, and James K. Polk 731; for State senator, Henry Frey 1,133, and Mr. Norfleet 50; for representative, Peter C. Buck (Whig) 867, Dortch (Democrat) 816. The campaign in 1844 was a very enthusiastic and exciting one with both Democrats and Whigs, and resulted in Mr. Clay receiving 1,271 votes, and Mr. Polk 1,029. In 1845 the vote for Montgomery County was as follows: For governor, Aaron V. Brown 901, Foster 1,104; for Congress, Lucien B. Chase 898, Mr. Mathewson 1,109; for the State Senate, David Northington 876, Tyler 1,119; for representative, William Rogers 885, Munford 1,109, the Whig candidates having the majority in each case. In 1847 the vote of the county was as follows: Governor, A. V. Brown 988, Neill S. Brown 1,182; Congress, Lucien B. Chase 976, Swayne 1,181; State Senate, William Rogers 973, Tyler 1,191; Legislature, James T. Wynne 997, E. P. McGinty 1,128; Whigs in the majority. In the presidential election of 1848 Gen. Taylor received 1,288 votes, and Lewis Cass 969. The election in 1849 resulted as follows: Governor, Trousdale 953, Brown 1,069; Congress, I. G. Harris 945; Morris 1,043; State Senate, W. L. Norfleet 931, Kimble 1,045; representative, Lemuel Cherry 909, G. A. Harrel 1,065. In 1851 the State election resulted as follows: Governor, Trousdale 921, Campbell 1,132; Congress, Harris 906, Hornberger 1,096; Senate, Northington 814, Stark 1,177; Assembly, Henry 1,326, Collins 516. The same result is shown in the election of 1852, when Mr. Pierce received 992 votes for the presidency, and Gen. Scott 1,283, as was also the case in the presidential election of 1856, when Mr. Buchanan received 944 votes, and Mr. Fillmore 1,368. In 1857 the vote was as follows: Governor, Harris 993, Hatton 1,229; Congress, Quarles 1,038; Zollicoffer 1,145; State Senate, Thomas Menees 985, Stark 1,205; floater, Haywood 983, Maney 1,208; representative, R. H. Moody 888, Davie 1,289. The vote in 1859 was as follows: Governor, Isham G. Harris 1,043, Netherland 1,353; Congress, Dr.

Thomas Menees 1,015, Quarles 1,370; Senate, Yancey 1,043, Horn 1,340; floater, A. G. Merritt 1,022, Cheatham 1,347; representative, Samuel D. Power 979, Dudley 1,368. In the last presidential election before the war the vote was as follows: John Bell 1,426, John C. Breckinridge 1,042 and Stephen A. Douglas 95. Thus at this election, so fraught with momentous consequences, did Montgomery County still refuse to sustain the Democratic party. The Clarksville Jeffersonian, a strong supporter of Mr. Breckinridge, immediately after the announcement of the success of Mr. Lincoln, contained the following paragraph:

The vast majority of the American people, and indeed of the Southern people, are not prepared to disrupt this great confederation, and bring upon us the mighty train of disasters which would inevitably follow in the train of that event, for anything short of actual violation and disregard of their constitutional rights. The election of Mr. Lincoln is an act which the majority of the American people had the right to do, and they have done it under all the forms and sanctions of our laws and constitution. That of itself is certainly no invasion of the rights of the States. That his election will result in such invasion is not improbable, but until it is attempted there can be no substantial justification for resorting to secession.

On the 14th of January, 1861, a meeting of the people of the county was held, at which resolutions were adopted expressive of their views as to the proper course of Tennessee with regard to secession, which were substantially those adopted by the State convention of Kentucky, embracing the Crittenden compromise, with an amendment to the effect that if the Northern people refused to concede such guaranties as were required for the security of the South, Tennessee would then feel justified in withdrawing from the Union, or adopting such other measures for her own security as she might deem proper. On Saturday, February 9, 1861, Montgomery County voted on the question as to whether a convention should be held to determine as to the secession of Tennessee from the Union. The vote for the convention was 1,611; against it 389. Cave Johnson received on the same day 1,832 votes for senator, against 58 for G. A. Henry. John F. House received 1,854 votes for floater against 84 for W. S. Flippin.

These large majorities indicated the strength of the Union sentiment in the county, but when the news came of the conflict at Fort Sumter, the entire body of the people immediately became in favor of secession. A public meeting at the court house was addressed by N. H. Allen, J. F. House, H. S. Kimble, James E. Bailey and G. A. Henry, all in favor of secession unless all attempts at coercion were abandoned. As there was neither expectation nor hope that attempts at coercion would be abandoned, active preparations for war were at once made. On the 17th of April an independent company of Home Guards was organized with the following officers: Rev. J. B. Duncan, captain; John A. Bailey, first lieutenant; J. J. Crusman, second lieutenant; B. H. Pickering, third lieutenant; J. E. Wilcox, fourth lieutenant; Thomas H. Hyman, orderly sergeant; T. H. Jackson, second sergeant; Samuel Simpson, third sergeant; W. J. Ely, fourth sergeant, and H. M. Acree, fifth sergeant. Companies formed rapidly all over the county. Prof. William A. Forbes raised a company which went into camp on the fair grounds, which was named Camp Forbes. The entire female population of Clarksville was at once engaged in manufacturing clothing for the volunteers. Stephen Brandon raised a company of Irish volunteers, to whom Mrs. McCullough presented an elegant flag. Capt. M. G. Johnson brought in a company from Palmyra. On Wednesday, May 22, 1861, Company A was mustered into service with the following officers: William A Forbes, captain; W. W. Thompson, first lieutenant; B. W. Cartwright, second lieutenant; J. A. Waggoner, third lientenant; B. A. Sargent, orderly sergeant. Before the 1st of June four other companies had been mustered into service—those of Capts. Gholson, Brunson, Brandon and Beaumont. When the vote came to be taken on the 8th of June, on the question of separation from the Union, there were cast for it in the county 2,631, and for no separation, 33. In District No. 12, including Clarksville, 561 votes were for separation and only 1 opposed it, and the work of organizing military companies went forward with vigor. Capt. Forbes had been commissioned colonel, and his regiment of volunteers, the Fourteenth Tennessee, was organized and in Camp Quarles on June 20. The following were the officers of the regiment: Colonel, W. A. Forbes; lieutenant-colonel, M. G. Gholson; major, Nathan Brandon; acting adjutant, W. W. Thompson; acting sergeant. Maj. Richard Lyles; surgeon, J. F. Johnson; assistant surgeon, J. D. Martin; quartermaster-general, John Gorham, assistant quartermaster-general, A. J. Allensworth; commissary-general, G. D. Martin; asssistant commissary, John Goostree. Company officers: Company A—captain, G. A. Harrel; first lieutenant, W. W. Thompson; second lieutenant, R. W. Cartwright; third lieutenant, J. A. Waggoner. Company B—captain, W. G. Russell; first lieutenant, D. B. Martin; second lieutenant, T. W. Lewis; third lieutenant, W. J. Jennings. Company C—captain, Clay Roberts; first lieutenant, N. M. Morris; second lieutenant, R. B. Lisenby; third lieutenant, W.. E. Parker. Company D—captain, I. Brunson; first lieutenant, J. H. Johnson; second lieutenant, D. E. Outlaw; third lieutenant, J. P. Howard. Company E—captain, E. Hewett; first lieutenant, J. W. Mallory; second lieutenant, W. McCombs; third lieutenant, R. J. Brown. Company F—captain, W. E. Lowe. Company G—captain, H. C. Buckner; first lieutenant, J. W. Hazier; second lieutenant, E. D. Lester; third lieutenant, H. L. Hargis. Company H—captain, W. Lowe; second lieutenant, A. C. Dale; third lieutenant, J. B. Malloy. Company I—captain, W. P. Simmons; first lieutenant, J. S. Henry; second lieutenant, W. S. Winfield; third lieutenant, D. W. C. Randolph. Company I—captain, J. W. Lockert. Company K—"Clarksville Ninety-first," captain, F. S. Beaumont; first lieutenant, F. P. McWhirter; second lieutenant, J. J. Crusman; third lieutenant, W. S.

Moore. On the 12th of July, 1861, this regiment left Camp Quarles under marching orders, and was next heard of in Virginia.

At the beginning of the conflict the students of Stewart College were anxious to join Col. Forbes, of the Fourteenth Tennessee, but he would not permit them to do so. However, they were not required to wait long for an opportunity to prove their patriotism. A second call for troops was made, and James E. Bailey, of Clarksville, then upon the military board of the State, at Nashville, came home to raise a company. In a few days this was accomplished, a company of 121 being organized November 29, 1861, of which he was elected captain. December 6, following, this company left Clarksville, midst the waving of handkerchiefs by the ladies, the shouts of the citizens and the firing of the guns at the fort at the mouth of Red River. They descended the Cumberland River on a steam-boat and reached Fort Donelson that night This was the commencement of the organization of the Forty-ninth Tennessee, which when completed was officered as follows: James E. Bailey, colonel; Alfred Robb, lieutenant-colonel, D. A. Lynn, major; B. E. Douglass, adjutant, and Dr. W. B. Williams, surgeon. The companies were commanded as follows: Company A—Capt. James E. Bailey; Company B—Capt. T. K. Grigsby, of Dickson County; Company C—Capt M. V. Fyke, of Robertson; Company D—Capt. J. B. Cording, of Dickson; Company E—Capt J. M. Peacher, of Montgomery; Company F----Capt. D. A. Lynn, of Montgomery; Company G—Capt William F. Young, of Montgomery; Company H—Capt Pugh Haynes, of Montgomery; Company I—Capt T. A. Napier, of Benton; Company K—Capt. William Shaw, of Cheatham.

The regiment was reorganized in 1862, the Rev. James H. McNeilly appointed chaplain and Dr. L. L. Lindsey, surgeon. This regiment remained at Fort Donelson until the battle by that name under command of Col Bailey, during which Lieut-Col. Alfred Bobb was mortally wounded. On the 16th of February the regiment surrendered with the rest of the Confederate force, the field officers being sent to Fort Warren, other officers to Johnson's Island, and the private soldiers to Camp Douglas, Chicago, Ill. The regiment was reorganized at Clinton, Miss., September 29, 1862, when Col James E. Bailey was re-elected colonel. Later in the history of this regiment, Capt William F. Young was promoted to the colonelcy, and lost an arm July 28. 1864 Further reference to this regiment may be found in the general history of the State.

The Fiftieth Tennessee Regiment was partially raised in Montgomery County. McGavock's battalion was its nucleus. The Montgomery County companies were A and E, Of the former T. W. Beaumont was captain at the time of its organization and of Company E, Cyrus A. Sugg. Upon the organization of the regiment Capt George W. Stacker of Company B, from Stewart County, was elected colonel, and Cyrus A. Sugg of Company E, lieutenant-colonel. Col. Stacker resigned at the end of one month after his election, and Lieut-Col. Sugg was promoted to full colonel Lieut C. W. Robertson of Company A, was appointed adjutant This regiment was stationed at Fort Donelson, and during the battle remained most of the time in the fort. Capt. Beaumont's Company A, was detailed to man the heavy guns at the river and had a terrific artillery duel with the Federal gun-boats, preventing them from passing the fort. Lieut. W. C. Allen, of this company, was complimented in an official report for gallantry on this occasion. About midnight of February 15 the Confederate soldiers were ordered to evacuate the fort, and marched to Dover, about two miles, where they stood shivering in the cold for hours, while Gens. Buckner, Floyd and Pillow held a council of war in the hotel on the river bank, after which they were ordered back to the fort, and in a short time Col. Sugg, who was in immediate command, was ordered by Gen. Buckner to raise a white flag. Having surrendered the same disposition was made of the officers and men as in the case of the Forty-ninth Tennessee. They met again at Jackson, Miss., September

20, 1862, where the regiment was reorganized, and from which time its history may be found elsewhere. Besides these there were two cavalry companies organized within the county, Woodard's and Dortch's.

Besides raising soldiers for active operations in the field it was necessary to organize regiments of "Home Guards," or "Minute Men." May 17 the county court ordered that a tax of 3 cents on each $100 worth of taxable property be levied for the relief of the families of soldiers in actual service, and on the same day R. W. Humphreys was elected commander of the Home Guards or minute men of Montgomery County. On May 20 the companies of minute men composing the Home Guard of the Clarksville District were directed to complete their organization by the election of company officers, and the minute men of each civil district were directed to organize immediately and report to the county judge, the captains to report to Commander Humphreys, and furnish a roll of their men. All men between the ages of 18 and 45 were directed to be enrolled by the justices of the Clarksville District, and the names of over 300 were published as being thus enrolled. Soon after this "Order No. 7," was issued by Commander Humphreys directing the organization of the companies of the minute men into battalions as follows: Battalion No. 1, was to be composed of the companies from Districts No. 3, 4, 8 and 9; Battalion No. 2, was to be composed of those from Districts No. 1, 5, 10, 13, 14 and 15; Battalion No. 3, of those from Districts No. 2, 11, 6, 7 and 12, and Battalion No. 4, of those from 16, 17, 18, 19 and 20, and in case of organization into regiments the First Regiment was to be composed of Battalions Nos. 2 and 3, and the Second Regiment of Battalions Nos. 1 and 4. The money first appropriated ($2,000), for the arming of the minute men, was found insufficient and on October 7, 1861, the county court ordered an additional appropriation of $4,000. About this time the Montgomery County Soldiers' Aid Society, of which T. McCullough was president, sent a large quantity of clothing and various other supplies to the Fourteenth Regiment, which was then in Virginia. Thus did the people of the county labor in every way with hope, zeal and enthusiasm to aid the cause of the Confederate Government. These efforts continued until after the fall of Fort Donelson, Sunday, February 16, 1862, soon after which the city of Clarksville was taken possession of by Federal soldiers, and remained under their control, except for a very short time, until the cessation of hostilities in April, 1865.

The following is an imperfect list of Montgomery County Confederate soldiers killed in battle: Fourteenth Regiment, Col. William A. Forbes, Lieut.-Cols. G. A. Harrel, Robert Armistead, W. W. Thompson, Charles Mitchell, Gustavus Tompkins. Forty-ninth Regiment, J. C. Anderson, Robert Bringhurst, Fletcher Beaumont, Montgomery Bell, S. E. Cooke, George Elliott, John T. Farley, E. C. Goostree, J. S. Jarrell, Matt. Leggett, William B. Munford, Alfred Robb, Nathan Vick, Polk Wilcox, E. T. Coulter, E. G. Halliday, S. A. Wall, James B. Howard, T. J. Stone, Joseph W. Burnes, A. J. Cuthbertson, Thomas R. Coulter, James Norfleet, T. J. Barbee. Fiftieth Regiment, Col. Cyrus A. Sugg. Lieut.-Col. T. W. Beaumont. No means are now at hand for obtaining the names of even a majority of those who fell in battle, nor a satisfactory approximation even to the total number, but it is believed that of those who enlisted about 400 died.

On June 20, 1865, a meeting of citizens was held at the court house to elect delegates to the convention to be held at Columbia on the 24th. George W. Hampton was made chairman of the meeting, by whom, after the adoption of a series of resolutions approving of the policy of President Johnson, the following delegates were appointed to the Columbia convention: G. C. Breed, C. G. Smith, William Wines, Thomas McCullough, E. A. Fisher, W. E. Newell, L. M. Bently, Josiah Hoskins, W. H. Crouch, J. H. Wall, O. M. Blackman, G. H. Warfield, D. W. Nye "and all other Union men of the county, who will be governed by the spirit of the resolutions adopted at the meeting." On Thursday, August

3, an election for congressman was held, at which D. B. Thomas, the independent candidate, received 239 votes and S. M. Arnell 37.

A meeting of the citizens of the county was held September 30 to give expression to their sentiments on the state of the country. They expressed themselves as accepting the new position of things, as being desirous of peace between the sections, as looking upon the abolition of slavery as a fact, as sympathizing with the negro, and as approving President Johnson's policy. The Hon. R. B. Peart who had cast the only vote in Clarksville against separation in 1861, having died while a member of the Senate, an election was held March 31, 1866, to supply the vacancy, resulting in the selection of the Hon. Cave Johnson, who was not admitted to his seat.

At an election held August 5 (?), 1869, D. W. C. Senter received in this county 2,516 votes for governor to 1,464 for William B. Stokes. On Saturday, December 18, 1869, an election was held for delegates to a constitutional convention, with the following result: For the convention, 1,601; against the convention, 10. At the election held November 8, 1870, the vote was as follows: Governor—Gen. John C. Brown, 1,320 votes; W. H. Wisener, 1,261. At the presidential election of 1872 Horace Greeley received 2,157 votes to 2,035 for President Grant. There was considerable excitement in connection with the election that occurred in 1874, in consequence of the withdrawal of certain individuals from the Democratic party and joining the Republican party for the sake of being elected to office through the assistance of the negro vote. The result, however, was in favor of the Democratic candidates by the following votes: Governor—James D. Porter, 2,533; Horace B. Maynard, 1,753. The next election was that of President in 1876: Samuel J. Tilden, 2,813; R. B. Hayes, 2,096; Gov. James D. Porter, 2,391; D. B. Thomas, 2,483.

In 1878 there were three tickets in the field, Democratic, Republican and Independent. The result was as follows, candidates being named in the above order: Governor—Albert S. Marks, 1,911; R. M. Edwards, 918; E. M. Wight, 467. The election in 1880 was one in which great interest was taken, and after it was over the Democrats were exceedingly gratified at the result, which was as follows: President—Gen. W. S. Hancock, 2,846; James A. Garfield, 2,039. Governor—John V. Wright, 2,583; Alvin Hawkins, 1,498; Wilson, 838; R. M. Edwards, 17. The election in 1882 was one in which great interest was taken on account of the debt question involved. The result was as follows: Governor—William B. Bate, 2,451 votes; Alvin Hawkins, 1,800; Joseph H. Fussell, 399, and John R. Beasley, 148. The votes at the presidential election of 1884 were as follows: Cleveland, 2,517; Blaine, 1,922; St. John, 9. Governor—W. B. Bate, 2,483; Reid, 1,939.

The first county officers elected after the war were as follows: Sheriff, Berry Lyle, for two years from March 6, 1864; register, B. M. Clifton, four years from same time. Clerk of county court—W. E. Newell, four years. On February 7, 1865, an election was held for the remainder of the county officers, and the list was completed as follows: Coroner— W. K. Cummins; county trustee, H. M. Acree; surveyor, A. A. Powers; notary public, George B. Faxon; circuit court clerk, G. C. Breed. In 1878 the following officers were elected by the majorities appended to their respective names: County trustee—John S. Neblett, 289; attorney-general—R. H. Burney, 2,851; county judge—C. W. Tyler, 1,382: circuit court judge—James E. Rice, 2,290; circuit court clerk—C. D. Bailey, 1,804; county court clerk—R. D. Moseley, 927; sheriff—J. M. Rogers, 2,838; register—J. E. Moseley, 1,450. The present county officers are as follows: County court clerk, B. D. Moseley; register, J. M. Rogers; circuit court clerk, C. D. Bailey; county trustee, B. H. Pickering; sheriff, J. M. Collier; surveyor, E. Shelton; coroner, J. T. Staton. The voting population of Montgomery County in 1841 was 2,033. This would indicate a white population of about 11,000. In 1851 the population was as follows: Whites—males, 6,151; females, 5,749, Colored—slaves, 9,071; free, 74; total population, 21,045. In 1860 the white population was 11,235, and the colored, 9,660. In 1870 the population was as follows: White, 13,077; black, 11,760. In 1880, white, 14. 786; black, 13,694; Indian, 1; males, 14,103; females, 14,378; over twenty-one years of age, 6,386. The assessed valuation of real estate was, in 1880, $3,997,880, and of personal property, $522,745. Taxation was as follows: State tax, $13,050; county, $35,652; city, $20,006. The bonded debt of the county was $357,423, and the floating debt. $8,443.

Previous to the late civil war, the iron industry was the most important of any in the county. Timber was abundant for making charcoal and the iron ore being of superior quality, the iron manufactured at the numerous furnaces was in great demand and commanded a high price. Many of those who established furnaces and forges, realized handsome fortunes. By the war all this was changed, and now there are no furnaces in operation. The first "iron works" started in Montgomery County, were doubtless, those known in the early days as Dr. Morgan Brown's. They were built in 1805 and operated by him for a number of years. They were located three and one-half miles from the mouth of Yellow Creek, and were washed away by the great flood of 1836, a short time after having been purchased by Steel & Sox, who, it is believed changed the name of the works to the "Yellow Creek Furnace." Steel & Sox rebuilt the furnace and ran it up to the war, or the latter part of 1862, when it was burned down by the Federal soldiers, and Mr. Steel himself killed. In 1852, Yellow Creek Furnace was yielding about 700 tons of pig iron per annum, valued at $15,000; and Yellow Creek Forge about 500 tons of blooms, valued at $27,500. Mount Vernon Furnace was erected in 1830, by Baxter, Hicks & Mitchel. Soon afterward Mr. Mitchel retired and the firm became W. R. Hicks & Co., Edward Hicks becoming a partner. There were at this furnace two stacks, both of which were in blast for a short time, simultaneously, while making heavy castings for a rolling mill at Nashville, in which W. R. Hicks & Co. were interested. This furnace was run a great deal on hollow ware castings. In 1850 Mr. Baxter died, at which time he owned the furnace in whole, and about 20,000 acres of land besides. He was a molder by trade, came to this country in 1812, and became the head of the iron works system on the south side of the Cumberland; at his death all of his manufacturing interests came into the possession of his four sons-in-law: G. T. Abernathy, S. Watkins, A. Jackson and C. B. McKernan.

The Washington Furnace was built in 1830, by Barton Richmond and S. & J. Stacker. Soon after this Mr. Richmond sold his interest to the Stackers, who in 1832, sold to Col. George Pattison. In 1834 Col. Pattison attached to the furnace a steam forge and put in an engine of greater capacity, with which to run both works. In building the forge he located the refining fires so that the flues from the forge should pass under the boilers. When the forge was being operated this arrangement answered a good purpose, but when the forge fires were out the influx of cold air through the flues kept down the steam. The works suspended December, 1839. For a few months in 1840, Robert Baxter operated the furnace to work up the stock left on hand by Col. Pattison. Dr. W. I. Holmes then bought the property in 1846, converted the buildings into a granary and the land into a stock farm, and subsequently sold off the farm in tracts.

The Blooming Grove Furnace was started in 1834 by the Nebletts, John, Ben, Henry and Frank, and was located about five miles from the Cumberland River. The Nebletts bought the engine that had been used at the Washington Furnace, and in 1840 established a forge about three miles from the furnace. In 1844 both furnace and forge went into the hands of Newell & Co., and afterward into the hands of Newton, Newell & Co., who operated them until Mr. Newton was killed in 1846 or 1847, at which time they were suspended. In 1849 they were revived by S. E. Cook & Co., who operated them until the war.

The Webster Furnace was established in 1845 by Carter, Jackson & Co., who ran it until 1848, when they sold to Ellis, Oliphant & Co. This firm, after continuing it about a year, sold to J. L. James & Co., who changed its name to the "Phoenix," and ran it until 1855, when it went out of operation. In 1852 the product of this furnace was about 1,700 tons of pig iron per annum, valued at $37,400; it was located about three miles due south of Palmyra.

The Louisa Furnace was started in 1846 by Robert Baxter, and was operated by steam-power. In 1852 it was owned by Baxter, Abernathy & Co., and was probably the most productive of all the furnaces in the county, making about 1,800 tons of pig iron annually, valued at $39600. This furnace ceased to operate at the time of the war.

Lafayette Furnace was erected in 1826 by Samuel Vanleer. He sold out, in 1828, to S. & J. Stacker, who, in 1831, sold to Stewart & Co. Ward retired in 1835, and Stewart & Co. operated it very successfully until 1849. This furnace always made money, was in fact the bonanza of the iron furnaces in the county. The chief product was sugar kettles, which stood the heat better than any others carried to the New Orleans market. The annual yield was about 900 tons. The kettles sold at $1 per inch of the diameter at the top. The great income from this furnace was during the years from 1843 to 1849, from which the proprietors became rich. O. K. Furnace, afterward "Antonio," was built in 1853 by Geniren, Skates & Co. T. Y. Dixon purchased the interest of Mr. Skates. In 1860 the furnace ceased to operate.

The Montgomery Furnace started in August, 1853, by Steele, Bradley & Co. was located about one and a half miles south of Palmyra. In December of that year they sold out to Robinson, Hinson & Co., who ran it until 1855, when its operation was suspended. Red River Forge was established about the year 1815 by Dr. Samuel Watson. It was operated from 1830 to 1834 by Pattison & McCaslin, who about that time moved the hands to Washington Forge. Red River Forge then became a flouring-mill, owned by Peter Peacher, who added thereto a woolen factory. It afterward became the property of E. C. Hambaugh, who is now the owner. Valley Forge was built by Phillips, Welsh & Welker in 1850, and was operated by them until the war. Blooming Grove Rolling Mill was built about the year 1841 or 1842 by Jones & Co., who operated it, however, only a short time.

On the 12th of September, 1853, the president and directors of the Memphis, Clarksville & Louisville Railroad petitioned the County Court of Montgomery County to submit to the voters of the county a proposition to issue the bonds of the county for $250,000, having thirty years to mature, with coupons for semi-annual interest at the rate of 6 per cent per annum. The election was held October 20, 1853, with the result of there being east 1,145 votes for the proposition and 424 against it. On July 6, 1856, eighty-three of the bonds were issued and the balance July 6, 1858. The county received in exchange stock of the railway company to the same amount $250,000. About the time the last issue of bonds was made the county court offered to buy in the bonds at 80 cents on the dollar, payable in six equal annual installments with interest from January 1, 1859. The citizens of the county appear to have been dissatisfied with this proposition, and the railway company in view of this dissatisfaction made a proposition to the court that the county should pay the interest on the bonds. The court thereupon ordered that a tax of 1 per cent on the taxable property be levied, and that Henry Lyle be appointed collector of said tax. On the 3d of January, 1859, a tax of 12 cents on the $100 was levied for railroad purposes, and on February 11, 1860, the county clerk, William Rogers, produced his certificate of deposit with the Clarksville Branch of the Bank of Tennessee for $2,085 revenue for the railroad, collected upon privileges for the year ending January 1, 1860. The tax for 1862 was fixed at 2 per cent on the taxable property, and on the 31st of July, 1865, a railroad tax of 50 cents on the $100 was unanimously voted. In April, 1866, this tax was fixed at 35 cents, and in 1867 at one-half of 1 per cent. On the 20th of July, 1868, the clerk reported that he had collected since April 1 railroad tax to the amount of $1,760.69, the largest amount from any one class being from tipplers, $770.

An interesting case came before the county court for trial July 20, 1868, that of the Southern Telegraph Company vs. the Memphis, Clarksville & Louisville Railroad Company, the former company desiring to erect a telegraph line along the railroad. The question to be decided was that of the amount of damages to the property of the railroad company consequent upon the erection of said proposed telegraph line. The court appointed Robert H. Williams, H. C. Merritt and Polk G. Johnson commissioners to assess the damages, and on the 25th of the month these commissioners reported the damages to be 83 cents, or 1 cent per mile for the entire length of the line.

The amount of railroad tax collected in 1868 was $1,097.97. By this time the county realized that the railroad was a very expensive luxury. It could not avoid paying out taxes every year on account of interest on its bonds, and it could not collect any interest on the railroad stock it held. On the 4th of January W. A. Queries was authorized to sell the stock of the county in the railroad, the amount of original stock being $250,000, and the amount of stock for accrued interest being about $50,000, on the condition that the county should realize at least 20 per cent upon the stock, the balance realized to be equally divided between the county and Gen. Queries. About this time the chancery court at Nashville ordered the Memphis, Clarksville & Louisville Railroad to be sold for a minimum of $1,700,000. and the Louisville & Nashville Railroad Company became the purchaser. After this purchase Montgomery County and Clarksville employed agents to sell the stock of the city and county. These agents after making unsuccessful efforts in other directions finally sold the stock to the Louisville & Nashville Railroad Company. This company agreed to pay for the stock $300,000, and tendered in payment $100,000 worth of its own stock to be taken by the county at the value of $113,860, and in the agreement for the purchase stipulated not to discriminate in its freights against the city of Clarksville. This agreement was ratified by the Montgomery County Court by a vote of thirty-four to none. On the 10th of October, 1872. an elaborate report was made by a committee appointed for the purpose the summary of which was as follows:

We find that our bonded debt is as follows:

236 original railroad bonds @ $1,000 $ 236,000 00
225 funded bonds @ 180 40,500 00
Total bonded debt $ 276.500 00
Judgment on 60 coupons 11,190 00
Interest on funded bonds 658 80
Total liabilities, bonds and interest $ 288,348 80

The committee also reported further that the railroad had cost the county in all up to that date, including outstanding indebtedness, cash paid on bonds and interest and incidental expenses, the enormous sum of $495,024.45. The committee also reported that on account of the depreciation of assessed values from $9,987,011 in 1868 to $5,146,985 in 1872, it was necessary to increase the rate of taxation from 10 cents on $100 to 50 cents, and advised the establishment of a sinking fund to pay the bonds at maturity.

With regard to the sale of the county's stock in the Memphis, Clarksville & Louisville Railroad the attorneys reported that they had received in payment $100,000 in the Louisville & Nashville Railroad valued at $113,860, and $186,140 in Tennessee bonds. The committee closed its report with a statement of the assets and liabilities of the county on account of railroad investment—the liabilities being $288,348.80, and the assets $247,058.50. This was after setting apart to Clarksville its share. On the 2d of January, 1882, a committee appointed to sell the State bonds reported the sale of all the bonds at from 71 to 74 cents, the net proceeds being $82,043.68. The interest-funding bonds of 1866 had all been paid but four.

The Louisville & Nashville Railroad stock taken in part payment for the county's stock in the Memphis, Clarksville & Louisville Railroad was sold in 1881 for 42 cents on $1, and the proceeds credited to the sinking fund, and used in payment on the debt of the county and in the erection of the new court house.

The Indiana, Alabama & Texas Railroad was projected in 1881. In 1882 active work was begun in soliciting subscription, holding meetings, etc. At these meetings Judge Smith, of Clarksville, was one of the principal speakers. On February 1, 1882, an enthusiastic meeting was held at Princeton, Ky., the proposed southern terminus of the road. Clarksville & Princeton Railroad was the name by which the road was known for some time. When the subscription books were opened at the Clarksville Bank, March 11, 1882, subscriptions were made that day for $1,312,500, the principal amount being taken by the Gordon family. A stockholder's meeting was then held and a board of directors elected for the next twelve months as follows: Eugene C. Gordon, Walter S. Gordon, W. B. Wood, C. G. Smith, W. J. Wood, D. N. Kennedy, A. Howell, G. B. Wilson and H. C. Merritt. The directors then chose the following officers: Eugene C. Gordon, president; W. B. Wood, vice-president; W. S. Gordon, treasurer, and H. C. Merritt, secretary. Resolutions were then adopted consolidating the Mobile, Clarksville & Evansville Company with the Indiana, Alabama & Texas Company, the Princeton & Ohio Company and the Clarksville & Princeton Company, under the name of the Indiana, Alabama & Texas Railroad Company, this name being adopted because the termini of the road were to be in Indiana and Texas. Texas was added because the road was to connect with the Georgia Pacific running from Atlanta to Texarkana. The sum of $340,000 was asked to be subscribed by seven counties in Kentucky which were to be immediately benefitted by the construction of the road. Since then the road has been built from Clarksville to Newstead, Ky., at a total cost of $337,998.03. The design is to connect the Kentucky coal fields with the Montgomery County iron ore beds, and thus present an opportunity for the resumption of the manufacture of iron. Efforts are now being made for the completion of the road to Princeton, Ky.

The first court house was a rude log one, erected on the public square and possessed but the most primitive conveniences. It was succeeded in 1811 by a new brick building also upon the public square, which had a stone foundation, was forty-four feet square and two stories high. This building served as a court house until 1843, when it was sold to John D. Everett and a new one erected on Poverty Row, which was destroyed on the night of April 13, 1878, by the great fire. This building had stood in a very unsatisfactory location, and it was then determined to purchase the lot of Mrs. Jennie E. Glass, fronting on Second and Third Streets and also on Commerce Street, upon which to erect the new court house. This new building is one of the handsomest court houses in the State. The exterior is of pressed brick with stone trimmings. The first story above the basement has large and convenient rooms for the county clerk, trustee, register, circuit and criminal court clerk, county judge and two rooms for the chancery clerk. In the second story are the court rooms, jury room, witness room, etc. The entire cost of the building with the furniture and grounds was $100,000.

The county asylum is located in Civil District No. 10, near the Cheatham County line. The farm consists of 200 acres, on which are the superintendent's house and the houses for the inmates, all located on a sightly elevation. The superintendent is allowed the free use of the farm and an annual salary of $200. He is not permitted to work the inmates without their consent. All supplies and medicines needed are furnished by the commissioners appointed for the purpose, of whom J. E. Ramsdell is chairman. The inmates are for the most part persons of feeble mind, or those suffering from some mild form of insanity. Previous to 1870 the asylum was located in South Clarksville, and in that year it was moved to its present location. The present superintendent is J. D. Burney.

Until recently the Montgomery County Jail, like most of the other county jails in Tennessee, was a totally unfit place for the keeping of prisoners; but with the past seven or eight years great improvements have been made in its interior and other appurtenances and arrangements as well as management. There is room in it now for about forty prisoners, which is about double the number on hand. There are four rooms designed for prisoners of the better class, and in the upper story a large steel cage for desperate criminals. Every room is lighted, heated by steam and contains running water. The jailer is allowed an annual salary and the management of the jail is in the hands of a commission composed at present of Charles W. Tyler (the county judge), J. H. Achey, H. R. Rogers and Gr. W. Armstrong. By this commission all food, clothing, medicine and other needed supplies are purchased and paid, and taken altogether this is one of the best managed jails in Tennessee, the commission being governed by humane motives.

One of the earliest settlements in the county was made at Idaho Springs, the waters of which were early sought for their medical virtues. No effort was made to entertain boarders there, however, until 1858, when a number of cabins were built with a view of erecting a large hotel. The civil war coming on caused an abandonment of the project, and the property lay comparatively unoccupied until the present incumbent, J. A. Tate, purchased it in 1879, and employed a skillful Irishman to assist him in opening up the long slumbering streams. Finding traces of iron water he followed them to their source, and discovered fine chalybeate waters, till then entirely unknown here. He also found the strongest sulphur water, dark in appearance, and discovering a change in the taste of the water at different times, inferred that there were several waters Mended. After much labor and expense the different waters were entirely separated, the strongest water becoming as clear as crystal. There are now three distinct varieties of sulphur water, white, red and black, as well as a strong chalybeate and a silvery sparkling water of little mineral taste, making as fine a collection of mineral waters as can be found in any State. Rheumatism, dyspepsia, chronic diarrhoea, all cutaneous and blood diseases, diabetes and gravel yield promptly to their influence, and in consequence this is becoming an exceedingly popular resort, especially in connection with Dunbar's Cave.

Dunbar's Cave is situated about three miles from Clarksville on the Russellville pike. Though inferior in size to the Mammoth Cave, in Kentucky, it is second in beauty to none in the country. The mouth of the cave is fifteen feet wide and eight feet high, and from the cave is emitted a stiff, uniform breeze, from which fact it is known as a "blowing cave." Here a temperature of from fifty to seventy-five degrees is maintained the summer through. Among the places of note and objects within the cave are the following: "Counterfeiters' Room," so named from having been occupied by a band of counterfeiters in 1842; " Music Hall," which is about half an acre in extent, and from fifteen to thirty feet high; the "Ball Room," which is 50 by 400 feet in extent; "Dunbar's Coffin," "Spray Hall," "Rocky Mountain" and the "Cathedral," the "Saltpeter Mine," "Lovers' Leap," "Peterson's Leap," "Relief Hall," "Great Relief Hall" and "Independence Hall." In the latter hall, which embraces about two acres in extent, and contains hundreds of columns interspersed throughout in all kinds of fantastic shapes, are "Solomon's Porch," "Jacob's Well," "Rebecca's Seat," the "Happy Dutch Family," the "Elephant," the "Monkey," the "Petrified Coon," the "Irish Potatoes" and the "Willapus Wallapus." Eight different caverns lead from this hall, the "Crystal Palace" being by far the most beautiful. It is in three stories, the roof of each being studded profusely with white and colored stalactites. The "Ice Pond" and the Diamond Grotto" are named from their similiarity to the objects after which they are named.

Montgomery County Farmers' Association was organized July 21, 1883. A meeting was called at the court house by G. H. Slaughter, vice-president of the Middle Tennessee Farmers' Association. At this meeting it was agreed that all persons more interested in agriculture than any other pursuits should be entitled to membership. Thirty-seven names were then enrolled. C. P. Warfield was elected president of the association; M. V. Ingram, secretary, and B. R. Burchett, treasurer. One vice-president was chosen for each civil district in the county, and the following executive committee appointed: G. H. Slaughter, T. L. Mabry, H. E. Rogers, Griffin Orgain, J. K. Ramey, W. P. Johnson and T. J. Swift. The officers of this new association felt the responsibility resting upon them, and determined on holding a grand picnic reunion of the farmers and everybody else who would attend, at Dunbar's Cave. This was also to be a county fair, at which the stock, farming implements and products of the county were to be exhibited. This reunion or fair was held August 21, 1883, and was a surprising success, about 2,500 people being present. By this success the farmers were so encouraged and inspirited that each succeeding reunion has been an improvement on all of its predecessors.

Dunbar's Cave proved to be admirably adapted to these gatherings in summer. The first seed show was held at the court house February 26, 1884. The second was held December 16 and 17, 1884, the ladies taking an active part in exhibiting samples of rare needle work, paintings and other works of art. The second reunion and stock show was held August 19 and 20, 1884, and the third August 25 and 26, 1885. The present officers of the association are C. P. Warfield, president; A. V. Goodpasture, vice-president; M. V. Ingram, secretary, and W. O. Brandon, treasurer. The executive committee are as follows: G. H. Slaughter (chairman), W. P. Johnson, Polk Prince, T. S. Mabry, W. L. Warfield, J. W. Pardue, Dr. N. L. Northington and Calvin Webb.

The county court of pleas and quarter sessions was instituted April 20, 1789, but, on account of the destruction of the early records of the county, it is not easy to give an account of the early justices constituting the court The first lawsuit, however, came on that day, the plaintiff in the case being no less a personage than Andrew Jackson, while the defendent was Philip Alston. The lawsuit was about a "sorrel horse, about fourteen hands high, known by the name of Samuel Martin's sorrel," for which Jackson paid £100. Upon the same day Sarah Stewart gave bond, with William Borin and Elkin Taylor as her securities, in the sum of £2,000, as "administratricks" of John Stewart, deceased. Bond was also given in the sum of £500 by Mary Jones and Thomas Lidle, as administrators of John Jones, deceased, George Nevill and Joseph Martin being securities. The court ordered jurors to be summoned as follows, to its next term, to be held on the third Monday in July, 1789, at Isaac Titsworth, Thomas French, William Williams, Stephen Borin, Isaac Wiling cox, Robert Edmonston, Charles Mcintosh, William Grimbs, Jesse Cain, Daniel Flournoy, Samuel Hauley, Jacob McCarty, Josiah Ramsey, William Gales, Caleb Winters, Francis Prince, James Stewart, William McClain, Isaac Pennington, James McFarland, John McFarland, John Wilcox, Hugh Lewis, John Codra, Archibald Mahon, John

Titsworth, William Conner, John Stanley, Richard Dodge, James Boyd, James Hollis, Sr., Charles Thompson and James Elliott The court levied taxes in 1792 as follows: 3 shillings on each poll; 1 shilling on each 100 acres of land, and 3 shillings on each £100 worth of property, and double these sums for the payment of arrearages due guards for escorting families from the Holston. The reputation of citizens was also guarded by this court, as the following will show. It is given verbatim et literatim;

I, John Irwin, of my free will and accord, do hereby acknowledge & certify the raskelly and scandoullus report, that I have Raised and Reported Concearned Miss Polly Mcfaddin, is faulse and Groundless; and that I had no Right, Reason or Cause to Believe the Same. Given under my hand, this 26 March, 1798.

[Signed]
JOHN IRWIN.

'Test: FRANCIS PRINCE,
ROBERT ASHLEY.

On the 16th of July, 1793, this court took action in reference to a certain law of the Territory. The act of Congress for the government of the Territory provided that the governor and judges, or a majority of them, should adopt and publish in the district such laws, civil and criminal, as might be necessary and best suited to the circumstances of the district. Under authority of this act, on March 13, 1793, Gov. William Blount and Judges David Campbell and Joseph Anderson passed an act requiring clerks and registers to give bond for the due Collection and payment of the moneys arising from fines, forfeitures and taxes. On July 16 the County Court of Pleas and Quarter Sessions of Tennessee County met; present: the Wpful. Francis Prince, chairman, and Joseph Philips, Isaac

Philips and John Montgomery, Isqrs. The following proceedings were had:

Anthony Crutcher, Esq., clerk of Tennessee County, came into court and offered James Adams, Hugh McCullom and Julius Sanders, his sureties for collecting fines and taxes on writs, etc., agreeable to a law passed by Gov. Blount and two of the judges, to wit: Anderson and Campbell. The court refused to have any security from the clerk, as they did consider the law made without authority, and they would pay no attention to it; and directed the clerk not to receive any of the taxes agreeable to that law. Also, Hugh Lewis, register for the county aforesaid, tendered security for receiving taxes on deeds, etc; but the court also refused, as above, and directed him not to receive any taxes on deeds, etc.

At a subsequent term the court reversed its decision and received the securities. The first records now in existence of the proceedings of the county court, are dated December 2, 1805. On that day a meeting was held at the court house in Clarksville, the following esquires being present: Shadrack Tribble, chairman; Joseph Woolfork and David Pritchard. The grand jury present on that occasion was composed as follows: Glidwell Killebrew, foreman; Hugh McCullom, Thomas Williams, Thomas Dunbar, Richard Whitehead, James M. Carroll, Samuel Bumpless, Robert Nowlen, William Randall, Isaac Martin, Peter Hubbard, Thomas Hunter, Jesse Sibley, Abraham Cocke and Allen Anderson. These persons attended three days and were then dismissed. As a portion of their proceedings the following items are given: John Kimbel was licensed to keep a tavern in his own house in Clarksville, giving James Boyd and John R. McFarling as securities in the sum of $500. William Ross, Sr., was licensed to erect a cotton-gin in Montgomery County, James Ross, Joseph Wray and David Enloe going on his bond in the sum of $500. Joseph Woolfork gave bonds in the sum of $2,000 for keeping a ferry across Red River and Sulphur Fork at their junction. On the next day Hugh McClure and Thomas Smith presented a commission from his excellency, John Sevier, as justices of the peace for Montgomery County, and they two, with Joseph Woolfork, Joseph Robertson and James Fentress, constituted the court.

Peter Brown was authorized to keep a ferry across the Cumberland River at the mouth of Red River. At this time John Cocke was sheriff, and, according to his report, delinquent taxes were due from sixty-seven owners of 51,538 acres of land, amounting to $264.78 and from owners of ninety-five town lots in Clarksville, amounting to $76.48. Ten bills of sale of negroes were proved and ordered to registration on the 6th day of the December term. On the next day the court appointed the following persons for the different captains' companies in Montgomery County as valuers of property taken for debt: For the town company, Hugh F. Bell and John Marshall; for Hundley's company, Andrew Stewart and David Weakley; Capt. Baker's company, David Rudder and William Barton; Enloe's company, Charles Stewart and Andrew Allen; McCrabb's company, John Trousall and Elisha Willis; Wilson's company, David Peoples and Francis Tompkins; Allen's company, Robert Wells and Abraham Cocke; Stephenson's company, Edwin Gibson and David McFadden; Craft's company, Benjamin Hawkins and Guthridge Lyons. At the March term, 1806, the Wpful. Robert Prince, Thomas Smith and James Lockart were the justices. March 26 Willie Blount Esq., produced a commission from the governor as justice of the peace, and the first case of assault and battery was tried that day—W. G. B. Prince vs. Aaron Jenkins, resulting in a verdict for the plaintiff of $150 damages. The first murder trial in the county, of which there is any record, occurred March 30, 1807. It was before a called court, consisting of the Wpful. Robert Prince, Thomas Smith, Hugh McClure, John Blair, Samuel Gattis, James Stewart, Esqrs., and Hugh F. Bell, Moses Oldham, Sr., James Hambleton and John Marshall, four free-holders, holding slaves. The person tried was a negro man named Moses. He was charged with the willful and malicious murder of Samuel Minott. Being led to the bar by the sheriff, arraigned and charged with the crime, he pleaded "not guilty." "The court then proceeded to well and truly try the prisoner, and having heard the evidence declared upon their oaths, that they found the negro man, Moses, guilty of willful murder, and it was considered by the said court that the said Moses be taken back to whence he came, and thence to be conveyed to the place of execution and there to be hung by the neck until he is dead, dead, dead; and then to have his head cut off and the head to be set upon a pole, and the sheriff of Montgomery County is directed to put this judgment into execution this day, between the hours of two and three o'clock." To this entry are appended the signatures of all the justices and the freeholders constituting the court. Moses was executed in the flat between Franklin and Main Streets, and the head placed upon a pole, set up on the corner of Main and Fourth Streets where it remained until the flesh disappeared and the skull became bleached with the sun. On the 19th of September James H. Russell was admitted to practice law in this court. The first case of trespass vi et armis was that of Samuel Vance and John Bradley, surviving partners of Vance, King and Bradley, vs. Samuel Thornton. The jury decided the defendant guilty, The first trial for disturbing the public worship was that of the State vs. Duncan Stewart July 19, 1810. The defendant pleaded "guilty" and was fined 1 cent and costs. The first slander case was that of Stephen Cocke vs. James Tribble, July 21, 1810. The defendant made default and the court decided that the plaintiff recover such damages as had been by him sustained by reason of the utterance of the several false, scandalous and opprobrious words, the damages to be assessed by a jury at the next term of court. The first case of a free colored person being bound out during minority was that of Ester Irwin April 16, 1811. She was of a bright mulatto color, about sixteen years old and was the daughter of a "free white woman." She was bound out as an apprentice to Elisha Willis. During the various terms of 1820, most of the criminal cases were for assault and battery and bastardy, and the civil business

consisted mainly in the ordering of the registration of deeds of convey-
ance of land. The first case of assumpsit was tried April 20, 1820. The
first case of indictment for keeping a tippling house was July 26, 1831,
against John B. Green, who was fined $5 and costs. Among the early
usury cases was that of the State vs. Asa W. Hooper, who was adjudged
guilty.

On the 10th of April, 1832, important action was taken in reference
to the classification of the roads of the county. Those of the first class
were as follows: That from Clarksville to Russellville; that from Clarksville to Hopkinsville; that from Clarksville by Simmon's ferry and the
Stubb's ferry road toward Reynoldsburg; from Clarksville to Charlotte;
from Clarksville to Nashville by Sanford Wilson's and Henry Williams';
from Clarksville to the Robertson County line at Shanklin's by way of
Joseph Ligon's; that from Hopkinsville to Nashville by way of Port Royal; that from Clarksville to Dover; from the mouth of Red River to
Wheatley's mill, and from the iron works to the Kentucky line; from
Clarksville to Port Royal by John Edmonston's old place, and that from
the Red River bridge to Benton; all other roads to be second class until
otherwise ordered by the court.

For a number of years after this court began to consist of more than
three justices of the peace it was customary, upon convening at the beginning of each quarter session, first to elect a chairman and then being
thus organized to elect a "court of quorum" to transact the business of
the court. For instance at the January term, 1848, N. F. Trice was elected
chairman, and himself together with Joseph Pollard and F. Ramey, were
chosen the "court of quorum." This arrangement lasted until the going
into effect of the law under which a county judge was elected, who since
then has taken the place of the "court of quorum." The first judge of the
county court was the Hon. Thomas W. Wisdom, who was elected at a
general election held all over the State for county judges, May 3, 1856.

Judge Wisdom's commission was signed by F. N. W. Burton, secretary of State, and by Andrew Johnson, governor, in May, and presented to the county court June 2, 1856. Judge Wisdom took the oath of office before the Hon. W. R. Turner, who was then judge of the criminal court. Judge Wisdom served as judge of this court until April 5, 1858, when he was succeeded by the Hon. H. S. Kimble who presided until February 8, 1862. This was the day on which the last session of the court was held under the old order of things, before the three years of chaos caused by the civil war.

The next meeting of this court was held February 6, 1865, upon which occasion the Hon. L. M. Bentley presided. The first business of the court under Judge Bentley was to receive from Berry Lyle his certificate of election as sheriff of the county, signed by I. O. Shackleford, special sheriff. The salary of the county judge was fixed October 23, 1865, at $1,200 per annum. The last day Judge Bentley presided over this court was April 16, 1866, and on the next day his successor, the Hon. Thomas W. King, took his place upon the bench with the same salary as his predecessor. Judge King presided over this court until his death, which occurred at Waukesha, Wis., July 22, 1873. In 1870 the criminal court was separated from the circuit court and the judge of the county court made judge of the criminal court. Judge King at his death was succeeded as judge of these two courts by the present judge, Hon. Charles W. Tyler, who was appointed to fill the vacancy and commissioned by Gov. John C. Brown, and who served for the first time August 4, 1873. Judge Tyler has been elected to this position since his appointment. The court of quarter sessions, composed of magistrates from each civil district hold sessions each quarter at Clarksville.

The Superior Court of Law and Equity for the District of Robertson under the law for the division of the District of Mero into three districts, held its first meeting at the court house in Clarksville, on the first Monday in December, 1806. The judges present were the Hons. David Campbell, Hugh L. White and John Overton. The district of Robertson was composed of the counties of Robertson, Dickson, Stewart and Montgomery. This court held a session at the court house in Clarksville on the first Monday in June, 1807. The judges were the Hons. David Campbell, John Overton and Thomas Emmerson. The first case was that of Martin Armstrong vs. Thomas Farmer, and the second that of Levi Noyes vs. John Boyd. Noyes and Boyd had played at hazard in Nashville November 23, 1801, and the latter won of the former $169. November 6, 1804, at Springfield, Robertson County, Noyes bound himself to pay $125, which Boyd promised to accept as a full settlement. At this term of this court Noyes filed a bill in equity to prevent Boyd from collecting this amount, setting up the statute against gambling as a defense. Boyd demurred and the court sustained the demurrer, assessing the costs against Noyes. At the December term 1807, David Campbell and Samuel Powell were the judges, and at the June term 1808, John Overton and Parry W. Humphreys.

The county court had jurisdiction in all cases up to 1809, when the circuit court system was put in operation in this State. The records of the circuit court for Montgomery County appear to have been lost previous to the August term, 1813. On the minutes for that term the first case is that of the State vs. Benjamin Menees; John Carr, prosecutor. There was but one day's session and the minutes were signed by " John F, Jack." On the third Monday of February, 1814, the Hon. Bennett Searcy, Esq., took his seat on the bench as judge of this court. Henry Minor, clerk, resigned, and Frederick W. Huling was appointed in his place. A grand jury was impaneled as follows: John Blair, foreman: Barney Duff, James McCarrell, David Peoples, James Boyd, John Boyd, Isham Trotter, Charles Barker, Matthew Rybourn, Thomas Batson. Francis Rolack, Stephen Cocke and John Lee. James Williams was sworn as bailiff. Henry Minor then presented his commission as solicitor-general of the Fifth Circuit. Then came the case of Thomas Washington vs. Joseph Gray, William Cherry and Henry Gibson. Bennett Searcy's last day on the bench was February 24, 1814. On the 15th of August Thomas Stewart, Esq., was the presiding judge. The first habeas corpus case came on that day. It was that of Taviner C. Oosman vs. John S. Williamson. Williamson, in obedience to the writ of habeas corpus issued by the court that day, brought into court Taviner C. Oosman and made known the cause of his "caption and detention." "On Monday, August 15, 1814, the said Taviner was duly and legally enlisted a soldier in the army of the United States, received the bounty, signed the enrollment and took the oath, all agreeable to the existing laws of the United States, and this I do certify to your honor to be the cause of said Taviner.'s detention and caption." The court decided that the said Oosman be remanded to the custody of said Williamson and pay the costs occasioned by the writ

The Hon. Nathaniel W. Williams was judge of this court at the term commencing February 20, 1815. Under Judge Williams another habeas corpus case came on for trial similar to the above. The title of the case was "William Outlaw vs. George W. Sommerville, lieutenant in the United States Army." The decision of Judge Williams was that William Outlaw be remanded to the custody of Lieut. Sommerville and pay the costs. Judge Williams' last day at this term was March 7, 1815. Archibald Roane, Esq., held the August term of this court. Judge Williams presided at the February term, 1816, and Judge Bennett Searcy at the August term; Judge Thomas Stewart at the February term, 1817. The first murder trial on the records of this court was on February 17, 1817, and was that of John Rutledge for the killing of William Logging. Rutledge was found guilty of murder, but not as charged in the indictment. He was remanded to prison and on the next day, when brought to the bar, prayed the benefit of clergy. The sentence of the court was that " the said John Rutledge be branded on the brawn of the left thumb with the letter

M, and be imprisoned for the term of two months." He having no property the State paid the costs. At the August term, 1817, Judge Nathaniel
W. Williams presided, and probably the first case of naturalization in
the county occurred at this term—that of Alexander McClure, a native of
Ireland. At the February term, 1818, the Hon. Parry W. Humphreys presided, being commissioned by Gov. Joseph McMinn. At the August term
Hon. Thomas Stewart was judge; at the February term, 1819, Alfred M.
Harris, and also at the August term. The Hon. Parry W. Humphreys
presided at the February term, 1820, and Alfred M. Harris at the succeeding August and February terms. The Hon. Parry W. Humphreys
presided again at the August term, 1821, and at the February term, 1822.
The Hon. Robert Mack, judge of the Sixth Judicial Circuit " under authority of the act passed at the last General Assembly," presided by interchange with the Hon. Parry W. Humphreys, because of his
incompetency occasioned by his connection with some of the causes in
the court. The Hon. Parry W. Humphreys presided at the August term,
1822; the Hon. Robert Mack at the February term, 1823; the Hon. Parry
W. Humphreys at the August term, 1823, and February term, 1824; and
the Hon. Robert Mack at the August term, 1824. The Hon. Thomas
Stewart at the February term, 1825, and the Hon. Parry W. Humphreys
at the August term. The Hon. John C. Hamilton presided at the February term, 1826, by interchange with Judge Humphreys, and also at the
August term. Judge Humphreys then presided three successive terms,
and at the August term, 1828; the Hon. Joshua Haskell presided by interchange with him. Judge Humphreys then presided at the February term,
1829, and at the August term also; and at the February term, 1830, the
Hon. William F. Turley, commissioned to hold court in the Tenth Circuit, held court in the fifth by special request of Judge Humphreys.

Judge Thomas Stewart presided at the court in August, 1830; and in
February, 1831, both judges, Humphreys and John C. Hamilton, each
held a part of the time. In August, 1831, the Hon. John C. Hamilton pre-

sided, and in February, 1832, the Hon. Parry W. Humphreys, as also in August, 1832, and February, 1833. In August, 1833, the Hon. John W. Cooke presided in interchange with Judge Humphreys, who himself presided in February, 1834, and both terms in 1835. At the May term, 1836, the Hon. John W. Cooke presided in interchange with the Hon. Mortimer A. Martin, and Charles Bailey became clerk of the court at this term. In September, 1836, Judge Martin presided, and in January, 1837, the Hon. William B. Harris in interchange with Mm. At the May term, 1837, the Hon. William T. Brown presided; at the September term the Hon. Abraham Caruthers; at the May term, 1838, the Hons. James Rucks and Valentine D. Barry, each a part of the term; at the September term the Hon. Benjamin C. Totten, all in interchange with Judge Martin, who himself presided from the January term, 1839, to August 22, 1845. The Hon. Mortimer A. Martin remained judge of this court until the Ml of 1850, and presided, except as other judges took his place by interchange, as was done by the Hon. Edmund Dillahunty from November 3 to 10, 1845, and on November 3, 1846; by the Hon. William Fitzgerald in July, 1846; and by the Hon. Elijah Walker in May, 1850. In September, 1850, the Hon. Cave Johnson was judge of the circuit court a short time. The Hon. W. W. Pepper became judge in May, 1852, and remained on this circuit until his death February 1, 1861. During the illness of Judge Pepper, in 1859, Gov. Isham G. Harris appointed the Hon. N. H. Allen special judge, and again for a similar reason in January, 1861. On May 13, 1861, the Hon. Thomas W. Wisdom became judge of the circuit court and so continued until January 28, 1862, the last day the court held session before the general interim caused by the war, and on that day no business was transacted.

This court again convened the second Monday in May, 1864. The Hon. Thomas W. Wisdom was still judge, and was present and presided on this occasion. He continued to serve as judge until May 11, 1865, and soon after this, on the 20th of July, he died. On the same day the Clarks-

ville bar met and adopted resolutions of respect, in which his character
and ability were highly praised. He was succeeded on the bench of the
circuit court by Hon. John A. Campbell, who first presided January 8.
1866. The criminal court, having been abolished June 5, 1865, was now
again merged with the circuit court. Judge Campbell's term lasted until
May 10, 1869. He was succeeded by the Hon. James E. Rice, who remained judge until January 26, 1878. During his incumbency the criminal court was again separated from the circuit court. From May 10,
1878, the Hon. A. G. Goodlett was for a short time special judge, and on
the 2d of September, 1878, the Hon. Joseph C. Stark, the present judge
presided for the first time.

The criminal court was separated from the circuit court and established as an independent court by an act of the Legislature passed in
about 1847. The first session held in this county was on March 13. 1848,
the Hon. W. K. Turner having been appointed to hold a special term of
said criminal court for the county of Montgomery. There were transferred from the circuit court to this court the following cases: Assault
and battery, 16; affrays, 6; gaming, 94; horse racing, 1; felony, 13; road
overseer, 1; malicious stabbing, 1; disturbing public worship, 1; scire
facias, 13; selling liquor to a slave, 2; tippling, 6; riot, 1; perjury, 1; passing counterfeit money, 1; betting on election, 2. The first case tried was
that of the State vs. John Ripley, assault and battery, nolle prosequied,
and the second was against the same individual for passing counterfeit
money, and was disposed of in the same way. The June term commenced on the 7th of the month, and opened with the indictment of
Franklin C. Trice for killing Andrew McNichol on the 13th of July,
1845. was found guilty of murder in the second degree and sentenced to
the penitentiary for fourteen years. A new trial was, however, granted,
and he was bound over to the next term of court in the sum of $7,500.
On the 5th of February, 1850, William Emerson was sentenced to elev-
en years in the penitentiary for stealing a slave. From the 6th of October,

1851, the Hon. Cave Johnson, one of the judges of the circuit court of the State, commenced a term of this court which lasted until October 14, 1851, by special request and interchange with Judge Turner. The transactions of this court appear to have little historic interest during the first few years after its establishment. At a general election for judges and attorney-general held in the State May 25, 1854, the Hon. William K. Turner was again elected judge of this court. He was commissioned June 2, by Andrew Johnson, governor. The district was then composed of Davidson, Rutherford and Montgomery Counties. The first day of the term was June 6. The attorney-general was James M. Quarles, but Thomas W. Wisdom was appointed attorney-general pro tem in all cases in which Mr. Quarles had been employed to defend.

Tuesday, January 28, 1862, was the last day Judge Turner presided in this court. He was followed by Judge Thomas W. Wisdom, who presided January 29, 1862, and this was the last day this court was in session before the breaking up of all business in this county by the war. This court met for the first time after the war, Monday, May 22, 1865, the time appointed by law for holding the criminal court in Montgomery County. Present and presiding the Hon. J. O. Shackelford, by special request and interchange with the Hon. Theodore N. Frazier. No attorney-general being present, J. E. Rice was appointed attorney-general pro tem. This was May 24, 1865. On the next day Judge Shackelford presided in this court for the last time, and was succeeded on the second Monday in September, 1865, by the Hon. John A. Campbell, who on January 8, 1866, became also judge of the circuit court.

This court was again established by an act of the Legislature passed July 6, 1870. The first section of this act provided for the establishment of the Criminal Court of Montgomery County, and fixed its jurisdiction as co-extensive with the limits of the county. The second section of this act provided "that the said court has all the jurisdiction given to the circuits courts of the State, the trial and presentment of crimes and offenses against the State within the said county of Montgomery, to the exclusion of the circuit of said county." The third section provides for the transfer of all bills of indictment and presentment and all papers and proceedings appertaining to criminal matters. On the 7th of September. 1870, the Hon. T. W. King presented his commission as judge of this court, having been commissioned September 1, by Gov. D. W. C. Senter, and elected August 4, preceding. During Judge King's term, on February 1, 1871, the judge of the Criminal Court of Montgomery County, was authorized by the Legislature to hold circuit court in Houston, which authority lasted until March 26, 1877, when Houston County was placed back in the Tenth Judicial Circuit. Judge King's last day on the bench of this court was February 20, 1873. The Hon. James B. Rice held court by interchange with Judge King from April 28 to May 23, and the present judge, Hon. Charles W. Tyler's first term began October 6, 1873.

The most important murder trials in the history of the county occurred during Judge Tyler's term. Jim Brown (colored) was killed in 1877, for which crime Dr. Peter F. Bellamy, son-in-law of Ransom Morrow, was tried in 1878 and acquitted. Tom Sleigh was killed in 1878, and Dick Overton (colored) in August, 1883. For this last murder William and Charles Morrow, brothers, and sons of Ransom Morrow, were given preliminary trials in 1884, and Ransom Morrow and his son William had their examining trial for the killing of Jim Brown. Dr. Bellamy was again arrested and held without bail, charged with being an accessory to the murder of Brown, These arrests and charges were telegraphed all over the country, and attracted the attention of Ben Morrow, who had been living in Seneca, Kas., since the killing of Tom Sleigh in 1878. Ben wrote his father, the letter was intercepted, his hiding place thus found out, and he was brought back to Montgomery County and lodged in jail with his father, brother William (Charles Morrow having been admitted to bail), and brother in-law, Dr. Bellamy. The trial of William Morrow for the murder of Jim Brown, and of Ransom Morrow and Dr. Bellamy, as accessories, came first, Judge Charles W. Tyler on the bench. A severance being denied all three were tried together. Jim Brown, who was an old and decrepit colored man, lived with his wife about 300 yards from Dr. Bellamy's house; Dr. Bellamy wanted the house in which Brown lived, but Brown refused to move until the end of the year. While at work in the "coalings" Brown was approached by William Morrow, who asked him if he had seen any yearlings, and then told him he was going to kill him. He immediately shot Brown in the head and then in the neck, after which shot he fell. He then fired four more bullets into the fallen man's head. This was according to the testimony of James Pacaud, to whom Morrow had related the circumstances. The reason assigned for the murder was an attempted outrage on the person of the wife of Dr. Bellamy, Morrow's sister. The verdict of the jury in this case was "guilty," as to all three, and they were sentenced to imprisonment for life. An appeal was taken to the supreme court, which remanded the case to this court on account of the refusal to grant a severance. Shortly after the disposition of this case Ben Morrow was tried for the murder of Tom Sleigh, and was acquitted on the ground of self-defense. He at once returned to his family in Kansas.

Then came the trial of William, Charles and Ransom Morrow for the murder of Dick Overton in August, 1883. Dick Overton, a young negro, had been working for some time for Ransom Morrow, who owed him about $65. Of this Morrow paid $10, with which Overton bought some new clothes. A few days afterward Overton disappeared, and the Morrows said he had gone to Alabama, as he had said upon attempting to settle with Morrow that he desired to go to that State. Nothing was heard of him for eight months, or until May, 1884, when a skeleton was discovered in "Hell's Hole," a deep cavity, at the bottom of which a bold and rapid stream runs, about forty feet within Bellamy's Cave. From William Morrow's own confession it appeared that he had asked Overton to remain with his children on the day of the murder, while he and his wife went to church, but that he, pretending to be sick, returned to the house where he heard a noise, and opening the door came to the conclusion that Overton had attempted an outrage on the person of his (Morrow's) three-year old daughter. Morrow thereupon knocked him down, bound him with a rope and marched him to the mouth of Bellamy's Cave, about a mile distant, where he shot him to death. The next afternoon he and his brother Charles hurled the body down the rude slide that runs along the right side of the funnel shaped entrance to the cave, and thence down the slippery incline around the jutting rocks into "Hell's Hole." A point of the jutting rocks caught the coat on Overton's body as it hurried along on the slippery slide and held it fast until it was discovered by Deputy Sheriff Taylor, who brought it to the light of day, when it was identified by the new clothing bought just before the commission of the horrible crime. The trial of the three persons being concluded the judge instructed that as to Ransom and Charles Morrow there was no evidence of their having been accessories before the fact, and the case went to the jury as to William Morrow. Their verdict was "guilty of murder in the first degree," and Morrow was sentenced to be hanged January 30, 1885. He appealed to the supreme court, which sustained the finding of this court, and the day of execution was fixed for May 17. Gov. Bate granted a respite until June 19, 1885, on which day he was hanged. This was the first execution of a white man in Montgomery County. There had been four legal executions before this, all of colored men. Besides these legal executions there have been two cases of lynching, both of negroes. The first was just before the war, and was that of William Gray, who had murdered his employer, William Harris, an employe of a Richmond, Va., firm, who was putting up tobacco in a factory near Frice's Landing. Gray was taken out of the Clarksville jail by a number of unmasked citizens of New Providence, a jury of twelve men improvised, which found him guilty and sentenced him to death. The other case was that of Winston Anderson, an old colored man, who attempted an outrage upon the daughter of a highly respected farmer living some distance east of Clarksville. Notwithstanding the attempt failed and the flight of Anderson to Robertson, he was pursued, captured, brought back, put in the Clarksville jail, taken out by a mob of from 200 to 300 men, and hanged about two miles out on the Nashville pike. This was in 1878.

The chancery court was established in Montgomery County under an act of the Legislature passed January 24, 1840. The first session held in Montgomery County was September 21, 1840. The chancellor was the Hon. Andrew McCampbell; P. Priestly was clerk and master, and J. N. Johnson, deputy clerk. The first case before this court was that of John James and wife vs. Axum, Wallace et al. The first appeal was that of Mary P. Persons vs. Benjamin P. Persons, for divorce, the complainant taking an appeal on the pauper's oath. The first judgment rendered was in the case of Richard Browder vs. D. Hoozer. The judgment was against the complainant and Thomas Green, his security, for $154.93. The session lasted two days, on the first of which there were six cases and on the second nineteen. The first case in which a widow was allowed dower was that of Priscilla Parker vs. William Parker and Thomas Myers. The first trial by jury was March 25, 1842, in the case of Benjamin E. Orgain and Griffin Orgain vs. A. D. Ramey et al. The first chancellor, Hon. Andrew McCampbell was succeeded by the Hon. Terry H. Cahal, in April, 1846, who was chancellor until April 29, 1848, and during the next term, commencing October 28, 1848, the Hon. Bromfield L. Ridly sat by interchange with Chancellor Cahal. The Hon. A. O. P. Nicholson then, April 23, 1849, presented his commission, signed by Gov. Neill S. Brown, and served until April 28, following; Chancellor Cahal then held court from October 18, 1849, to April 26, 1850. The Hon. A. O. P. Nicholson then served from October 24, 1850, until April 26, 1851, and was then succeeded by the Hon. John S. Brien, chancellor of the middle division of Tennessee from December 15, 1851 to October

22, 1853. The Hon. Samuel D. Frierson was the chancellor from April 20, 1854, to April 21, 1860, and was succeeded by the Hon. Joseph C. Guild, who served from October 15, 1860, to October 21, 1861. There was then no chancery court until after the war, and then the Hon. J. O. Shackelford, who was commissioned by Gov. Brownlow for the Seventh Chancery Division, held court commencing April 15, 1865. On that day the Clarksville bar held a meeting in the chancery court room and adopted a series of resolutions expressive of their feelings of profound sorrow for the death of Abraham Lincoln. The Hon. Thomas Barry was chancellor from October 16, 1865, to December 3, 1867. The Hon. J. F. Lauck was commissioned chancellor by Gov. Brownlow, and held court one day, April 20, 1868. His election was contested and set aside and a new election ordered, and the Hon. J. O. Shackelford of the Thirteenth Chancery Division held court from October 23, 1868, to November 10, following. The Hon. Charles G. Smith was elected in August, 1869, and was chancellor until December 7, 1874, when he resigned, having been re-elected in the meantime, February 27, 1871. He was succeeded by the Hon. Horace H. Lurton, who was appointed by the governor and held his first day's session April 27, 1875, and served until August 6, 1877, when he resigned. Hon. B. J. Tarber was appointed by Gov. Porter January 3, 1878, and held his first session February 4, and served until July 19, 1878. He was followed by the present chancellor, the Hon. George E. Seay, who was commissioned September 1, 1878, and held his first term of court commencing February 10, 1879.

The first clerk and master, P. Priestley, served until May 1, 1852, on which day he was succeeded by Thomas J. Mumford, who served until October 19, 1865. William T. Shackelford became clerk and master on that day and was succeeded by the present incumbent, Polk G. Johnson, who was first appointed by the Hon. Charles G. Smith, July 8, 1870. He was reappointed February 27, 1871, by Chancellor Smith, and again on the 6th of August, 1877, for six years, by Chancellor Tarber, and for the fourth time on the 21st of February, 1883, by the present chancellor. The deputy clerks have been as follows: J. N. Johnson, appointed September 21, 1840; Lafayette Priestley, March 25, 1842; O. C. Smith, January 11, 1871; C. W. Crozier, September 1, 1879, and A. B. Gholson, August 1, 1885.

The principal lawsuit to which Montgomery County has ever been a party is known as W. C. McClure et al. vs. the Louisville & Nashville Railroad Company and County of Montgomery, and was brought in the chancery court at Nashville, at the October term in 1875. This suit arose out of the sale by the State of Tennessee of the Memphis, Clarksville & Louisville Railroad to the Louisville & Nashville Railroad Company in 1871, for $1,700,000. McClure, as receiver for the Bank of Memphis, had received a judgment in the circuit court of Montgomery County against the Memphis, Clarksville & Louisville Railroad Company for $75,680.30 and costs $15.35. Other plaintiffs to this suit had received judgments in the same circuit court against the same railroad company for various amounts aggregating $27,871.27, and costs aggregating $80.34. Executions had been issued in each case, and in each case returned by the sheriff nulla bona, there being no property found in the county out of which to make the money. These various parties, therefore, after the sale of the railroad, brought suit to have the sale set aside, claiming that the decree for the sale was a decree for the State's debt against the road and that alone; not authorizing a sale of the road, road bed, rolling stock or franchises, but simply the mortgage debt of the State; and charging that when the pretended sale was effected, it was by a private agreement between the contracting parties of the two roads that the said Louisville & Nashville Railroad Company should not buy the debt of the State but the road itself, and that when they did buy they would buy the stock of Montgomery County and Clarksville; and that a compromise had been effected with the second mortgage bond holders by which they were to remain neutral, and to receive for their neutrality

$500,000, of which they were to pay to Montgomery County $250,000, and to Clarksville $100,000, and the balance was to go to the second mortgage bond holders. Numerous other charges were made, the substance of all being that the plaintiffs as creditors of the Memphis, Clarksville & Louisville Railroad Company had been defrauded out of their just claims against said company. With reference to the position in which it was sought to place Montgomery County as to the above mentioned judgment claims, the following extract is sufficient to set it forth: "Your orators further insist that the said County of Montgomery, having received $250,000 for the assets of the said Memphis, Clarksville & Louisville Railroad, is bound for the payment of the debts of the creditors of said road to the amount they have received for their stock, and that they have also the right to recover the stock of the Louisville & Nashville Railroad transferred to them in part payment for their stock in the said Memphis, Clarksville & Louisville Railroad, which is in effect the assets of said railroad." Having considered all the premises, the plaintiffs petitioned the court that the Louisville & Nashville Railroad Company, and the Memphis, Clarksville & Louisville Railroad Company be made parties defendant to the suit; that Robert Meek, D. N. Kennedy, W. A. Quarles and John F. House be made parties defendant, and that the county of Montgomery, or its justices of the peace, be also made parties defendant, and that the said county of Montgomery be held liable for the payment of the debts against the said Memphis, Clarksville & Louisyille Railroad to the amount of money received or to be received from the Louisville & Nashville Railroad Company.

The answer of the Louisville & Nashville Railroad Company to the above allegations and petitions was filed October 2, 1875; that of J. E. Bailey, John F. House, W. A. Quarles, W. M. Daniel, H. H. Lurton, B. W. McCrae and others October 20, and that of Montgomery County, also, on October 20, 1875, and the answer of Clarksville to the amended and supplemental bill, October 23, 1875. January 3, 1876, the Hon. William F. Cooper, chancellor, before whom the case was tried, decreed that the complainants had wholly failed to establish a state of facts which implicated the defendants in any fraudulent combination to their injury, or any fraudulent combination whatever, or which gives them any claim whatever upon the Louisville & Nashville Railroad Company, or upon any one of the defendants individually by reason of fraud. It was also the opinion of the court that Montgomery County and the city of Clarksville had only offered to sell their stock in the Memphis, Clarksville & Louisville Railroad, which they had a right to sell, and which the Louisville & Nashville Railroad Company had a right to buy; hence the creditors of the former road had not been aggrieved by what had been done by the defendants, and hence that so much of said bills as sought a decree against any of the defendants, or to subject the $300,000 paid or agreed to be paid by the Louisville & Nashville Railroad Company to Montgomery County and Clarksville under the contract of July 18, 1871, be dismissed with costs.

All the Baptist churches in this part of Tennessee compare the date of their origin with that of the Red River Baptist Church, organized near the line of Montgomery County, in Robertson County, in 1791. The first Baptist church organized in Montgomery County was the Spring Creek Church, in 1808. Their meeting-house was near Spring Creek, a tributary of the West Fork of Red River, a short distance south of the Kentucky State line. Among the first members of this church were Barbara Barker, Mary Meriwether and Mary D. Barker. The meetinghouse was built of large poplar logs with spaces between them. In summer time it was airy and pleasant, but in winter time it was bleak and cold enough. It was erected in 1804, and on Saturday, October 3, 1807, it was, on motion, "ordered that there be a chimney erected to this meetinghouse." This church until this time was a branch of the old Red River Church or Fort Meeting-house Church, as it was originally called, and when this branch desired to be fully constituted into an independent body, Elders Jesse Brooks, Josiah Horn, Josiah Fort and others were sent there as a presbytery, and effected the desired organization. This was on Saturday, April 2, 1808. In the following June it was named "Spring Creek Church of the West Fork," and on the same day the newly organized and named body petitioned for admission into the Red River Association. On Saturday before the first Sunday in November, 1809, Elder Reuben Ross was invited to become pastor, and on Saturday before the first Sunday in March, 1810, Elder Ross accepted the invitation and labored in this connection about twenty-nine years. In the pulpit of this church were also seen and heard all the distinguished Baptist divines who did not live too far away. Elder Moore was often there, and took great delight in dealing ceaseless warfare against Arminianism. Elders Todevine, Fort and Brooks were also there as occasion seemed to require. Elder Isaac Hodgen preached there a memorable sermon from the text "If any man love not the Lord Jesus Christ let him be anathema maranatha."

It is not remembered when the first Baptist preacher visited Clarksville, but it was at a very early day, and Elder Reuben Ross was at least one of the first, preaching for the most part in private houses. The Baptists had so increased in Clarksville by 1831 that it was decided to organize a church. The order for this organization was made by the Spring Creek Church in July, 1831, upon the petition of Isham Watkins, Jesse Ely, William Killebrew, Joshua Brown and others, the Clarksville Church having been, previous to this time, a branch of the Spring Creek Church. In 1841 there were forty-one members of the Clarksville Baptist Church. Up to this time Elder Reuben Ross had been the pastor, visiting the congregation monthly, according to the custom in those times. He was succeeded by the Rev. William Shelton. Soon afterward Rev. Mr. Shelton was succeeded by the Rev. Joseph Manton, and he by the Rev. Mr. Duncan, who continued his pastorate until the breaking out of the civil war, by which the church and congregation suffered greatly.

During the war the Rev. W. G. Inman preached to the congregation twice each month, but he had great difficulty in keeping the members together. In 1866 the Rev. Dr. A. D. Sears accepted the care of the church. In 1847 there were 61 members in the church, and in 1855, 81; but at the beginning of the pastorate of Dr. Sears, there were but 25. This small body possessed very limited means, and only three-fifths of them were animated with proper religious activity. It became necessary in order that the church might have a proper start in the great work contemplated, that a reorganization should be effected. This was accomplished at the church meeting Saturday, September 1, 1866. From the organization of the church in 1831, colored persons professing faith in Christ and being immersed were received into fellowship as members. Up to the war they had increased even more rapidly than the white members. During or immediately after the war they organized themselves into an independent church, and since the reorganization of the first church no colored members have been admitted. They, however, have been signally successful in establishing and sustaining church organizations of their own, having now (1886) four separate churches, with about 1,200 members, and constituting nearly two-thirds of all the colored Christians of Clarksville.

After the reorganization of the first church it entered upon a career of slow but solid and permanent prosperity. It regularly contributes to all the leading benevolent objects of Southern Baptists, and has a Sunday-school well conducted and numbering 120 members. The church at this time has 211 members. In the spring of 1867, when there were but 100 members, the enterprise of erecting a new church edifice was entered upon, the building to cost $25,000. This enterprise was successfully carried forward to completion, with the exception of the spire, which has not yet been erected. The church stands on the corner of Madison and Fourth Streets. The present pastor, Rev. A. D. Sears, has been with the church for twenty years, during which time fifty members of the body have died.

Methodism has materially assisted in the growth of Christianity in this county. The circuit rider in early days carried the gospel to every neighborhood. For many years services were conducted in private houses, afterward in small log or frame "meeting-houses." Camp-meetings were wonderfully efficient in those days in promoting the Evangelistic work of the church. The old camp-grounds at Antioch, White Bluff and Clarksville are well remembered by many Methodists still living. Previous to the completion of the brick court house, in 1811, Clarksville had no place set apart for public worship. From that time to about 1830, this court house was used by any and all denominations. If tradition is reliable there were some pretty hard cases in Montgomery County in early days. James Ross in his exceedingly entertaining "Life and Times of Elder Reuben Ross," relates an incident which is confirmative of the above statement. It was in this court house "that Parson N., a good old Methodist brother, had his feelings so much outraged. While describing the lower regions in the most dismal colors, and exhorting his hearers in the most earnest and affectionate manner to repent of their sins and reform their lives in order to escape it, a half-drunken fellow arose and said, 'Parson, I don't think there is any such place as that, or somebody would have heard of it before.' This sounded so droll and was so unexpected that the audience could not help laughing. The Parson soon brought his remarks to a close, and as he passed the door he was observed to move his feet slightly, as if to shake the dust from them, and never preached there again, but left them to be convinced when too late that there is such a place, or ought to be."

The exact date of the organization of "Clarksville Station," is not now remembered but it was at a very early date. The first Methodist Church building, however, was erected in 1831. This was occupied by them until

1841. The first sermon preached therein was in 1832 by the Rev. John B. McFerrin, D. D. In the year last named this church edifice was sold to the Cumberland Presbyterian Church, and another was erected by the Methodists on the corner of Franklin and Fifth Streets, which, like the first one, was sold to the Cumberland Presbyterians in 1882. On Tuesday, September 26, 1882, they laid the corner-stone of their present elegant and substantial brick church on Madison Street, which is now nearly completed. It is in the Gothic style of architecture, with Corinthian columns on the sides of entrance; has two towers—one 145, the other 120 feet high. The roof is supported by iron bridge-trusses, and the main audience room is 76 feet by 51 feet 6 inches in size, having a capacity of seating about 600 persons. It is one of the most complete and elegant church buildings in the State.

Since 1841 the pastors have been as follows: Rev. E. Hatcher, appointed November, 1841; John W. Hammer, November, 1842; Milton Ramey, November, 1843, but remained only a short time, and Joseph E. Douglas, appointed to fill the vacancy; Joseph B. Walker appointed November, 1844; Adam S. Riggs, November, 1845; Alexander R. Erwin, November, 1846; Lewis C. Bryan, November, 1847; Samuel D. Baldwin, October, 1848; Thomas Maddin, October, 1850; Thomas W. Handle, October, 1852; Alexander R. Erwin, October, 1854; A. Mizell, October, 1855; Joseph B. West, October, 1857; W. D. F. Sawrie, October, 1859; W. G. Dorris, October, 1861; R. S. Hunter, October, 1865; Wellborn Mooney, October, 1866; J. R. Plummer, October, 1868; J. P. McFerrin, October, 1870; W. M. Green, October, 1873; J. R. Plummer, 1874; R. K. Brown, 1875; James D. Barhee, 1879; T. J. Moody, 1883; W. R. Peebles, present pastor, 1885.

Montgomery County is well supplied with Methodist Churches, there being twenty-seven organizations of this denomination, with 2,716 communicants. They have twenty-seven church edifices with

5,700 sittings, and the value of the property is $53,500. There are, in the county, 1,235 Sunday-school scholars of this denomination. Prior to the late civil war this church labored extensively among the negro slaves and large numbers were enrolled as its communicants. Since the war the colored people have organized churches of their own, which are served by ministers of their own color. Of these there are in Clarksville the following: Clarksville African Methodist Episcopal, located on Franklin Street near College Avenue; Saint Peter's Chapel African Methodist Episcopal, on Franklin Street near Fourth Street; Zion African Methodist Episcopal, on Commerce Street near Fourth.

The first preaching for what afterward became the Clarksville Presbyterian Church was by Dr. Gideon Blackburn, an eloquent divine. While he was himself a Presbyterian his hearers were of all denominations. His sermons were ordinarily three hours long, and extraordinarily four hours; but his eloquence was so thrilling that no one left and no one went to sleep. This was in 1822. On the 25th of May, of this year, fourteen persons were constituted the Presbyterian Church of Clarksville. The moderator of this meeting was Rev. Lyman Whitney, of Connecticut; and on the same day two members, upon examination, were received into the newly organized church—John Patton and Ann Maria Patillo. Five months afterward the Rev. Mr. Blackburn returned to see this church, administered the sacrament, witnessed the admission of eight new members and went his way, never to return. The church, however, grew and prospered, holding meetings in private houses, in Masonic Hall, but most frequently in the court house. It had no regular minister. Ministers from other places made it occasional visits. After 1835 preaching became more regular. The Rev. Consider Parish, Rev. William A. Shaw and Rev. A. W. Kilpatriek were among those who preached before 1840, in which year Rev. Mr. Shaw was appointed stated supply. In 1885 a subscription had been raised for the building of a house of worship, but it was not built until 1840. It stood on the site of the present building, on the northwest corner of Main and Third Streets. The first pastor in the new church was Rev. Andrew H. Kerr, who received a salary of $800 per year. He was succeeded in 1846 by the Rev. John T. Hendrick, who remained until dismissed to Paducah, Ky., in 1858, by the Nashville Presbytery. Dr. T. D. Wardlaw and Dr. D. O. Davies then ministered to the church until the calling of the present pastor, Rev. J. W. Lupton, from Virginia, in 1872. At the time he began his labors, September 1, 1872, there were 165 members. In 1877 the old gray church was removed and the present spacious and elegant building erected. The corner-stone was laid May 19, 1876, and the finished building was dedicated by Dr. Palmer, of New Orleans, May 26, 1878. It is of pressed brick, with white stone trimmings; interior beautifully finished and furnished, and it contains a fine full-toned organ. The cost of this edifice was $43,000; and when it was dedicated the society was out of debt. Since September 1, 1872, 372 new members have been added, the membership at present being about 340.

There are four missions connected with this church, one of which is the Colored Presbyterian Church, which sprang out of a Sunday-school started about twelve years since, by Profs. Dinwiddie and Coffman, of the university. A church has been erected for this body at a cost of about $650. There is also a church building at Macedonia, which cost, exclusive of gifts of ground and labor, $500; and there is a prospect of each of the other missions having a house of worship built in the spring of 1886. During the pastorate of the Rev. Mr. Lupton the Presbyterian Church of Clarksville has raised for all purposes $110,000.

The McAdoo Presbyterian Church was organized in 1807 or 1808, by the Rev. Finis Ewing, as an Old School Presbyterian Church. Its first elders were James Hutchison, William Morrow and William and Wylie Hogan. Regular annual camp-meetings were kept up for many years. In 1810, when the Cumberland Presbyterian Church was organized, it was placed under the care of Anderson Presbytery, of that church, and its first pastor after this change of relation was the Rev. Mr. Bonds, who served several years. His successors were the Revs. Mr. Daniel, D. Stephens, William Casky, J. C. Provine, James Frazier, A. H. Berry, H. L. Burney (the latter pastor entering upon his duties in 1856 and remaining until 1874), J. N. McDonald, J. M. Martin and the present pastor, Rev. Mr. Welburn. The present membership is about 140.

The Bethel Church, located four miles distant, is an outgrowth of this church. Besides these two there are, in the county, Liberty, Shiloh, White Chapel and Clarksville Cumberland Presbyterian Churches. The latter church was organized about the year 1843, by the Rev. Elijah Knight, and a house of worship was built on the corner of Main and Third Streets, which continued to be used until 1882, when it was sold to Dr. Hendricks, who converted it into a residence. The old Methodist house and lot, on Franklin and Fifth Streets, were then purchased and are now used for religious purposes. The present membership of the church is fifty-seven, and the pastor is the Rev. D. A. Brigham. The property is worth about $6,000, the value of the other church buildings in the county being as follows: McAdoo, $2,000; Bethel, $2,000; Liberty, $1,500; Shiloh, $500, and White Chapel, $300. About 1830 the first Catholic priest visited this place in the person of Father Allemany, late Archbishop of California. The first church building was erected in 1844 on College Street, between Fourth and Fifth, by Rev. Father Schat, who was succeeded by Rev. L. Orengo, Rev. Louis Hoste, Rev. Father Marshall, Rev. Father A. I. Ryan, well known as the "Poet-Priest of the South," Rev. Father Repis, Rev. Father Thoma, Rev. Father Molloy, Rev. P. Ryan, Rev. Father O'Brien and Rev. P. J. Gleeson, under whom the church property on Franklin Street was purchased in 1876, and a new church erected in 1880, at a total cost of $15,000. A Sisters' school by the name of St. Aloysius, was established and is under the care of the Sisters of Nazareth. The congregation aggregates about sixty families and the school attendance averages fifty pupils. The present pastor is the Rev Father Vaghie. The oldest Catholic families resident in Clarksville are those of Mr. Dunlavy and Mr. Boylan.

Trinity Episcopal Church, Clarksville, was organized as a parish in 1831, with a few members. Occasional services were held by Rev. Norman Nash, and afterward by Rev. George R. Gildings, of Hopkinsville, Ky. The Rev. Albert A. Muller was called by the vestry as first rector, September 11, 1833, and on September 10, 1834, the foundation of the first church building was laid. As this building approached completion the walls were found to be unsafe, and had to be taken down and re-erected. Thomas W. Frazier had this work done at his own expense, and also built the parsonage which still stands adjoining the church. The church edifice was consecrated June 23, 1838, by the Rt. Rev. James H. Otey, bishop of this diocese, assisted by the Rev. Leonidas Polk, of Columbia, Tenn. The Rev. Mr. Polk was afterward bishop of Louisiana, and during the civil war was lieutenant-general in the Confederate Army and was killed at the battle of Pine Mountain, Ga.

Dr. Muller resigned August 20, 1841, and Rev. Edward Cressy was called December 14, following. The Rev. Mr. Cressy resigned April 1, 1845, and during the same month the Rev. William C. Crane succeeded to the rectorship. The Rev. Mr. Crane remained until Easter Sunday, 1850, when he resigned to accept a call to Jackson, Miss. The Rev. William Pise was rector from November, 1850, to January, 1853; and on the first Sunday in November following he was succeeded by the Rev. Joseph James Ridley, who remained until June 25, 1860, when he resigned on account of having been elected president of the East Tennessee University at Knoxville. The Rev. Mr. Cannon was then rector for a short time, and during the civil war the parish was for most of the time without a rector. The Rev. Samuel Ringgold who had officiated as often as he could, was chosen rector in October, 1864, and on November 3 entered upon his duties. He remained the zealous rector of the parish nearly ten years, confirming during that time 231 persons. His resignation occurred July 31, 1874, and he was succeeded, November 1, 1875, by the Rev. Philip A. Fitts, of Birmingham, Ala., the present rector. In 1875 the old church was taken down, and on June 30, 1875, the cornerstone of the present edifice was laid. The building stands on Franklin Street, just east of Third, and is one of the finest ornaments to the city. The material of which it is constructed was obtained from the natural formation of blue limestone which is found in the vicinity of the city, near the mouth of Red River, and the trimming stone from the Bowling Green quarries. The edifice is of the Gothic style of architecture, is 106 feet long, and is a substantial and elegant structure. Its spire is surmounted by a cross 160 feet above the ground. Its cost, exclusive of the organ, was $41,474.18, including the stone from the old church, valued at $2,000. The beautiful organ in this church was awarded the first premium for excellence of tone at the Centennial Exposition in 1876. The church was consecrated December 1, 1881, by the bishop of Alabama. Connected with Trinity Church are two missions, White Chapel, located in District No. 1, and St. Andrew's, in South Clarksville, both of which have been in existence about ten years, and are now in a prosperous condition. Edward Boss was commissioned deacon of White Chapel in December, 1885.

The Christian Church at Clarksville was organized in December, 1842, when W. F. Fall and wife, Leolin Edding and wife, F. B. Everett and wife, John Thurston, Caroline Barker, Mrs. Black, Henrietta Fall, Mary A. Kinney and Amelia Love met and resolved to take the Bible as their only rule of faith and practice. Having no meeting-house they met at various private residences each Sunday for worship, and for some time occupied a schoolhouse on Main Street, and then a small house standing where the residence of B. D. Moseley now stands on Madison Street They were visited occasionally by such preachers as John T. Johnson, Jesse Ferguson, John Ferguson, C. M. Day, Henry T. Anderson, T.

Fanning and others, on which occasion meetings were held at the court house, or at the Masonic Hall. In 1851 the number of members had so increased that a church building became necessary, and to this end a lot was secured on the corner of Third and Madison Streets, upon which the present church edifice was erected, in which Elder John Ferguson and others preached occasionally. In 1858 Elder W. C. Bodgers was called as resident preacher and remained until 1861. During the war the organization was maintained and regular worship held, A. L. Johnson preaching occasionally. In 1866 Elder J. E. Myles was called and remained their preacher until his death in 1871. Since that time Elders E. B.———, J. M. Streator, W. A. Broadhurst, I. J. Spencer, N. R. Dall and W. T. Donaldson the present pastor, have served the church in the order named. During the past few years the membership has been much reduced by removals and deaths until at present the membership is but 175. From this church at Clarksville the churches at New Providence and South Clarksville are supplied.

Besides these churches there is a Christian Church at Oakwood established some years before the war, which has a neat frame edifice costing about $1,200. There is also one at Oakland started in about 1860, the edifice costing about $1,000, and one at Hazlewood which cost about the same amount. There is also a number of Christians who attend the church of their denomination at Guthrie, Ky.

Before the war all the schools in the county were private institutions. One of the first, of a grade higher than primary, that was established was a "Classical and Mathematical Academy" which opened January 1, 1834, by the Rev. C. Parish, A. M., "late Professor of Languages in Nashville University." This school under different instructors has been continued until the present time, taking the name some years later of the Clarksville Female Academy. Some years after the establishment of this academy by Rev. Mr. Parish, Clarksville Male Academy was started and continued until the war. There were other private schools for scholars not qualified to enter either of these academies. After the war this system of education was continued until the establishment of the common school system.

In 1873 the following persons were teaching private schools in Clarksville: Mrs. Lizzie Bibb, Miss Sallie Howard, Mrs. Rufus Rhodes, Mrs. William Mooney and Mrs. Sallie Ely, and the Female Academy was also in session. Other schools were also in existence in different parts of the county as necessity required and ability permitted. Since the common school system has been in existence the number of such schools throughout the county has steadily increased until at the present time there are about seventy-five. The schoolhouses have been gradually improved and better adapted to the purposes for which they are used. The opposition which they at first encountered has practically ceased to exist, and now the people are giving attention to the selection of good men to the office of school directors, and in this way showing their appreciation of their advantages, and their determination to obtain from them what advantages they may possess. The attention of the directors is more and more being directed toward securing well qualified teachers, and to the establishment of graded schools. The financial condition of the schools is good, the fund being about $20,000.

One feature of the school system in this as well as other counties in this State is remarkable. After the passage of the "Four Mile Act," in 1875, prohibiting the sale of intoxicating liquors within four miles of any incorporated institution of learning; the people of Montgomery County availed themselves of the powers conferred upon them by this act to abolish saloons, by incorporating several "institutions of learning." The first of these was "St. Bethlehem Male and Female Academy," incorporated April 20, 1881; then followed "Palmyra Schoolhouse," incorporated July 11, 1883; "Base-Ball Hill Schoolhouse," November 30, 1883;

"Forest Hill Seminary," May 30, 1884, and "Oak Hill Male and Female Academy," October 27, 1884.

Although these five are the only institutions of learning thus far incorported the effect is the same as though the entire seventy-five commons were thus established, for under the law the power to incorporate is always present, and no man desiring to start a saloon is willing to pay $450 for a license and run the risk of having a school incorporated within the limit of four miles, and thus be compelled to abandon his saloon enterprise and lose his license fee.

The Clarksville public schools were graded in 1877, but not without considerable opposition on the part of a portion of the citizens. The first superintendent under this graded system was John C. Brooks. His first annual report showed an enrollment of 277 white children and 239 blacks. In the Twelfth District, outside the city, there were 50 white children enrolled and 106 blacks. The principal of the colored school during a part of the first year was J. W. Jackson, and the remainder of the year J. W. White. The schools were divided into nine grades, included in the primary, intermediate, grammar and high school departments. Two buildings were provided, one for white scholars and one for black, both on Franklin Street; the first named the Howell School Building, after A. Howell, between Fifth and Sixth Streets, and the latter at the limit of the corporation. The superintendent for the next three succeeding year was E. Perkins. J. W. White was the principal of the colored school for the years 1878-79, and H. S. Merry, 1880-81. At the end of the year 1880-81, the superintendent's report showed an enrollment of 377 white children, and 470 blacks. H. C. Weber was superintendent of the schools. His report showed an enumeration of 2,154 school children in the district, and an enrollment of 1,075—whites, 503; blacks, 572. For the year ending in 1884 the enrollment was in the Howell School 532, and in the colored school 661. The former had then been classified into ten grades, in the highest grade there being 7 scholars enrolled, while in the colored school there were only eight grades the number of scholars in the highest grade being 5. The report of the superintendent for 1884-85 showed an enrollment of 1,218, both white and colored. This was in the entire school district which is co-extensive with Civil District No. 12. This report also gave the scholastic population of Clarksville as 602 whites, and 505 for 1885; for the district outside the city, whites, 387; blacks, 638; making a total of 2,152. The value of the school property is as follows: Houses, $18,000; lots, $6,000; furniture $1,659; total, $25,659. J. W. Graham is the present superintendent, and C. M. Watson principal of the colored school.

The Southwestern Presbyterian University had its inception in 1848, in which year the Masonic Grand Lodge of the State of Tennessee determined to establish a first-class institution of learning in the town of Clarksville. The Masonic fraternity of Montgomery County united to erect a suitable edifice, and obtained from non-Masonic friends munificent donations to aid them in the enterprise. The college was organized January 5, 1849, and went into operation January 8, following. The building was erected in 1849, but before it was fully completed the Grand Lodge of Tennessee directed the appropriation made for the support of this college at its establishment into an entirely different channel, thereby crippling the institution in the very beginning. The Masonic bodies of Clarksville, in order to prevent further dissension in the Grand Lodge, asked that the connection between the college and the Grand Lodge be dissolved and determined themselves to carry out the original design of establishing a Masonic institution and thus keep faith with the donors, and the lodges of Montgomery County borrowed $6,000 to complete the building. The institution, therefore, was carried on from 1851 to 1855 under the auspices of the Masons of Montgomery County and was known as the Montgomery Masonic College. Its presidents during that time were W. T. Hopkins, T. M. Newell, W. A. Forbes and W. M. Stewart.

In 1855 it became evident that the institution could not succeed unless its debts were liquidated. On October 12, that year, the Synod of Nashville (Presbyterian), held a meeting at Florence, Ala., at which the transfer of the college to that synod was discussed and finally determined upon. A board of trustees was appointed, consisting of W. M. Stewart, John Stacker, W. B. Munford, Bryce Stewart, J. E. Bailey, A. Robb, W. P. Hume, John McKeage, C. R. Cooper, D. N. Kennedy, T. J. Pritchett, J. T. Hendrick, D. D., R. A. Lapsley, D. D., W. H. Mitchell, D. D., R. B. McMullen, D. D., and Duncan Brown, D. D., to receive the deed when executed and to take charge of and manage the college.

In consequence of the munificent donations of William M. Stewart, of his long continued and disinterested services, of his ardent and untiring devotion to science and of his high moral and Christian character, the college was named in his honor "Stewart College." In the transfer when finally made certain of, the trustees bound themselves by signing an obligation February 5, 1856, to pay $7,000 of the indebtedness of the institution, provided the Synod of Nashville would pay $5,000. These trustees were as follows: John McKeage, D. N. Kennedy, Bryce Stewart, W. P. Hume, A. Robb, W. B. Munford, T. J. Pritehett and J. E. Bailey. W. M. Stewart's name does not appear on the minutes as one of the obligators, but nevertheless he was one of them in fact. The faculty was reorganized under W. M. Stewart as president, and the institution conducted by the board of trustees appointed by the Synod of Nashville, and named above. In 1858 he was succeeded as president by Rev. R. B. McMullen, D. D., in the meantime, however, continuing his labors as professor of natural sciences. The school was progressing in funds, patronage and appliances for teaching when the civil war came on and caused a cessation of its work. At this time Dr. McMullen was conducting it under a special arrangement with the board of trustees. His second session under this arrangement commenced January 20, 1862, holding his session in the Presbyterian Church, the college building being used as a hospital for the Confederate soldiers. A few weeks only of the session had passed when Fort Donelson capitulated and Clarksville was occupied by the Federal soldiers. Upon their arrival in the city the Confederate soldiers were removed from the college and the building was used by them for a similar purpose. They thus occupied it about a month, leaving March 25. In April the Seventy-first Ohio Volunteer Infantry took possession of the building and occupied it as barracks until August 18, 1862. By them the work of demolition of library apparatus, furniture and cabinet was made complete, and of the building itself nothing was left but the bare walls and floors.

After the war a private school was taught about two years within the building, and in 1868-70 the work of putting the building in repair was completed at a cost of $8,000. In the meantime on June 15, 1869, a competent corps of professors was elected as follows: W. M. Stewart, professor of natural science; Rev. D. O. N. Davies, professor of logic, rhetoric and belles lettres, and D. M. Quarles, principal of preparatory department. After failures in other directions to elect a president, at length on August 25, 1869, Rev. J. B. Shearer, D. D., was elected to that position. Under this arrangement the institution prospered until 1873. For some time leading Presbyterian thinkers of the Southwest had been cherishing the idea of a great Presbyterian University, and it became evident that such an institution must be in a certain sense local. In furtherance of this idea active negotiations began among the synods of the Southwest, and a meeting was held in May, 1873, at Memphis, consisting of commissioners from the synods of Alabama, Mississippi, Arkansas, Nashville and Memphis. At this meeting a plan of union was adopted under which the university, when established, should be conducted. The plan set forth among other things that

The object and scope of the institution shall be not only to train our youth to enter upon one of the learned professions, but also to fit them for the ordinary vocations of life.

To this end it shall be a university in two senses: first, it shall offer the largest facilities for thorough culture and for a high standard of graduation; and second, the organization shall be made on the plan of separate and co-ordinate schools and elective courses.

There were numerous competitive locations for the university, the principal among them, besides Clarksville being Jackson, Tenn., and Huntsville, Ala. In many cases the propositions were extremely liberal, but after a careful examination of all, the board, in May, 1874, decided upon Ciarksville, which city gave $50,000, besides $15,000 toward the erection of the "Stewart Cabinet Building." The faculty of Stewart College was continued provisionally, and the school conducted on the same scale as before. In June, 1879, the board of directors abolished the curriculum and reorganized the institution on the plan given above. Rev. J. N. Waddel, D. D., LL. D., was elected chancellor and professor of philosophy; James Dinwiddie, professor of mathematics; John W. Caldwell, professor of natural science; Samuel J. Coffman, of modern languages; and Rev. J. B. Shearer, of history, English literature and rhetoric. The name was changed to the Southwestern Presbyterian University. The university is now under the care of six synods, that of Texas having been added to the original number. Thirteen schools are provided in the departments of sciences, literature and the arts. There is a special endowment known as the McComb professorship of $30,000, named after the endower, J. J. McComb, of "cotton tie" fame. Besides this the general endowment fund consists of $110,412.22. The university has twenty-four acres of land well situated for grounds and college buildings, ample for class-room purposes for a large attendance of students, of whom there are at present (January, 1886) 106 in attendance. The present faculty is as follows: John N. Waddel, D. D., LL. D., chancellor and professor of philosophy; Rev. J. B. Shearer, D. D., professor of Biblical instruction, S. J. Coffman, A. M., professor of modern languages; James A. Lyon, Ph. D., Stewart professor of natural science; E. B. Massie, A. M., professor of mathematics; G. F. Nicholassen, A. M., Ph. D., professor of ancient languages; Rev. Robert Price, D. D., professor of history, English literature and rhetoric; N. Smylie, assistant instructor; Rev. J. R. Wilson, D. D., professor of theology and homiletics; Rev. J. W. Lupton, D. D., professor of practical theology.

Clarksville, the county seat of Montgomery County, is usually described as being situated on the north bank of the Cumberland River. Generally speaking this is correct, as the city is on the north side of that river, but strictly speaking, the city is on the east bank of the river because the river runs in a northerly direction as it passes that city. The east bank of the river at this point is in several places seventy-five or eighty feet above the usual level of the water. These several places are seven in number and hence Clarksville is said to be seated on her "seven hills." Six hundred and forty acres of land were included in the grant from North Carolina to John Montgomery and Martin Armstrong "upon the consideration of the payment of £10 for every 100 acres of land hereby granted." This tract of land contained 640 acres and was described as "lying and being within the county of Davidson on the north side of the Cumberland River at the mouth of the Red River, running thence up the Cumberland according to its meanders to a hickory on the bank: east 217 poles to a poplar and dogwood; north 350 poles to a hickory on the bank of Red River, and down the same according to its meanders to the mouth." This grant was signed by Richard Caswell, governor captain-general and commander-in-chief at Kingston, N. G, September 22, 1784, agreeable to a warrant, No. 147. This entry was made January 16, 1784. "I have surveyed for John Montgomery and Martin Armstrong 640 acres of land described in the above grant."

This survey was made in the fall of 1784, and Martin Armstrong drew the plan of the town. Lots were soon sold and the purchasers desiring that a town should be established by legislative authority, the General Assembly of North Carolina, in accordance with their wishes, in November, 1785, enacted "that 200 acres of land lying in the fork of Cumberland River and Red River, on the east side thereof, belonging to John Montgomery and Martin Armstrong, who have signified their consent for this purpose, be established a town and a town common, agreeable to a plan laid off by the said Martin Armstrong, Esq., by the name of Clarksville." By this act John Montgomery, Anthony Bledsoe, Anthony Crutcher, William Polk and Lardner Clark were appointed commissioners. The name Clarksville was conferred upon the new town in honor of Gen. George Rogers Clark, a distinguished officer, known to all early pioneers. At that time the principal inhabitants of Clarksville were John Montgomery, Anthony and William Crutcher, Amos Bird, George Bell, Robert Nelson and Æneas McCallister.

On the 19th of October, 1790, John Montgomery, Lardner Clark and Anthony Crutcher sold to James Adams Lot No. 18, containing half an acre of land for £10. Some time in 1791, John Boyd bought Lot No. 71 for £10. On September 20, 1791, Phebe McClure bought Lot No. 16 for £10. On October 19, 1791, Robert Dennehy bought Lot No. 2, containing three acres for £10 and also one "out-lot," containing three acres, also for £10. Mr. Dennehy also bought Lots No. 3 and 4, each containing three acres, giving £10 for each lot. On the 17th of November, George Bell sold to James Adams Lot No. 18, containing one-half acre for £10, and on January 18, 1792, Martha Curtis bought Lot No, 51, also paying £10. On the 18th of April, 1792, John Montgomery, Anthony Crutcher and Robert Nelson "of the county of Tennessee, and Territory of the United States south of the river Ohio," sold to Elijah Robertson, "of the county of Davidson" Lot No. 80 for £10, and on March 18, 1793, George and William Briscoe "of the county of Tennessee, and Territory of the

United States south of the river Ohio," sold to Rober Dunning of the same county and Territory for £40, one lot No. 53, containing one-half acre of land. Though not within the limits of the town another sale of land is here added. On April 17, 1793, John Montgomery sold to James Davis seven acres of land north of the Red River for £100.

An act to enlarge the town of Clarksville was passed by the Legislature October 25, 1797. The addition consisted of fifty-six town lots and fifty-six out-lots "to be laid off on the lands of Peter D. Roberts, with proper streets and alleys, and to be contained within the following boundaries: beginning at a sweet gum and hickory on the margin of Cumberland River, the southwest corner of the aforesaid town; thence east 3,108 feet; thence south 5 degrees east 1,344 feet; thence west to the aforesaid river; thence down the said river to the beginning. Each town lot shall be 2471/2 feet long and 88 feet in breadth, containing one-half acre, and each out-lot shall be 476 feet long and 911/2| feet in breadth, containing one acre, the longest sides of which lot shall be east and west."

It is believed that the original settlers scarcely contemplated anything more than a county seat and a few houses for trading purposes. The place was difficult of access by water, as even John Fitch's steamboat on the Delaware was not invented and in practical operation until 1790, and Robert Fulton's on the Hudson until 1807, and for about fifty years after this last named date the railroad did not come to Clarksville. The people were surrounded by a dense wilderness, and were content to build on the narrow strip of land on the river bank for nearly twenty-five years after the founding of the city in 1785. They had no commerce, none of the luxuries and few of the comforts of life, but they were hardy pioneers, spent their time in their own peculiar way, hunting "Ingens," deer, buffalo and other "varmints," and failed to miss what they had never enjoyed. Court days and muster days were the great events of the times. Horse-racing, cock-fighting, whiskey-drinking, fiddling and dancing, and pugilistic contests were in those days innocent amusements. Calico cost $1 per yard, salt from $5 to $6 and sometimes, but seldom, as high as $16 per bushel, and whisky packed through from Kentucky on horseback in kegs sold at varying prices; merchants packed specie to Philadelphia in payment for goods. "Kauphy" was very dear and could only be used by the wealthiest families, and by them only on Sunday. Sugar was worth 50 cents per pound, and wheat flour was almost entirely unknown. Bacon and greens were the principal articles of food.

In 1805 the town commenced to grow and "to climb the hills." About this time the first brick house was built. In 1808 the entire distance from the public square to the mouth of Red River was a magnificent forest of tall and beautiful trees, owned principally by Hon. James B. Reynolds, or "Count Reynolds," as he was called. He was at one time a member of Congress, and named this fine property "Grattan's Grove." Its glory has long since departed, as the ground on which once stood the stately trees is now largely occupied by the shanties of "American citizens of African descent." In 1811 the few unpretending houses in the town were quite thrown in the shade by the new brick court house, just completed by Capt. C. Duvall upon the public square.

"About the year 1819, a noted land jobber (or land pirate as he was known), Patrick Darby, Esq., resurrected an obsolete claim against the original owner of the town plat, and hoisted Clarksville up for sale by the sheriff at the court house door. It was knocked off to the plaintiff for $14, but being a cash sale and he minus the cash, it was bid off by a well known citizen, who generously acted for the benefit of the town. But he, being highly incensed against the offender, rushed upon him with a drawn knife, and would have cut his jugular vein had he not been prevented by a citizen throwing up his arm. Patrick left instanter for parts unknown. This transaction caused the passage of the statute now in force known as Darby's Law, confirming titles, with seven years' peace-aable possession, subject to certain restrictions."

In 1826 there was but one vehicle in the town, and that an ancient one-horse cart, used for every purpose for which it could be used—carting criminals to the gallows, and good citizens to the grave. At this time there were 215 white people in Clarksville, consisting of forty families. Of the entire number there were sixty-five unmarried men, eight unmarried women and fifty-five children. There were fifty buildings then in the place, of which one was a commission warehouse. Steamboats as yet rarely ascended the river, and it was still more rare that they stopped at Clarksville. There was no artificial landing or levee, but there were two hotels. The days of pioneer glory lasted until about 1829, when a rude structure yclept a bridge was constructed across Red River. Then strangers commenced settling in the place, private dwellings were erected, and stores and warehouses, and a new and brighter face began to be put on all things, and innovations began to creep steadily into all departments of business and social customs. Down to 1837 there were none but general stores, but in this year a regular grocery store was opened, which was both wholesale and retail. A general classification of stores also soon followed, and in 1839, when the first turnpike was complete a new impetus was given to the business of the town.

In 1831 the first permanent church edifice in the town was erected, viz., the Methodist, on the corner of Main and Fourth Streets; the Episcopal, in 1833, and the Presbyterian in 1842. In 1846 Clarksville had a population of 2,128, one-third of that number being free blacks and slaves. In 1859 the city contained 400 houses and 5,000 inhabitants. The tobacco stemming business had become very large, there being then nine stemmeries in active operation, beside two immense tobacco warehouses. There was one pork house and several commission and forwarding houses. The wholesale grocery business was rapidly increasing, as was also the retail dry goods business, and in short all mercantile pursuits were rapidly improving. The public buildings consisted of a court house, jail, market house, seven churches, a Masonic Hall, two hotels, a male academy, female academy, public school building and four banks, and the Memphis, Clarksville & Louisville Railroad being nearly completed, it was considered that Clarksville was in a very flourishing condition. Theatrical entertainments had been frequent for over twenty years, and also lectures on literary and scientific subjects, by the best talent in the country, showing that society had advanced from its primitive condition in the early days of the century to a gratifying state of intelligence and refinement. The single antiquated cart of 1826 had been supplanted by numerous elegant carriages for pleasure and various kinds of vehicles for general teaming. And it was thought Clarksville was a very pious community if all were Christians who went to church. Still there was one drawback to the growth of the city, and that was its lack of manufacturing and mechanical industries.

This was before the war, which for some time checked the prosperity of the city. Since then its growth has been steady and permanent, and is the result of natural causes and the industry, energy and intelligence of the citizens. There is now an excellent system of water-works, established in 1879, the streets are lighted with gas, as are many of the public buildings and private houses. There is a telephone exchange, and lines leading to Nashville, Hopkinsville and Russellville, Ky. The streets are well paved with broken limestone, of which there is an abundance in the vicinity.

Since the war the town has steadily grown, having met with but one serious drawback, viz., the great fire of April 13 and 14, 1878. This fire broke out in the rear of Kincannon's store on Franklin Street, between Second and Third Streets. The alarm was given about 11:30 P. M., but it was found impossible to check the progress of the flames, which spread until they had destroyed most of the business portion of the city. There were over eighty sufferers from this fire, their losses ranging from $50 up to $32,000, the aggregate loss being in round numbers $500,000, which was reduced by insurance to the amount of $165,000. The principal buildings destroyed were the court house, chancery clerk's office, Melodeon Hall, The Tobacco Leaf office and the Franklin Bank. The district burned was bounded as follows: on the east by Third Street, on the west by the Hillman Block, on Franklin between Second and Third; on the north by Strawberry Alley, and on the south by Commerce Street Since this great calamity the city has been rebuilt, and is now in as good condition as before the fire. Business has resumed its wonted activity, the population has increased, and the prospect is as flattering as could be desired. At the present time the population, including the suburbs, is about 7,000.

Clarksville remained a "town" until 1855. However, at least as early as 1840 it had ceased to be governed by commissioners, their place being supplied by a mayor and aldermen. On the 29th of January, 1840, the boundaries of the town were redescribed as follows: "Commencing on the line of the south boundary of the town on the Cumberland River as heretofore established, running east with Robert's line to the corner of Robert's Addition; thence to Elder's Spring, so as to include the same; thence northeastwardly to a point on the Nashville road so as to include the residence of Eli Lockert; thence north so as to include the lots and houses now occupied by Jesse Harrison and George B. Wilson to a point on the old Russellville road, where the turnpike leaves the same; thence west of north to the northeast boundary of said corporation as heretofore established, and thence northeastwardly in a straight line to Red River bridge; thence down Red River to the mouth of the same; thence up the Cumberland at low water mark with its meanders to the beginning. This act gave the mayor and aldermen of the town of Clarksville power and authority to regulate the police, to enforce the collection of taxes, etc., in accordance with the several laws of the State incorporating the town of Clarksville. In 1846 a new act of the Legislature incorporated the town under the style of the mayor and aldermen of Clarksville, under which name the town was governed until December 20, 1855, when an act was passed which changed and simplified the boundary lines, and gave to the corporation the name of the City of Clarksville. The boundaries were fixed as follows:

"Beginning at the line of the south boundary of the town as heretofore established at the Cumberland River; running east with Roberts' line to the corner of Roberts' Addition; thence to Elder's spring so as to include the same; thence northeastwardly to a point in the Nashville road so as to include the brick building of John Bullard's east of and adjoining the present residence of E. R. W. Thomas; thence north to a point in the old Russellville road where the turnpike leaves the same; thence to the lower Red River bridge; thence to the middle of the river; thence down said river to the middle of the Cumberland; thence up the middle of the Cumberland to a point opposite the beginning and thence to the beginning." In December, 1855, the name "City of Clarksville" was conferred on what had previously been the town of Clarksville. Since the organization under this charter a complete list of officers and aldermen has been preserved, but of those previous to that time only a few of the mayors can now be recalled, as follows: Samuel McFall, William B. Bringhurst, Dr. Isaac Harris and C. L. Wilcox. At the time the charter of 1855 went into effect the city was divided into eight wards, and the city government consisted of a mayor, and one alderman from each ward.

The mayors have been as follows: Charles M. Hiter, 1856-58; George Smith, 1859-62. During 1863 and 1864 there was no regular government. Joshua Cobb, 1865; John A. Bailey, 1866; Joshua Cobb, 1867-68; Henry Freeh, 1869; H. C. Merritt, 1870-71; George Harris, 1872-73; G. A. Ligon, 1874; M. Sullivan, 1875-77; G. A. Ligon, 1878-79; J. J. Crusman, 1880-81; A. Howell, 1882-85 inclusive. James H. Smith elected January 16, 1886. Recorders.—T. W. Beaumont, 1856-57; C. G. Smith, 1858-60; B. A. Rogers, 1861; J. A. Bailey, 1862; D. W. Nye, 1865; L. G. Williams, 1866-68; Samuel J. Powers, 1869; H. M. Doak, 1870-71; J. O'Brien, 1872-76; W. A. Jackson, 1877-79; R. D. Bead, 1880-83 inclusive; Charles H. Bailey, 1884-85. Attorneys.—Thomas W. King, 1856-62, assisted in 1857 by G. A. Harel; J. E. Bailey. 1865-68, inclusive; J. W. Jones, 1869; John P. Campbell, 1870-71; B. D. Johnson, 1872; A. H. Munford, 1873-77, inclusive; Rufus N. Rhodes, 1878-81, inclusive; John J. West, 1882-85. Treasurers.—W. P. Hume 1856-70, inclusive;. John W. Farm, 1871; W. P. Hume, 1872-85. Marshals.—J. E. Marshal, succeeded by E. Withers, 1856; E. Withers, 1857-62; J. W. Wright, 1865; J. J. Rawls, 1866-68, inclusive; M. Carkuff, 1869; B. B. Walthal, 1870; E. S. Bringhurst, 1871; B. B. Walthal, 1872-81, inclusive; B. H. Williams, 1882-85. Chiefs of Police.—J. M. Moore, 1856-57; A. D. Smith, 1858; J. M. Moore, 1861-62; James Welch, 1869; Frank Phillips, 1874; M. W. Carkuff, 1875-83.

The Northern Bank of Tennessee was organized in 1854, with a capital of $50,000. The officers were then D. N. Kennedy, president, and James L. Glenn, cashier, and no change has occured in these offices since that time. The bank occupied a building on the square from 1854 to 1885. On the 14th of December of the latter year it moved to a new banking house on the southwest corner of Franklin and Second Streets, built expressly for its use. It is a three-story brick and cost about $15,000. It was a bank of issue up to the war, and redeemed its notes in gold until United States notes were made a legal tender when it redeemed in them until all its notes were retired.

The First National Bank of Clarksville was organized in 1865, its charter dating from September 5, of that year. There were only two national banks organized in Tennessee earlier than this, viz.: the First National Bank of Nashville, whose certificate is numbered 150, and the First National Bank of Memphis, whose certificate is numbered 336. That of this bank is 1,603. Among the first stockholders, were George H. Warfield, Theodore Cobb, S. W. Dawson, Thomas F. Pettus. S. F. Beaumont, Joseph W. Edwards, Mrs. M. C. Allen, Benjamin Caudle, Henry Frech, W. P. Hume, and J. P. Y. Whitfield. The first board of directors and officers were as follows: S. F. Beaumont, president; George H. Warfield, Thomas F. Pettus, Joseph W. Edwards and Guy W. Wines; W. P. Hume, cashier. The original capital of this bank was $50,000, which on July 1, 1867, was increased to $100,000. It had on January 1, 1886, an accumulated surplus and undivided profits amounting to $27,600, thus making the entire capital and surplus $127,600. It has paid regular semi-annual dividends for twenty years without intermission. Its present directors and officers are as follows: S. F. Beaumont, president; B, W. McCrae, cashier; J. P. Y. Whitfield, Dr. S. W. Dawson, E. B. Ely, and William F. Taylor. The general management of the bank has been in very nearly the same hands for twenty years, S. P. Beaumont having been its president since its organization, and B. W. McCrae, director and vice-president, and then cashier since 1867.

The Franklin Bank was organized in 1868, its first stockholders being T. F. Pettus, P. C. Hambaugh, W. S. Poindexter and V. A. Garnett, who were also the first board of directors. The first officers were T. F. Pettus, president, and W. S. Poindexter, cashier. Its original capital was $40,000. From its organization to 1876 it was located at New Providence; in the latter year it moved to Clarksville, and in 1878 increased its capital stock to $52,000, which is the present capital, the surplus on January 1, 1886, being $10,400. The only change in its officers has been in the presidency, P. C. Hambaugh succeeding to that office.

The Clarksville National Bank was organized in 1868, as the Montgomery Savings Institution, by B. O. Keesee, H. C. Merritt, John F.

House, C. G. Smith, and B. H. Williams. The original capital was $40000.Mr. Keesee was the president of the institution until his death in 1875, since when Mr. Merritt has been president. Joseph E. Broadus was cashier one year, and since 1869 A. Howell has been cashier. In 1875 the name was changed to the Bank of Clarksville, and in 1882 this name gave place to that of the Clarksville National Bank. The capital of the bank was increased to $50,000, and on January 1, 1886, the surplus was $10,000 and undivided profits $5,700. The first building occupied was the one recently vacated by the Northern Bank, and in 1870 they moved into the building formerly occupied by the Clarksville branch of the Bank of Tennessee.

The Farmers and Merchants National Bank was organized September 23, 1884, under its charter obtained August 25, of the same year. The original stockholders were about ninety in number, residing both in Tennessee and Kentucky. The first and present board of directors and officers were as follows: H. H. Lurton, president; James H. Smith, vice-president; John W. Faxon, cashier; T. Herndon, B. Y. Johnson, B. F. Gill, T. J. Edwards, C. T. Young, G. W. Jessup and J. J. Garrott; and Frank T. Hodgson, book-keeper. The original authorized capital of this bank was $500,000; and the paid up capital $100,000. The surplus on January 1, 1886, was $2,000, after declaring a dividend of 3 per cent. On January 1, 1885, the deposits amounted to $58,000, and January 1, 1886, they amounted to $113,000. The building in which this bank transacts business is an elegant two-story brick, built expressly for its occupancy on the northwest corner of Franklin and Second Streets, and contains a very secure vault, one of Hall's latest improved burglar-proof safes and one of Sargent & Greenleaf's most modern time locks. This bank has an arrangement by which it can sell exchange on any city in Europe.

The *Clarksville Chronicle* was started in 1808 or 1809. The files for a number of the first years of its existence have been destroyed, and for a number of these first years it changed its name and proprietors frequently, indicating an unsettled state of its affairs, and as each new proprietor commenced with Volume I of a paper with a new name, it can in strictness hardly be said that the *Chronicle* was started so early as the years mentioned above. A copy of The *Clarksville Recorder,* bearing date July 27, 1815, is preserved, published by Crutcher & McLean, marked Vol. I, No. 45. A copy of the *Chronicle* dated January 21, 1818, is in existence, marked Vol. IV, No. 33, published by Wells & Peebles. The *Clarksville Gazette* was published in 1819 by John Fitzgerald, and in 1820 by Thomas S. Shannon &, Co., a copy dated April 22, of that year being marked Vol. I, No. 38. The *Tennessee Watchman* was published in 1833 by Francis Richardson & Co., a copy dated December 19, that year being marked Vol. I, No. 29. In 1836, on November 5, No. 5 of Vol. I, of The *Clarksville Chronicle* was published by the same firm. No-6 of Vol II appeared November 24, 1837, published by E. P. McGinty, who continued its publication until June, 1849, when he sold out to R. W. Thomas, who continued to publish it until 1857. Mr. Thomas sold the paper to J. S. Neblett and J. A. Grant, who continued the publication with Mr. Thomas as editor until the death of the latter in 1876. Dr. D. F. Wright was then editor three years; then Ed C. Campbell nearly two years, and in 1881 the present editor, R. H. Yancey, succeeded Mr. Campbell. In 1878 W. P. Titus bought the interest of Mr. Grant and the publication firm was then Neblett & Titus until 1885, when Mr. Neblett sold his interest to Mr. Titus, who thus became sole proprietor. The *Chronicle* is a nine-column four-page paper, and its presses have been run by water-motor since 1885. The *Daily Evening Chronicle* has been issued for some time with success.

The *Clarksville Tobacco Leaf* was established by M. V. Ingram, the first issue appearing February 11, 1869. The Louisville press and tobacco trade had been trying to prevent the re-establishment of the tobacco trade of Clarksville, crippled by the war, and the Robertson *Register,* published at Springfield, came to the defense of Clarksville, which so pleased the enterprising young men of this city that they held out inducements to, and finally prevailed upon, Mr. Ingram to move his paper to Clarksville. The merchants advanced $900, to be received back in advertising and job printing, and the three banks then in the city each loaned $300. With this money the outfit was purchased, the Franklin Type Foundry giving credit for the balance of the $4,000, Mr. Ingram having no money, not even enough to move his family to Clarksville. A Cottrell & Babcock power press was purchased, the first brought to Tennessee, outside of cities publishing daily papers. The paper started as a four-page, nine-column sheet, with a circulation of 1,500; and with liberal advertising patronage, Mr. Ingram doing all the work, editorial, mechanical and financial, requiring eighteen hours each day; but finding the burden too heavy, he engaged Charles O. Faxon to write political editorials. It was reconstruction time and the *Leaf* made it red-hot for carpet-baggers who attempted to run the town and country. W. M. Doak was soon engaged as political editor, and in December, 1869, admitted to partnership, which lasted five years. The first year's profits of the paper were $4,000. The organization of the Clarksville Tobacco Board of Trade was advocated, as well as the building of the Clarksville & Princeton Railroad. In 1872 William N. Barksdale entered the office as an apprentice, and is now one of the proprietors of the establishment In 1873 the paper, now enlarged to an eight-page, six-column sheet, agitated the organization of the Iron Wagon Manufacturing Company, which remains a well organized company, with a good wagon establishment, although the iron wagon proved a failure. Mr. Ingram sold his interest in the paper to Mr. Doak February 11, 1874 One year later Mr. Ingram bought the paper back. N. O. Brandon, then employed as foreman, soon afterward became business manager. The great fire of April 13 and 14, 1878, destroyed the entire establishment, except the imposing-stone, the form of four pages which had been issued, and a table and desk. The office and the building on the corner of Third and Franklin Streets were worth $6,000; insurance on all, $3,200. A new outfit was ordered, at a cost of $4,200. In 1879 The *Semi-weekly Tobacco Leaf* took the place of the weekly, and has since maintained its existence, continuing to prosper. T. M. Riley was engaged as assistant editor in 1874 and remained connected with the paper in that capacity until 1879, when Mr. Ingram being attacked with rheumatism, Mr. Biley became editor. Mr. Ingram sold an interest, in 1880, to Clay Stacker, the firm of Ingram & Stacker continuing about one year, when Mr. Ingram sold his remaining interest to Stacker. Mr. Stacker immediately sold the entire establishment to the present proprietors, Brandon & Barksdale.

The *Clarksville Democrat* was founded in June, 1882, as a campaign paper, by M. V. Ingram. It was in favor of a low tax, both the other papers favoring the payment of the entire State debt, with interest at 6 per cent. At the close of the campaign it was resolved to continue its publication. Mr. Ingram sold out, in 1883, to Messrs. Hall & De Graffenried, who managed it until September, 1884, when Mr. Hall sold out to his partner. Mr. Graffenried employed G. M. Bell to edit the paper, and' finally, on account of ill health, sold out, April 1, 1885, to Mr. Bell, who still continues its publication. Previous to the war there were a number of papers in existence besides the *Chronicle*, that being the only one to survive that conflict. The most prominent of them was The *Clarksville Jeffersonian*, which was started by C. O. Faxon, May 25, 1844, and continued to be published by him until the city was taken possession of by the Federal soldiers immediately after the fall of Fort Donelson.

The first meeting of the business men of Clarksville, having in view the organization of an association to promote their mutual interests, was held February 7, 1870. A temporary organization was effected by the election of E. H. Lewis, president, and M. V. Ingram, secretary. Twelve of the leading business men were chosen a board of directors, as follows: J. P. Y. Whitfield, L. Bloch, J. H. Schrodt, W. H. Turnley, F. P. Gracey,

F. F. Fox, D. Kincannon, B. O. Keesee, G. B. Wilson, W. Roach, H. H. Poston and J. J. Crusman. The objects of the movement were stated and commented upon by Judge Humphreys, W. A. Quarles and others, and a committee appointed to wait upon the railroad managers with a view to obtaining a reduction of freights, etc. This committee consisted of F. P. Gracey, W. H. Turnley, J. J. Crusman, G. B. Wilson, B. O. Keesee, W. C. Barksdale, D. Kincannon and L. Bloch.

The next evening a constitution and by-laws was adopted. The constitution provided for monthly and annual meetings, for certain officers, for two standing committees—"the committee of arbitration" and the "committee of appeals," which was to have a "committee of finance," and prescribed the duties of officers and members. The objects of the newly organized board were to improve the commerce of Clarksville, to build up or to encourage the building up of manufactories, to exercise as much control as was necessary or practical over the railroads, and to make Clarksville a large city. At this meeting John W. Faxon was appointed temporary treasurer. On the 15th of February the following gentlemen were elected permanent officers of the board: President, the Hon. D. N. Kennedy; vice-presidents, B. H. Lewis, F. P. Gracey, J. J. Crusman, J. P. Y. Whitfield and A. F. Smith; secretary, M. V. Ingram; assistant secretary, Poston Couts; treasurer, John W. Faxon. The following gentlemen were elected directors: W. A. Quarles, C. A. Baker, B. O. Keesee, L. Bloch, W. T. Dortch, J. H. Schrodt, F. F. Fox, Winfield Roach, W. H. Turnley and H. H. Poston. The following standing committees were elected: On Arbitration—E. H. Lewis, H. H. Lurton, George H. Conover, L. R. Clark and W. W. Kirby; Committee of Appeals—J. J. Crusman, F. P. Gracey, W. M. Daniel, H. C. Merritt, J. J. Hamlett, J. F. Couts and H. P. Dorris. On the 1st of March, 1870, there were sixty-eight members of the board. The meetings of the board were held for some time at the Southern Hotel, the free use of a room having been tendered by the proprietors, Messrs. Roach & Raimey. Under the auspices of the board a "tobacco fair" was held June 15, 1870, which was a complete success and materially enhanced the tobacco trade of the city. From time to time such questions were discussed as the building up of an agricultural implement manufactory, of proposed railroads, of procuring changes in the law pertaining to the inspection of tobacco, of desired changes in the running of trains over the Louisville & Nashville Railroad, building a plow factory, building the Southern Pacific Railroad, etc., until March 5, 1872, when the last meeting of the board occurred for a number of years. After a seven years' dormancy the Board of Trade held a called meeting April 17, 1879, for the purpose of considering the railroad connections of Clarksville. The project of a canal from Seven Mile Island to Red River was discussed, as also that of lighting the city with gas, and of sewerage. W. O. Brandon was made secretary pro tern, at this time. On July 8, 1879, the feasibility of the city's purchase of the water-works was discussed and much feeling developed. The board was reorganized October 14, 1879. On the 2d of October, 1885, the following officers were elected: President, D. W. Kennedy; vice-presidents, J. J. Crusman, Thomas Herndon, M. H. Clark, F. P. Gracey and A. Howell; secretary, W. O. Brandon; treasurer, John W. Faxon. The last important action of the board was the entertainment of North-western excursionists in November.

The Clarksville Tobacco Board of Trade was originally established as the Tobacco Exchange in 1858, all the leading tobacco buyers being members, about twenty in number. The exchange was reorganized in 1866 and continued on until 1870, when the Tobacco Board of Trade was formed, with the following officers: S. F. Beaumont, president; W. H. Crouch, first vice-president; P. C. Hambaugh, second vice-president; M. H. Clark, secretary; W. J. Ely, assistant secretary, and James H. Smith, treasurer. This board was regularly incorporated under the laws of Tennessee by a charter obtained May 16, 1878, with a capital of $50,000. In 1879 they commenced the erection of a tobacco exchange building, in which to transact business, which was completed at a cost of nearly $30,000. It is a four-story brick, standing on the corner of Main Street and the public square, and is completely appointed with all the modern conveniences. The present officers of the board are Thomas Herndon, president; E. N. Flack, first vice-president; L. T. Gold, second vice-president; M. H. Clark, secretary; W. J. Ely, assistant secretary, and R. E. McCullough, treasurer. For a number of years the sales of tobacco in this market ranged from 14,000 to 20,000 hogsheads, but in 1885 the number 27,907 was reached.

The tobacco warehousemen in Clarksville are as follows: Herndon, Young & Co.; Parrish, Buckner & Co.; Kendrick, Pettus & Co.; Hancock, Fraser & Bagsdale; Smith & Anderson; Shelby & Rudolph, and R. H. Walker & Co. The prominent buyers on the board are as follows: M. H. Clark & Bro., W. H. Crouch & Son, S. F. Beaumont & Co., Jarrett & Co., John Kropp, B. K. Gold, P. C. Hambaugh, L. T. Gold, E. M. Flack, T. D. Luckett & Co., R. R. Neale, T. L. Harvie, Buck & Morrow and Julius Spicer.

There are seven tobacco stemmeries outside the Board of Trade. These are owned by T. D. Luckett & Co., R. R. Neale, Allan Gilmour, S. F. Beaumont, T. L. Harvie, Hamilton & Co. and G. W. Bryarly. The usual out-turn of these factories is from 1,500 to 4,000 hogsheads, which is shipped to foreign markets, mainly to Europe, but some to Australia.

Clarksville is well supplied with benevolent institutions. Clarksville Lodge, No. 89, A. F, & A. M., was organized October 11, 1839, and reorganized December 6, 1866. Tannehill Lodge, No. 116, was organized in October, 1846, and was discontinued about the time of the breaking out of the war. Clarksville Chapter, No. 3, R. A. M., organized December 8, 1866. Clarksville Council, No. 4, Royal and Select Master Masons was organized in October, 1847. Clarksville Commandery, No. 8, was organized in October, 1867. Pythagoras Lodge, No. 23, I. O. O. F., was instituted January 27, 1847, and their hall was dedicated December 26, 1849. Young Encampment was organized March 24, 1869. Cumberland Lodge, No. 17, K. of P., was instituted May 14, 1874. Endowment Rank, Section No. 28, was organized in 1876. Clarksville Lodge, No. 232, K of H. was organized September 5, 1876. Sublime Order of Wise Men was organized about February 1, 1870. Warfield Lodge, No. 9, A. F. and A. M. (colored) was instituted lately. Mt. Vernon Lodge, No. 1644, G. U. O. O. F. (colored), was instituted September 28, 1874. Hebron Lodge, No. 1711, G. U. O. O. F. (colored), was instituted December 27, 1875. Ark of Safety Lodge, No. 1731, G. U. O. O. F. (colored), was instituted in May, 1876. Sons of Union (colored) was instituted a short time ago.

The Clarksville Marine Insurance and Life and Trust Company was organized January 15, 1840. The Clarksville Gas Company was incorporated in 1858, and organized April 6, 1859. Its capital stock was $35,000. The company as incorporated consisted of D. N. Kennedy, William Munford, John S. Hart, B. Stewart, G. A. Henry, Ed Thomas, C. Faxon, W. Vance, R. Moore and C. M. Hiter. The Clarksville Gas Light Company was chartered April 30, 1881, the following named persons being the company, as chartered: J. E. Bailey, B. H. Owen, F. P. Gracey, A. Howell, Henry Frech, Charles G. Smith, D. Kineannon, D. N. Kennedy, T. C. Hopper and Alfred Hopper. November 26, 1883, a contract was made between the city of Clarksville and this company to light the streets with gas. Union Wharf Company was incorporated in 1854 as the successor of Montgomery Wharf Company, incorporated February 5, 1842; the Franklin Wharf Company, incorporated January 15, 1844, and the Middle Wharf Company, which was acting without a charter. The individuals comprising the Union Wharf Company when incorporated were the following: George S. H. Warfield, Joshua Elder, Starkey Norfleet and others who owned the stock in the Montgomery Wharf Company; Robert Bryson, Alfred Robb and others who owned the stock in the Franklin Wharf Company, and O. H. Smith, George A. Harrel and Samuel B. Seat who owned the stock in the Middle Wharf Company.

The present business and manufacturing interests of Clarksville are represented by the following firms: Groceries—C. M. Barker, E. Cross, Crusman & Howard, Cunningham Bros., Dixon & Martin, Dority & Herndon, W. C. Hester, Hurst & Co., A. Jackson, Keesee & Northington, Mrs. J. M. Kelty, T. V. Kilgore, G. W. Leigh, M. Mattill, J. R. Sensing, E. H. Wilkinson and Wood & Abbott. Dry Goods—Bloch Bros., R. S. Broaddus, Coulter Bros., Gerhart's Cash Store, E. Glick, A. R. Hall & Son, Simon Katz, P. Sieber, R. W. Roach, S. Shyer and C. D. White. General Stores—G. Eleazar, M. Gorham and J. W. Wade. Boots and Shoes—Bloch Bros., Bowling & Wilson, A. R. Hall & Son, S. Katz, J. Rick and M. A. Stratton. Clothing—Bloch Bros., Gerhart's Cash Store, A. R. Hall & Son, J. G. Joseph, Pitman & Lewis, R. W. Roach and Simon Katz. China, Glass and Queensware—G. W. Hendrick, Kincannon, Son & Co. and J. F. Wood. Drug Stores—Lockert & Reynolds, S. B. Stewart and Owen Moore, Hardware and Agricultural Implements—J. S. Elder, Fox & Smith and Kin, cannon, Son & Co. Coal, Coke and Wood—Bringhurst & Stacker, F. P. Gracey & Bro. and Keesee & Northington. Dress-making and Millinery—A. R. Hall & Son, Hodgson & McGuire, the Misses McAllister and Mrs. W. Rosenfield. Harnessmakers—G. W. Cooper, M. L. Joslin and John Young. Tobacco Salesmen—Herndon Young & Co., and Kendrick Pettus & Co. Warehouses —The Bailey Warehouse, Central Warehouse, Elephant Warehouse, Gracey Warehouse, Grange Warehouse, The People's Warehouse and Smith & Anderson. Jewelers—C. L. Cooke, L. Gauchat and T. Rohner. Hotels----Lehman's European Hotel and the Franklin House. Flouring Mills—The Anchor Mills, Lafayette Flouring-Mills, Meriwether & Gilmer and T. J. Munford. Planing-Mills—Clarksville Planing-Mill, Smith, Clark & Co. and G. B. Wilson & Co. Whitfield, Bates & Co., manufacturers of engines, proprietors of foundry, saw-mill and sugarmill, and manufacturers of tobacco screws. Wagon Manufacturers—I. Alward, The Clarksville Wagon Company and J. B. Jarrell. Merchant Tailor—A. B. Pugh. Furniture Dealers—Q. C. Atkinson and J. F. Couts. Photographers—H. E. Dibble and J. W. McCormac. Blacksmiths—C. Dinneen, W. M. Frazier, E. Gaisser & Son, M. Gorham, J. Henry and J. McDonald. Steamboat Owners and Agents—F. P. Gracey & Bro. There are the following physicians: C. W. Bailey, N. L. Carney, B. N. Herring, T. D. Johnson, J. M. Larkin, C. E. L. McCauley, T. H. Marable, W. G. Patrick, A. M. Trawick and D. F. Wright.

Evergreen Lodge is a floral and nursery garden formed from the old Shackelford property and a tract between that and the Hopkinsville Turnpike. While owned by the Shackelfords, Mrs. Shackelford, who had a taste for horticulture, had planted the Norway spruce and hemlock, from which it derived its appellation. Some years since A. Weill bought the Shackelford place, and in 1879 sold it to the present proprietor, Capt. J. J. Crusman, who purchased it for a place of residence for himself and sister, Mrs. Champlin, whose death occurred shortly after the purchase was made. Capt. Crusman then employed Mr. Munro to take charge of it as a floral establishment, since which time Clarksville, which had previously depended on Louisville and Nashville for flowering plants, has found a constant supply at home, and a foreign demand has sprung up from a number of the neighboring States. Nursery operations are also carried on here on a large scale, and the cultivation of the grape is receiving that attention it deserves. The products of the nursery are fruit trees and ornamental trees and shrubs, rose trees, fuschias, verbenas, heliotropes, a very large variety of ferns, lilies of the valley and violets, bulbous roots, as hyacinths, tulips, ivies, narcissus, etc., as well as fresh fruits and vegetables in their seasons. This establishment taken altogether is of great benefit to the city of Clarksville, and a great credit to the enterprise and taste of the proprietor and manager, who at present is James Morton.

The Clarksville Street Railway Company was chartered August 5, 1885, and organized September 25, 1885. Following are the names of the stockholders, directors and officers of the company: stockholders—John F. Shelton, H. H. Tharpe, F. P. Gracey, D. Kincannon, A. B. Masey, Mrs. S. M. Snow, John W. Faxon, S. B. Stewart, H. C. Merritt, B. F. Gill, W. H. Lanier, M. C. Northington, M. A. Stratton, B. W. Boach and J. M. Pardue. Directors and officers—John F. Shelton, president; John N. Faxon, secretary and treasurer; H. H. Tharpe, F. P. Gracey and D. Kincannon. The railway was built during November and December, 1885, being completed and the cars started on the 15th of the latter month. This was a free day, and on the 16th the amount of fare collected was $37.07. The track is one mile long, extending from the public square up Franklin Street to Tenth, and thence to the Louisville & Nashville Railroad Depot, and has a turn-table at each end. At present the company has two cars.

Palmyra is situated on the Louisville & Nashville Railroad twelve miles below Clarksville. It is one of the oldest towns in the county, having been incorporated by the Legislature April 20, 1796. It was laid off by Dr. Morgan Brown on both sides of Deacon Creek, on the south bank of the Cumberland, and contained 246 lots. For this reason and WHEREAS, Establishment of the same [the town] will promote the public good by extending the settlements lower down the Cumberland River, and by facilitating trade and commerce to the District of Mero: Be it enacted, etc., that the spot of ground laid off into a town containing two hundred and forty-six lots numbered from 1 to 246, inclusive, with the necessary streets, is hereby established a town by the name of Palmyra." Dr. Morgan Brown, Robert Prince, Richard Miles, Benjamin Thomas and Isaac Titsworth were by the same act appointed commissioners of the town, and on November 2, 1809, Samuel Vance, John Summerville, Adam Harman, Burrell M. Williamson, William Clements, Sr., James Wheeling and Thomas K. McAlrath were appointed additional commissioners for Palmyra. The town grew and prospered, and at one time became a formidable competitor for the capital of the State of Tennessee. In the year 1880 there were only forty-eight inhabitants in the town. B. W. Owens is the present postmaster.

Port Royal is situated on the south bank of Red River, about thirteen miles east of Clarksville. It was incorporated by the Legislature October 25, 1797, and is thus but little more than a year younger than Palmyra. It had been laid off on lands owned by Samuel Wilcox, and at the time of incorporation a considerable number of lots had been sold to various parties, who were desirous that a town should be established by legislative authority. The plan of the town contained thirty acres. There were in the plan thirty-six lots of one-half acres each, together with a square of two acres, necessary streets, alleys, etc. Francis Prince, Jonathan Stephenson, John Baker, William Mitcherson and William Connell were appointed commissioners for the "designing building and improving said town." This town has had a history somewhat similar to that of Palmyra. Its superior advantages for water-power have not been utilized, and now there is scarcely any thing but a postoffice.

New Providence is a flourishing town on the Cumberland River, two miles below Clarksville. It was incorporated by the county January 28, 1854. The petition for this incorporation was signed by thirty-eight individuals. The boundaries were set as follows: "Beginning at the mouth of the Tanyard Spring Branch, and to run thence up the Cumberland River 100 poles to T. W. Atkinson's southeast corner of the tract on which he now lives; thence with his western boundary line, including J. S. Slaten's and John T. Shelton's lots, and continuing on Atkinson's line so as to include Darby's house and lot; thence westwardly to Meacham's east boundary line including Mrs. Trevesthaus' old house; thence south with Meacham's line to a corner on Meacham's line; thence east with Meacham's line so as to include the Methodist Meeting-house; thence southwardly with N. F. Trice's line to the branch, and down the branch to the beginning." The population of New Providence is now about 700, and it is a point for some manufacturing. It has telephone connection with Clarksville and Hopkinsville, Ky., and receives mail six times per week from Clarksville and from Ringgold, three times from Dover and Hopkinsville, and twice from Dotsonville. The present postmaster at New Providence is Samuel Buckley. Meachamsville was incorporated by the county court on the same day as New Providence. This incorporation was effected in consequence of a spirit of rivalry between the places, the people of Meachamsville being very much opposed to being included in the corporate limits of New Providence. Their corporation has since been abandoned.

Bald Hornet is a small interior place known also as Poplar Spring Furnace. It is fifteen miles from Clarksville and four miles from Carbondale. Very little business is done in the village. Carbondale is on the Louisville & Nashville Railroad, two miles from Palmyra. The Western Union Telegraph Company maintains an office here; T. B. Etheridge, operator and agent for the railroad. R. G. Watwood is agent for the Southern Express Company, while Burrell J. Corban is the postmaster. Four miles northwest is the famous "Bellamy's Cave," one of the largest in the State, and largely visited by sight-seers. Carmel is a small place in the southeastern part of the county. Mail is received on Mondays, Wednesdays and Fridays. A small business is done. Dotsonville also known as Central Point, is situated about five miles north of Palmyra. Carbondale is its express, railroad and telegraph office. Mail is received semi-weekly from New Providence. J. E. Outlaw is the postmaster. Grantville is situated ten miles southeast of Clarksville, whence it receives mail three times per week, and also as frequently from Ashland

City. L. P. Stewart is postmaster. Hampton Station is situated on the Louisville & Nashville Railroad, nine miles northeast of Clarksville. It is also known as Doe River Cave. C. B, McMurray is postmaster and express agent Jordan Springs is located in the northwestern part of the county, fifteen miles from Clarksville. Its mail is received every Tuesday and Saturday from Woodlawn. McAllister's Cross Roads, otherwise known as Batson's Mills, is sixteen miles south from Clarksville. Its mail is received semi-weekly from Cumberland Furnace, Dickson County. John B. Batson is postmaster. Maggie is a farmer's postoffice ten miles from Clarksville. I. Z. Grant is postmaster. Oakwood is thirteen miles west of Clarksville. It receives its mail on alternate days from Clarksville and Dover. John H. Buck is postmaster. Foster's Cave is one and one-half miles from this place. Orgain's Cross Roads is a small interior post-office, eight miles from Clarksville, whence it receives its mail on Tuesdays, Thursdays and Saturdays. Peacher's Mills is situated on the Big West Fork, eight miles north of Clarksville. It is a milling point of some consequence. Mail is received on Tuesday, Thursday and Saturday. H. O. Hambaugh is postmaster. Pleasant Mound is a country postoffice, nearly eight miles southeast from Clarksville, and about four miles from the Cumberland River. Lewis Lowe is postmaster.

Rex is a small postoffice receiving mail semi-weekly from St Bethlehem. Riggins, otherwise known as Sailor's Best Furnace, is in the southwest part of the county. Ringgold lies on the Little West Fork of Red River, nearly eight miles northwest of Clarksville. J. P. Parrish is postmaster. Boss View, also known as McMurry's store, is eight miles from Clarksville and four miles south from Hampton's Station. Mail is received semi-weekly. W. W. McMurry is the postmaster. Sailor's Best is a landing on the Cumberland River and a station on the Louisville & Nashville Railroad, nineteen miles below Clarksville. Considerable grain and tobacco are shipped from this point. John Miner is the postmaster. St. Bethlehem is a postoffice four and one-half miles from Clarksville.

The railroad station is known as Cherry's. It has telephone connection with Clarksville and Guthrie; has an office of the Southern Express Company. G. H. Slaughter is the postmaster. Sango is a small country postoffice nine miles from Clarksville. S. T. Halliburton is postmaster. Shiloh lies sixteen miles southwest of Clarksville and seven miles south of Carbandale. J. D, Fletcher is postmaster. Southside, formerly Collins-ville, is twelve miles from Olarksville and nearly south. W. L. Lyle is postmaster. Steele is a postoffice on the Louisville & Nashville Railroad, six miles from Clarksville. J. E. Steele is postmaster. Woodford is a country postoffice about ten miles from Clarksville. B. E. Miller is post-master. Woodlawn is a country postoffice ten miles west of Clarksville. It receives mail from New Providence on Tuesdays, Thursdays and Saturdays.

Figure 1. A. G. Goodlett

PART TWO

BIOGRAPHIES

Gilbert T. Abernathy, a native of Tennessee, was born May 21, 1820. His father, Charles C. Abernathy, was a native of Virginia, and was born in 1790. When but sixteen years of age he immigrated to Tennessee with his father. He was educated at the university at Nashville, then known as Cumberland College. He was clerk of the circuit court in Giles County, this State, for thirty years. Our subject's mother was Susan W. Harris, a native of Tennessee, born in 1800, and was married to Charles C. Abernathy in 1815. In 1840 Mrs. Abernathy died; then Mr. Abernathy was married the second time to Miss Elizabeth Dickson, a native of Tennessee, born in 1817. Mr. Abernathy died in 1877 and Mrs. Abernathy in 1878. Our subject was united in marriage January 8, 1839, to Miss Ann L. Baxter, born in Tennessee May 9, 1821. Her father was Robert Baxter, a native of New Jersey, and her mother was Rebecca Boon, a native of Kentucky. To our subject and wife were born two children: Rebecca S. and Mary E. September 18, 1848, he had the misfortune to lose his wife, and on the 15th of December, 1853, he married for his second wife Miss Emily B. Talley, a native of North Carolina, born March 4, 1839. The fruits of this union were eleven children: Charley G. (deceased), Emily P., Gilbert T., Ann L. (deceased), Alfred H., Elenora S., John C., George S., Andrew J., Harriet N. and Sarah M. Our subject was reared on a farm, and educated at the Nashville University. At the early age of sixteen he volunteered and went with the Tennessee Brigade to the Creek nation, and thence to Florida to fight the Indians, where he remained seven months. About two years of his life he spent in studying law. In 1840 he was employed as book-keeper at the Tennessee Iron Works, then owned by his father-in-law, Robert Baxter. At Mr. Baxter's death our subject and three brothers-in-law purchased and ran it and two others successfully until the breaking out of the war, when they closed all but the Mount Vernon Furnace, which they continued to run up to 1862. Our subject remained near the furnace for several years farming and making shingles, but as he was almost ruined financially by the war he went to teaching school, and is so occupied at the present time. He has a fine farm and a large residence. Politically he is a Democrat.

Florence F. Abbott, junior member of the firm of Wood & Abbott, was born in Clarksville, Tenn., March 13, 1862, son of Florence and Julia (Sullivan) Abbott, and is of Irish extraction. Both parents were born in the "Emerald Isle." They came to the United States about 1850, settling in Troy, N. Y., where they were afterward united in matrimony. Later they moved to Kentucky, and a few years before the breaking out of the late war purchased a permanent home in Clarksville, where they have resided ever since, and there the father died in 1875. Our subject was educated in the Clarksville schools, and graduated from tike Nashville Commercial College in 1879, and the same year accepted a position as book-keeper for the firm then known as Dority, Wood & Co., and in this capacity continued three years. In 1883 he engaged in the wholesale and retail grocery business in partnership with A. S. Wood, and has succeeded well in his undertakings. He is a Democrat, a member of the Catholic Church, and is a shrewd young business man. His father was for many years a prominent man of the city.

James W. Adams was born in Robertson County, Tenn., March 7, 1848, and is of French and English lineage. He is a son of William G. and Henrietta (Payne) Adams, born in Tennessee and North Carolina, respectively. The mother came to Tennessee when a child, and has borne her husband seven children, our subject being the fourth, and the oldest now living. The father died in 1855, and the mother in 1875. James W. came with his mother to Montgomery County in 1865, and in the latter county he received his education. In 1869 he purchased and moved upon the farm where he now lives. In May, 1874, the nuptials of his marriage with Eudora Nichols were celebrated. She is a native of Dickson County, Tenn., and daughter of William H. and Fannie Nichols, both now dead. The father was killed in the public road near his residence by guerrillas during the war. No children have been born to our subject and his wife. His farm is said to be one of the oldest in the county, and at the time he purchased it had been farmed until it was supposed to be worn out and almost worthless. By proper cultivation he so improved it that it is now one of the most productive farms in the county. Tobacco is his staple crop, and he is now preparing to plant about 100 acres of corn. He is a Democrat in politics and a member of the Baptist Church.

Daniel D. Allen, farmer, was born in Montgomery County, Tenn., September 11, 1827, and is the son of Nathaniel H. and Lucy A. (Neblett) Allen. His father was born in North Carolina, January 8, 1793, and died January 2, 1871. His mother was born in Virginia, August 27, 1799, and died August 7, 1867. They both came to Tennessee with their parents when quite young. Our subject is of English descent, and was educated in the country schools of the county. He was united in marriage to Miss Mary A. Barney, born in Montgomery County, June 27, 1830, and the daughter of Thomas and Susan (Orgain) Barney. There were three children born to the subject of this sketch and his wife, viz.: Charles S., Clara B. and Thomas H. July 17, 1865, Mrs. Allen delivered her body to the dust and her soul to its Creator. Mr. Allen's second wife was Miss Mattie T. Lowe, born January 22, 1839, and a native of Tennessee. She is the daughter of Louis and Mary E. (Sumner) Lowe. Mr. Lowe is a sprightly man of seventy years, and is a minister of the gospel. Mrs. Lowe died in the year 1851. To our subject and wife were born five children, viz.: Carrie E., Daniel S., Nathaniel H., Louis L. and Mattie E. Mr. Allen is a member of the Methodist Episcopal Church, a Democrat, and a well-to-do farmer. He lives on the farm where he was reared, which is situated on the south bank of the Cumberland River. He raises but little stock, and that of an extra breed.

John M. Anderson is a native of Green County, Ky., and was born September 15, 1832. He is the eldest of five children born to Peter and L. J. (Montgomery) Anderson. Peter Anderson was born in the year 1808, and died January 17, 1876. He was a native of Virginia. L. J. (Montgomery) Anderson was born in 1811, and died November 17, 1885. She was a native of Kentucky. Our subject was united in marriage, January 29, 1868, to Miss Mary H. Bahannon, who was a native of Kentucky, and was born August 17, 1843. She is the third of a family of thirteen children. Her parents are natives of Virginia and Kentucky, respectively. To this union was born one child, viz.: Annie M., born April 13, 1873. In 1854 Mr. John Anderson moved to Montgomery County, Tenn., and settled on a portion of the farm on which he now lives. He has an elegant residence, and it is beautifully situated. In 1861 he enlisted in Company K, First Kentucky Regiment. This company organized at Bowling Green, Ky., and composed the right wing of A. S. Johnston's army, stationed at Glasgow. After the fall of Fort Donelson they moved to Nashville, and from there to several different places until after the battle of Shiloh; they were then ordered to Chattanooga, and the regiment was reorganized. Our subject was here taken sick, and was given a furlough on which he returned home, remaining there six months. He then returned to the army, and was transferred to the Second Kentucky Regiment. In the battle of Chattanooga he was knocked from his horse by a piece of shell, but was not seriously hurt. He was in Johnston's retreat when he fell back to Atlanta. His division was transferred to Gen. Joseph E. Wheeler's cavalry and made a raid into Tennessee, where he was captured between Pulaski and Columbia and taken to Johnson's Island, where he remained eleven months, or till the close of the war, when he returned to his farm where he now lives. In 1877 he was elected justice of the peace, and this office he holds at the present time.

W. W. Anderson, M. D., the son of J. M. and Martha (Crawford) Anderson, was born February 19, 1850. J. M. Anderson was a native of

Virginia, and came to Tennessee when quite young. He settled near Keysburgh, Ky., and was by occupation a cabinet-maker. He was married to Miss Martha Crawford, of North Carolina, and to them were born thirteen children, three of whom died; those living are J. W., C. R., S. J., D. W., J. H., W. W., T. J., A. J., C. G. and R. E. After his boys grew up he purchased a farm in Kentucky and lived there for a short time. He then moved to Robertson County, Tenn., and died near Springfield, July 4, 1864. W. W. Anderson is a practicing physician and dealer in general merchandise at Jordan Springs, Tenn. He was educated at Springfield, Tenn., and the Commercial College of Clarksville, Tenn., until the year 1880, when he went to the Vanderbilt University, and there graduated with honor in the year 1881. He then went to Jordan Springs, when he began the practice of medicine in April, 1882. In August, 1884, he began the mercantile business at the same place. He was married, February 4, 1874, to Miss Sarah T. Longford, of Port Royal, Tenn., and to this union have been born four children: Florence E., E. E., Thomas J. and Mary E. Dr. Anderson is a member of the Baptist Church, and is a good citizen.

W. H. Anderson was born February 10, 1818, in Humphreys County, Tenn., and when a child moved with his parents to Montgomery County, where he still lives. His father, Richard Anderson, was born in Montgomery County, in 1791, and there has always lived with the exception of a short time spent in Humphreys County, where our subject was born. The father, who was a useful citizen, married Margaret Rudolph, who was born in 1791, and to them were born six children. The subject of this sketch was educated at home and in the common schools, attending the latter only a few weeks. He learned the carpenter's trade when young, and worked at that occupation a few years. He then followed farming, and acted as constable until 1847. He then purchased the White Oak mills, and carried on milling for five years. He then sold his property and returned to Montgomery County, where he has since resided and farmed. In October, 1843, he married Margaret E. Smith, who was born in Montgomery County, August 30, 1825. She was a daughter of John Smith, who was of German descent, and died about 1851. Mr. and Mrs. Anderson became the parents of the following children: Ellen C., Margaret E. and Missouri A. Mrs. Anderson died in 1851. Our subject was a Whig as long as that party existed, and since that time has been independent. He has been magistrate of Montgomery County for twenty years and is at present magistrate of his civil district. He is a member of the Presbyterian Church, as was his wife. Mr. Anderson has taken such an active part in public life that he is now an exceptionally well-informed and intelligent man.

Hon. James E. Bailey was one of the most distinguished men of Montgomery County, of which he was a native, having been born August 15, 1822. His grandfather immigrated to North Carolina, and his father, Charles Bailey, was born in Simpson County, in that State. In early life he came to Montgomery County and was for forty years clerk of the circuit court. Hon. James E. Bailey's mother was Mary Bryan, a native of Robertson County and the daughter of Col. James H. Bryan. She was a woman of much natural ability and strength of character. The subject of this sketch obtained a liberal education at the old Clarksville Academy, and afterward at the University of Nashville. In July, 1842, he was admitted to the bar and entered into partnership with George C. Boyd, upon whose death he succeeded to the law business of the firm. In 1853 he was elected to the General Assembly of Tennessee. Previous to the civil war he was a Whig, and remained an earnest Union man as long as he could perceive any hope of its maintenance. In January, 1861, he was elected, with the Hon. Cave Johnson and the Hon. John F. House, a Union delegate to a proposed convention to consider the attitude of his State. After the breaking out of the war, he in common with the great majority of the people of his State, warmly espoused the cause of the South. He was elected colonel of the Forty-ninth Tennessee on Christmas day, 1861, and upon the surrender of Fort Donelson was sent as a prisoner of war to Fort Warren. Being exchanged in September, 1862, he rejoined his regiment at Vicksburg, Miss., and remained with it until the following spring, when on account of failing health, he was appointed a member of the military court of Gen. Hardee, holding this position until the close of the war. After the failure of the Southern cause he returned to Clarksville and resumed the practice of the law. He was twice appointed to fill temporary vacancies on the supreme bench of the State, and acted as chief justice in the place of A. O. P. Nicholson. In 1877 he was elected United States Senator to fill the unexpired term of Andrew Johnson. The divisions in the Democratic party upon the State debt question prevented his re-election to the Senate. During his service in the Senate his health began to fail, and for some months prior to his decease he was a great and constant sufferer. His death occurred December 29, 1885. He was married November 7, 1849, to Miss Elizabeth Lusk, of Nashville, who survives him together with five children—four sons and a daughter. The Hon. James E. Bailey was universally regarded as a just man, and a good citizen. He was an affectionate father and husband; and the bar, the county and the State are justly proud of his record, his life and his name.

J. W. Bartee was born May 22, 1819, in Dickson County, Tenn., and is the son of Jesse and Sarah (Harkleroad) Bartee. Jesse Bartee was born in East Tennessee in 1783, and was engaged in the iron business there for a number of years. He died in Dickson County in 1826. In early life he was married to Miss Sarah Harkleroad, to which union were born thirteen children. The only ones now living are Mary, James, Jesse W. and G. W. Mrs. Sarah Bartee died in 1873, in her ninetieth year. Our subject, J. W. Bartee, was educated in the country schools, and the first business in which he engaged was farm work; his health failing he went into the mercantile business at the mouth of Harpeth River, in Dickson County; here he remained twelve months; he then went to Charlotte, Tenn., and began the grocery business, but only engaged in that business for a short time. After moving about for some time he settled at last in the Eighth District. He was married February 22, 1852, to Miss Lucy A. Bullock. To this union were born six children, three of whom are now alive, respectively: J. B., J. H. and E. L. In politics he is a Democrat, casting his first vote for Martin Van Buren. Mr. Bartee is a member of the F. & A. M., joining this body at the age of twenty-one. He and his wife are members of the Methodist Episcopal Church, and he is one of the well known citizens of the county.

J. B. Bartee is a farmer of Montgomery County, Tenn. (For history of parents see sketch of J. W. Bartee.) Our subject was born October 25, 1857, in this county, getting his education as his brother did, in the country schools. In the year 1872 he went to Central Point Academy, where he remained ten months. He then came home and went to farming in the Eighth District. December 19, 1877, he was married to Miss Willie Fletcher, and by this union had three children: William B., Lucy M. and Jessie Chilton. In 1884 our subject was elected justice of the peace and still holds the office. He is a Democrat, easting his first vote for Tilden and Hendricks. Mr. Bartee is the possessor of a fine tract of land, and is a man highly respected for his many good traits.

Alexander Baynham is the son of W. J. G. Baynham and M. A. C. (Smith) Baynham. The family is of English descent. W. J. Gr. Baynham was born in Virginia in 1821, and immigrated to Tennessee in early life, settling in Stewart County. He was married to Miss M. A. C. Smith, and by her became the father of six children—three boys and three girls, viz.: Alexander, John W., Forest, Victoria, Isabella and Rebecca After remaining in Stewart County for fifteen years Mr. W. J. G. Baynham removed to Montgomery County, where he remained on his farm until the negroes were freed; from there he went to Lafayette, Ky., and went into the furniture and undertaking business. He died suddenly in Lafayette, Ky., in the year 1881. While on his way from church he was taken suddenly ill and died of hemorrhage of the lungs a short time after reaching home. Alexander Baynham was born December 10, 1842, in Stewart County, Tenn., getting his education in the country schools. When the war broke out he enlisted in the Fiftieth Tennessee Regiment. Our subject was in the battle of Fort Donelson, and was with his regiment until it surrendered in February, 1862. In the year 1866 he was united in marriage to Miss E. J. Rossetter, of Kentucky, and to them were born seven children: Selwyn, Cora B., Carrie T., Walter A., Etha, Harry and Nick. Mr. Baynham was elected justice of the peace in the year 1882, and still holds the office. He possesses two fine tracts of land in the Fourth District, and is one of the leading men.

William Beaty, contractor, was born in Canada West, Prince Edward's County, in 1841, and is a son of James and Elizabeth (Martin) Beaty, and of Scotch-Irish descent. The parents were born in the "Emerald Isle," and in early life moved to Canada, where our subject received a common school education, and, at the age of fourteen, began a four-years' apprenticeship at the carpenter's trade. He came to the United States in 1863, and located in Illinois, where he resided for some time, and then moved to Cincinnati, Ohio, where he remained six years. He came to Clarksville, Tenn., in 1867, and here has since resided. He began the contracting business in 1874, and has since continued it. He helped build the tobacco exchange, court house, Presbyterian church, the cabinet buildings at university place, and many private residences, being one of the leading contractors in the city. He was married, October 10, 1871, to Mary C. P. Scott, of Clarksville, Tenn., daughter of J. M. and Parthena (Norsworthy) Scott, natives of Dickson County, Tenn., and descendants of Virginia and North Carolina families. They have three children: William Herbert, the eldest, was born in Clarksville, Tenn., August 29, 1872; Charles Angelos, born May 4, 1874, and Parthena Alma, their only daughter, born April 15, 1877. Mr. Beaty is a Democrat and belongs to the Masonic and K. of P. fraternities. His wife belongs to the Methodist

Episcopal Church. Gilmer M. Bell, a leading member of the Clarksville bar, and editor of the Clarksville Democrat, is a native of Christian County, Ky., born December 27, 1859, son of Darwin and Mary W. (Merriwether) Bell, and is of Scotch-Irish origin. The father of Mr. Bell is a native of the same county as himself, and was born in 1830. The paternal grandfather, Dr. J. F. Bell, was a Virginian, who came to Kentucky in 1810, and effected a settlement in Shelby County. In 1818 the family removed to Christian County, where Dr. Bell died in 1878. The father of our subject is a prominent "tiller of the soil," and one of the first men of the county in which he resides (Christian County, Ky.). The early life of Gilmer M. Bell was spent on the farm. He received a common school education and began the study of law in 1878, under the direction of his illustrious uncle, Gen. W. A. Quarles, in Clarksville. In 1880 he entered the law department of the Cumberland University, at Lebanon, and graduated from that institution the following year, June 1, 1881. He was admitted to the bar the same year, and in 1881 formed a partnership in the law practice with the late Judge James E. Rice, and their union continued until the latter's death in 1883. For two years Mr. Bell practiced alone, and then he became associated with A. S. Major, the firm being known as Bell & Major. In 1884 Mr. Bell became editor of the Clarksville Democrat, and the April following became proprietor also. He is a Democrat and a prominent young man.

John T. Bellamy, farmer, was born September 13, 1840, in Montgomery County, Tenn. His father, Robert D. Bellamy, is a native of Lexington, Ky., born December 14, 1818. In 1839 he married Miss Sarah A. Northington, a native of Montgomery County, and daughter of John and Mary Northington. Mrs. Bellamy died December 17, 1852, but Mr. Robert D. Bellamy is still living in Todd County, Ky. Our subject received his education in the common schools of his native county, and also in the Montgomery Institute. After the death of his mother he and his sisters were reared by his grandmother, Mary Northington, and in

1861 he married Miss Bettie Wimberley, a native of this county and a daughter of George S. and Charlotte Wimberley. To this union five children were born: Ella N. (deceased), Mary (deceased), Robert S., Lizzie (deceased) and Douglas. In August, 1873, the mother of these children died, and in October, 1874, our subject married Miss Nannie L. Keesee, a native of Tennessee and a daughter of Reuben C. and Judith P. Keesee. To this union two children were born: E. Ross and Reuben K. Our subject possesses a fine farm in District No. 6, and also another in District No. 1. In politics he is a Democrat, and he and wife are members of the Methodist Episcopal Church.

Robert B. Bigger was born April 7, 1839, in Montgomery County, Tenn., and was educated in the common schools. He has always followed the occupation of farming in the same locality where he now resides. After becoming a man he married Victoria T., daughter of William and Nancy Wall, who were born in Tennessee, the father in 1802. Mrs. Bigger was born in Montgomery County, September 9, 1840, and bore her husband the following children: David C, born in 1869; Harriet L., born in 1870; Robert E., born in 1872; William, born in 1873; Samuel T., born in 1875; Eudora E., born in 1876; Eva H., born in 1878; Nannie, born in 1880 (deceased), and Charles C., born in 1884. Mr. Bigger was a soldier in the Forty-second Regiment Tennessee Volunteers, and served four years. He was in the battles of Fort Donelson, Port Hudson, Jackson, Miss., New Hope Church, Marietta, Atlanta, Jonesboro and Franklin. He was originally a Whig. Since the war he has been a Democrat He is a member of the A. F. & A. M., and has held many offices in his lodge. His wife is a member of the Methodist Episcopal Church. His parents were Thompson and Eliza (Nicholson) Bigger, natives of North Carolina and Tennessee, respectively. The father was born in 1793, and was of French and Irish lineage. He came to Tennessee when a small boy, and worked at tanning and farming. He was married in 1835, and died in 1865. The mother was of English descent, and died in 1868.

Leopold Bloch was born in Hechingen, Hohenzollern, South Prussia, July 24, 1823. His parents were also natives of Germany, and lived and died in their native country. Leopold Bloch received a liberal education in the schools of Germany, and came to America in 1852, and located in Stewart County, Tenn. Mr. Bloch engaged in the general merchandise business in Dover, and continued in that place until 1863, when he came to Clarksville, and has since followed the same business in this city. His is probably the oldest dry goods house in Clarksville, and the firm is composed of Leopold and Simon Bloch, tried and reliable business men, and their house is one of the most substantial in the State. Simon Bloch is junior member of the firm, and was born in Germany in 1838. The great success which the firm has attained is due to the energy and labor of years. Our subject, Leopold, is a Democrat, and has been a member of the city council for years. He has taken great interest in the public schools of Clarksville, and is now secretary and treasurer of the school board. Mr. Bloch became a Mason in 1853, and is one of the prominent, generous and cultivated gentlemen of the city.

Thomas Bourne, superintendent of the Clarksville Gas and Water Company, is a native of County Kent, England, born forty miles from the World's Metropolis, March 21, 1850. The parents were John and Frances (Hopper) Bourne, natives of England. The father was born June 18, 1818, and both died in England in 1874. Our subject was educated in the schools of England and came to the United States in 1866, locating in Philadelphia where he followed the machinists trade, serving a regular apprenticeship. Subsequently he became connected with the American Gas and Meter Company of that city as machinist, and continued in this capacity more or less until 1882. He then came to Clarksville and in December of that year took charge of the gas works, and it is owing to his energy and enterprise that the city of Clarksville is so well lighted. In 1883 he was made superintendent of the Clarksville Water Company and is one of the most enterprising of its citizens. He was married in 1873 to Miss A. A. Lavender, a native of London, England. They have four children: Frances E., Amelia E., John E. and Horatio T. In politics Mr. Bourne is independent. He belongs to the F. & A. M., I. O. O. F. and K. of P., and he and wife are members of the Protestant Episcopal Church.

Charlemagne Bourne, farmer, was born November 15, 1851, in Montgomery County, Tenn., in the neighborhood where he has always lived. His father, A. D. Bourne, was a native of Woodford County, Ky., and was born in the year 1805 and is of Scotch extraction. He married Miss Sallie Whitfield, a native of this county, and to them were born twelve children, of which our subject is the eleventh. Mr. A. D. Bourne was a farmer and subsequently engaged in buying and selling stock, in which latter business he was extensively engaged. He was appointed by the county court as tobacco inspector and served a number of years as such. He died in the year 1878 and his wife in 1857. Our subject was educated in the country schools of his native county and his life business has been that of farming. February 13, 1884, he married Miss Lucy Pollard Peterson, a native of Montgomery County, and daughter of James B. and Catharine Peterson. To Mr. Bourne and wife one child, William Henry, has been born. Our subject owns a farm near Cherry Station and the productions from it are, corn, tobacco and wheat. He also raises the different grasses indigenous to this soil. Politically he is a Democrat.

Dr. George S. Bowling, ice manufacturer and one of the prominent business men of the county, was born near Hopkinsville, Ky., February 20, 1853, and is the eldest son of Dr. Henry G. and Sallie L. (Snadon) Bowling. He is of English descent and the nephew of Dr. William K. Bowling, an eminent physician of Nashville, and the grandson of Dr.

James B. Bowling. Our subject's juvenile days were passed on the farm. At the age of sixteen he entered Bethel College at Russellville, Ky., where he remained some time and then became a student at Warren College, Bowling Green, Ky. He was a student in the medical department of the Vanderbilt University at Nashville for some time, but later abandoned that profession and turned his attention to business. From 1875 to 1880 he carried on farming in Christian County, Ky., and at the latter date came to Clarksville and engaged in the manufacture of ice, at which he has since continued. He has one of the most extensive and complete factories in Tennessee, and ships extensively to all the principal places within a radius of 100 miles. He was married in 1876 to Lady S. Bugg, of Nashville, daughter of Samuel and Catharine Bugg. In 1886 Mr. Bowling was elected a director of the Farmers and Merchants' National Bank at Clarksville. He is a Democrat and cast his first vote for S. J. Tilden. He and wife are members of the Presbyterian Church and he is one of the very first business men of the city of Clarksville.

James M. Bowling was born in Christian County Ky., November 5, 1854, son of Dr. H. G. and Sarah L. (Snadon) Bowling, who were born in the "blue-grass State" in 1828 and 1832, respectively. The grandfather, Dr. James B. Bowling, was a Virginian who came to Clarksville when quite young, but after remaining a short time removed to Adairsville, Ky., and there resided until his death. James M. Bowling was educated at the private schools in Hopkinsville, Ky.; Bethel College at Russellville, Ky., and Warren College, at Bowling Green, Ky., where he completed his school life. For four years after returning from college his time was divided between settling his father's estate (who died soon after he quit school) and as salesman in a shoe store. He came to Clarksville in 1879 and engaged in the boot and shoe business, at which he has since continued and been quite successful. Since 1882 he has been engaged in the manufacture of ice, and in January, 1886, he enlarged his factory and furnished it with new machinery. It has a capacity of ten tons per day.

He was married, in 1878, to Sallie Sugg, a Tennesseean, born in 1858, daughter of Col. Cyrus F. Sugg, a soldier in the late war, killed at the battle of Mission Ridge. Mr. and Mrs. Bowling have two children: Mattie B., and George M. Mr. Bowling is a Democrat and a man identified with the interests of the city. He and wife are members of the Methodist Episcopal Church.

William G. Brawner was born in Todd County, Ky., February 28, 1847. His father, James H. Brawner, was a native of Hardin County, Ky., and was of German and Scotch-Irish descent. When a young man he immigrated to Todd County, where he married Lucy A. McAllister, a native of that county, and to them were born nine children, our subject being the second. In 1852 the family came to Montgomery County, Tenn., where the parents are yet residing. William G. obtained most of his education by private study at home. Much credit, he says, is due to his mother, who instilled in him a love for knowledge. He has mastered the common English branches, natural philosophy, chemistry, mental philosophy, rhetoric, and has made himself familiar with the higher mathematics. He has also learned to speak, read and write the German language. He was a teacher for a number of years and had excellent success as an educator. April 7, 1871, he married Sophia F. Freeh, a native of Cincinnati, Ohio; of German descent. To them were born these children: Hattie E., Beulah, Edgar A. and Eva. Since 1881 Mr. Brawner has devoted his time and attention to farming and stock raising. His home is about eight miles from Clarksville and he makes a specialty of raising tobacco and some of the best thorough-bred stock in the county. He is a Democrat and an elder in the Cumberland Presbyterian Church, of which his wife and eldest daughter are also members.

Edmund L. Brewer was born at Thomasville, Cheatham Co., Tenn., June 20, 1850. His father, Sterling Brewer, Jr. was born in Dickson County, Tenn., in 1811. He was of Welsh descent and a son of Sterling

Brewer, Sr., a native of North Carolina, who came to Tennessee about the beginning of the present century and engaged in farming and merchandising. He was representative for Dickson County, Tenn., in the State Legislature and served a number of years in the lower house, and was then elected State senator and was a member of that body for several years, a portion of that time serving as speaker of the Senate, and was a member of the State Legislature twelve years. He died in Nashville in July, 1852. Sterling Brewer, Jr., was educated in Nashville, and after attaining his majority engaged in the mercantile business until 1830. He was a minister of the Methodist Episcopal Church for eight years, and then taught school in Turnersville and other points for about thirty years. In 1839 he was married to Agnes J. Sanders, by whom he had one child, Letitia H., who died in infancy. His wife died in 1841, and in 1844 he wedded Virginia G. Glenn, and to them these children, James S., Lucy L., Edmund L., Mary L., and Sterling C., were born. Sterling Brewer was a farmer and died April 5, 1885. His widow is still living. Edmund L., our subject, was educated in his father's schools, which were graded, and consequently received a liberal education. He came to Montgomery County, Tenn., when nine years old and has always remained in that county and followed farming as an occupation. In February, 1877, he married Tennie W. Patrick, born in the county October 28, 1855, daughter of James H. Patrick, a native of Tennessee. To Mr. and Mrs. Brewer have been born these children: Lewis V., Charles A. (deceased), James P. and Glenn. Our subject is a Democrat and holds the office of magistrate of District No. 10. He and wife are members of the Methodist Episcopal Church.

J. L. Brodie is the son of Alexander and Mary (Oldham) Brodie, and was born March 4, 1839. The family originally came from North Carolina and were among the early settlers of this State, to which they came in the year 1813, settling in the Fourth District of this county. Mr. Alexander Brodie was born November 13, 1794, in North Carolina, and came with the family to this State. He was a farmer by occupation and bought a tract of land in Montgomery County. In the year 1822 he was united in marriage to Miss Mary Oldham, a native of this State, born in Williamson County, To them were born six children, two of whom are dead; those living are S., E. M., J. S. and E. M. Alexander Brodie was a member of the Methodist Episcopal Church for thirty or forty years, and was one of the old settlers of this county, who leaves a name behind him to be cherished in the memory of those who knew him. He died March 19, 1865, and his wife November 13, 1869. J. L. Brodie, the subject of this sketch, is a native of this State, and was born near Bose Hill In the early part of his life he turned his attention to farming, and this calling he still pursues. In 1866 he was united in matrimony to Miss A. A. Trahern, of Christian County, Ky., daughter of William Trahern. To this union were born two children, viz.: W. S. and R. E. When the war broke out he enlisted in the Fourteenth Tennessee Regiment under Col. Forbes, where he remained for ten months; he was then discharged on account of being physically disabled. He then enlisted in the First Kentucky Cavalry, in which regiment he remained for a short time, then joining the Second Kentucky under Morgan. He participated in the battles of Shiloh and Murfreesboro, and was slightly wounded in the battle of Marion. He remained with his regiment until it surrendered at Washington, Ga., May 10, 1865. Mr. Brodie owns a tract of land in the Fourth District, is a member of the Methodist Episcopal Church, a Democrat in politics and one of the leading farmers in the county.

George Watson Back, brick manufacturer, was born in Louisa County, Va., August 23, 1831, son of George Washington and Sallie E. (Estes) Buck, both born in Virginia—the father in 1801, the mother in 1808. The paternal grandfather was an Englishman and came to America when only eleven years of age, working his way on shipboard; he landed in Norfolk, Va., and died in that State about 1834. The family came to Tennessee in 1833, and after residing one year in Rutherford County came to Montgomery County, where the father died in 1866. George Watson grew to manhood on the farm and worked on the same until twenty-one years of age, when he learned the brick-maker's trade. In 1861 he enlisted in Company A, Forty-ninth Tennessee Confederate Regiment, Infantry, and was taken prisoner at Fort Donelson, and until September was a prisoner at Camp Douglas, Chicago. He was exchanged at Vicksburg. In 1864 he was taken prisoner at Nashville and was taken to Camp Chase, Ohio, and was released in May, 1865. Since that time he has been a brick manufacturer and makes on an average 1,000,000 bricks per season, and gives employment to twenty-five men. Mr. Buck is a Democrat and a prominent citizen of Montgomery County.

James T. Buckingham, farmer, was born in this State October 12, 1826, and is the son of William and Nancy (Gardner) Buckingham, born in the years 1802 and 1803, and died in 1857 and 1869, respectively. September 27, 1850, our subject was united in marriage to Miss Mary J. Balswell, born March 24, 1832. To this union three children were born: Annetta C., born August 10, 1853; Mary J., born November 3, 1856, and William J. B., born September 30, 1860. In the year 1863 Mrs. Buckingham died, and Mr. Buckingham took for his second wife Miss Nannie L. Cathey, who was born October 8, 1838, and is now living with her third husband. To Mr. and Mrs. Buckingham were born six children: John H., born October 18, 1866; Maggie A., born January 3, 1868; Alice J., born April 4, 1869; William A., born July 31, 1871; Thomas E., born December 11, 1872, and Sarah E., born February 20, 1875. In 1868 our subject moved from Stewart County, Tenn., and resumed his occupation of farming. He is a good citizen and is respected by all.

W. Frank Buckner, of the firm of Parish, Buckner & Co., tobacco commission merchants, was born at Oak Grove, Christian Co., Ky., June 15, 1843; son of Frank W. and Sarah E. (Gordon) Buckner, and the third of five children. His father was born in Virginia in 1809, and came to

Kentucky when a young man. He was married, in 1839, to Miss Gordon, a native of Christian County, Ky., born in 1819. Our subject spent his boyhood days on a farm, and was educated at Bethel College, Russellville, Ky., and at Stewart College, in this city. He was a student when the war broke out, and in June, 1861, joined the Oak Grove Rangers, which were raised by Capt. T. Woodward, and after the secession of Tennessee he came with his company and was sworn into the State (Tennessee) service and transferred to the First Kentucky Cavalry. In 1862 he was chosen second lieutenant in the Second Kentucky Cavalry, and held this position until the close of the war. After the close of the war he engaged in farming, and has since continued. In 1870 he removed to Hopkinsville, Ky., and then engaged in the tobacco business until 1883, when he returned to the farm. In 1885 he moved to New Providence, and there now resides. November 1, 1885, he engaged in the commission business in Clarksville. He is a man of sterling business qualities and unimpeachable character. He was married, in 1867, to Hattie E. Elliott, of Montgomery County, Tenn., born in 1846, daughter of Col. William H. Elliott. They have four children: Elliott, Gordon W., Annie and Lewis. Mr. Buckner is a Democrat, a Mason, K. of P. and K. of H., and his wife is a member of the Methodist Episcopal Church.

Robert H. Burney, attorney at law, was born in Davidson County, Tenn., October 31, 1854. His father, H. L. Burney, a Presbyterian minister, was born in Robertson County in 1816, and for about forty years was engaged in ministerial labors. Our subject's mother was formerly Miss Mary L. Vick, a native of Virginia, born in 1815, and died in Robertson County, Tenn., in 1874. Our subject's ancestors were of Scotch-Irish descent, born in North Carolina and came to Tennessee at an early period. Robert H. spent his early days on a farm and in attending the schools of Montgomery County, having come here in 1855. He also attended private schools and in 1875 entered the Cumberland University at Lebanon, Tenn., and graduated in 1876. In July of that year he located in Clarksville, where he has since resided and practiced law. In 1878 he was elected attorney-general for the Clarksville Criminal Courts and is identified with the Democratic party. February 10, 1880, he was united in marriage to Clara S. Kennedy, daughter of D. N. Kennedy. Mrs. Burney was born in Clarksville and is the mother of three children: Robert H. Jr., Sarah B. and Mary L. Mr. Burney is a member of the K. of P. fraternity and his wife belongs to the Presbyterian Church.

Dr. T. E. Cabaniss, dentist, was born in New Providence, Montgomery Co., Tenn., March 12, 1857, son of J. W. Cabaniss, who is a native of Christian County, Ky., born in 1829, and came to Clarksville, Tenn., about 1850. He studied dentistry under Dr. W. J. Castner, one of the most prominent men in the State in his profession, and then practiced in Clarksville for about twenty years, He died in October, 1884. Our subject's mother was Miss Lucy New, who was born in Todd County in 1836. Dr. Cabaniss is the only son of their three children. He was educated in Stewart College and began the study of dentistry in Clarksville and graduated from the dental department of the Vanderbilt University in 1880. He has since practiced in Clarksville, and has met with good success. July 13, 1880, he led to the hymeneal altar Miss Annie Anderson, a native of Paris, Ky. They are members of the Christian Church, and the Doctor is a Democrat in his political views.

Samuel A. Caldwell, justice of the peace and proprietor of Caldwell's livery, sale and feed stable at Clarksville, Tenn., was born November 10, 1825, son of Samuel and Nancy (Howell) Caldwell, and of Irish extraction. The father was born in Virginia in 1776. He was a soldier in the war of 1812. The mother was a native Tennesseean, born in 1804 Her ancestors were Virginians. The Caldwell family came to Tennessee in 1806, and here the father died in 1840 and the mother in 1856. Our subject's early days were spent on a farm and his education was obtained in private schools. At the age of nineteen he began life for himself, and in

1841 began clerking in a store in Palmyra, continuing seven years. About this time he engaged in the lumber business, but lost more than $2,000 worth of lumber, which was used in the construction of Fort Donelson. In 1862 he abandoned the lumber business, and from that time until the close of the war he was engaged in farming. In 1867 he came to Clarksville and engaged in the livery business, in which he has continued to the present time. He was formerly a Whig, but is now a Democrat. In 1875 he was elected justice of the peace and served by reelection. He is a leading man, one of the prominent citizens of Clarksville. In 1857 he was married to M. A. Neblett, born in this county in 1831, daughter of Dr. Neblett. They have five children: Richard D., Mary C., Lucy V., Hart M. and Cora L. Mr. Caldwell is a successful business man, and has made his own way in the world. He is a member of the Methodist Episcopal Church, and belongs to the Masons and K. of H.

Dr. L. B. Chilton is the son of Dr. L. F. Chilton and Minerva (Tribble) Chilton. L. F. Chilton was born in Hardin County, Ky., in 1814, and was educated at the Medical University of Louisville, Ky., beginning the practice of medicine at Pembroke, Ky. He was twice married, his second wife being Miss Sarah W. Killebrew, of Montgomery County, Tenn. He died in the year 1861. Dr. L. F. Chilton represented the county of Christian in the Legislature, and introduced a bill to build the insane asylum at Hopkinsville, which institution now stands a monument to his memory. Our subject was born April 15, 1889, and was educated in the country schools until the year 1858, when he went to "Shelby Medical College" of Nashville, graduating with honor in the year 1861. At the breaking out of the war he enlisted in the First Kentucky Cavalry; after being in his regiment one year he was placed in the Second Kentucky as assistant surgeon. In two years he was promoted to chief surgeon in the same regiment. After the war he came back to his home at Pembroke, Ky., where he remained only a short time. He practiced in different places until 1867, and married Miss Mattie D. Washburn. Two years after his marriage he moved to Woodlawn, in this county, where he has practiced medicine for fifteen years. He owns sixteen and three-fourths acres of land, and does a practice of about $3,000 per year, and is a member of the F. & A. M. He and wife are members of the Cumberland Presbyterian Church, and are highly respected by all who know them.

J. B. Clardy is the son of John and Elena (Thomas,) Clardy. The family was originally from Virginia. The grandfather of our subject immigrated to Tennessee in the early part of the present century. John Clardy was married to Miss Elena Thomas, and to them were born six children: L. M., J. W., J. B., M. I., Mary H. and Alice E. John Clardy died in 1883 at his home in the Fourth District; he was a member of the Methodist Episcopal Church the greater part of his life, a good man, and is now receiving his reward in that better world. J. B. Clardy was born July 7, 1856, in Christian County, Ky., and moved to Tennessee in 1863, settling in Montgomery County. In 1881 he was married to Miss M. O. Clardy and became the father of two children, viz.: R. L., and Lizzie A. M. O. Clardy died December 25, 1885, and was a member of the Methodist Church. Mr. Clardy lives on the farm with his mother and is one of the leading citizens.

Benjamin F. Clardy, deceased, was born in Tennessee, July 19, 1836, and was the son of James Clardy and Henrietta L. (Daniel) Clardy, married in 1809 and both natives of Virginia. His father was born in 1784 and immigrated to Tennessee in 1815, where he died September 30, 1846. His mother was born about 1794 and died November 17, 1867. Our subject was the youngest of a family of thirteen, and in the year 1868 was united in marriage to Miss Cosby C. Carlile, a relative of Hon. John G. Carlile, of Kentucky. She is a native of Virginia, and was born November 29, 1841. Her father, Daniel B. Carlile, was born in North Carolina, in 1812, and immigrated to Virginia, where he was married to

Amanda M. Hutsell, a native of Virginia, born January 28, 1818. Daniel B. Carlile died January 19, 1882. To our subject and wife was born one child, May B., her birth occurring August 15, 1869. Our subject was a country boy and was reared on a farm. In 1868 he purchased the Meadow Grove farm. It lies about six miles northwest of Clarksville and is a splendid stock farm. It is favorably situated and is near the public road leading from Clarksville to Lafayette. Since Mr. Clardy's death his wife assumed control of the farm and has it cultivated by tenants.

M. H. Clark & Bro., leaf tobacco brokers. This firm, for so many years prominently connected with the tobacco trade of Clarksville, is composed of Micajah Henry Clark and Lewis Rogers Clark, born in Richmond, Va., and who came to Clarksville in January, 1855, and November, 1857, respectively. They are the sons of Dr. Micajah Clark, one of the most distinguished physicians Virginia ever produced. His memory is still so revered by the profession at large that a few years ago, over thirty years after Ms death, the American Medical Association of the United States requested a sketch of his life, which is published in its annals. We make below extracts from that publication: Micajah Clark, M. D., of Richmond, Va., was born on his father's plantation in Albemarle County, Va., near the present railroad station, Keswick, of the Chesapeake & Ohio Railroad, on January 28, 1788; died at his residence, in the city of Richmond, August 19, 1849. His father was William Clark, and his mother a daughter of Col. Tarleton Cheadle, an officer in the English Army, who immigrated to Virginia before the revolutionary war. Dr. Clark was named after his paternal grandfather, Micajah Clark, one of the pioneer settlers of Albemarle County, buying from the State a body of land of 40,000 acres, which is still known in the old county maps as "Clark's Tract." From this courageous old pioneer sprang a large family, twelve children, to be men and women grown, the youngest of whom was William Clark, and whose youngest son was Micajah Clark, the subject of this sketch. Dr. Micajah Clark belongs to that historical family of Clarks, of this county, which has furnished so many adventurous spirits—soldiers, governors, legislators and professional men. Among them were Gen. George Rogers Clark, who conquered the Northwest Territory; Gov. William Clark, of Missouri; Merriwether Lewis (the two latter being the Lewis and Clark who made the Rocky Mountain expedition under Jefferson's administration), and many other prominent men during and after the Revolutionary war, and subsequently in the governments of the States of Kentucky, Missouri, Texas and other Southern States. Their blood was again well represented in our late civil war, on the Southern side; among the most prominent were Gens. John B. Clark and M. L. Clark, of Missouri, and Gen. James Clark Dearing, of Virginia. Young Micajah Clark, having a decided predilection for the profession of medicine, went to Richmond and commenced his studies with Dr. Adams, a talented and prominent physician. After the usual routine he entered the University of Pennsylvania at Philadelphia, and had the good fortune, through his credentials, to become an office student of the celebrated Dr. Physick, then in the zenith of his fame. Dr. Physick soon discovered his talents, his great love for his profession and thirst for knowledge, and before his graduation, in speaking of him, remarked that he thought "Physicians like poets were born, not made, and that Clark was a born physician," such an expression being a diploma in itself, and probably no other student of Dr. Physick's ever received a higher compliment from him. Dr. Clark graduated an M. D. April 26, 1811.

After his graduation he took an extended tour on horseback, riding through Pennsylvania, New Jersey, New York, Rhode Island, Connecticut and Massachusetts. On his return home, deciding to settle in New Orleans, he again mounted his horse August 25, 1811. His horseback tour was again a full one, riding through many parts of Kentucky and Tennessee, not on the direct line, but to see the country. Then through the Indian nations, striking the Mississippi River at Natchez, at which village he sold his horses and left January 5, 1812, for New Orleans, up-on the first steam-boat which went down the Mississippi River (owned by Fulton, Livingston & Co.), arriving in New Orleans January 12. Dr. Clark kept a full diary of his tour, which is quite interesting. Dr. Clark finding the climate very enervating to him decided to return to Virginia via New York, reaching Albemarle June 25, 1812. His final decision was to settle in Richmond, Va., and his career there was an uninterrupted success, his practice steadily and rapidly increased, and even with the small current fees of his time, $1 per visit, his practice averaged for many years $13,000 to $16,000 per annum. He was appointed surgeon in the army in the war of 1812, and served two enlistments with the troops at Craney Island. Dr. Micajah Clark was married on the 29th of December, 1819, to his second cousin, Miss Caroline Virginia Harris, eldest daughter of Benjamin James Harris, a prominent and wealthy tobacco merchant of Richmond, Va. His children were William James, Sarah Ellyson, Mary Elizabeth, Micajah Henry, Caroline Virginia, Ellen Douglas, Henry Auburn, Lewis Rogers, David Branch, Emily Auburn, and six others who died in infancy without names. His widow survived him many years, dying February 17, 1871. The paternal grandfather of the subjects of this sketch, was William Clark, who married Judith Cheadle. He raised three children: James, who married Margaret Lewis, raised a large family and moved from Albemarle to Pike County, Mo.; Jacob, who married and died young without issue, and Micajah. William Clark was a cavalry commander in the war of the Revolution. Arms captured in personal combat from some of Tarleton's cavalry were retained as trophies in the family for many years.

The great-grandfather of M. H. and L. R. Clark was Micajah Clark, who was born September 16, 1718, and married Judith Adams, who was born October, 1716. Their children were Christopher, Robert, Mourning, Micajah, John, Edward, Penelope, Judith, Bowling, Elizabeth, James and William. This old patriarch was a man of strong character, good attainments and devout piety, and was able to give each of his numerous children a handsome estate. He was a valued and trusted friend of Thomas Jefferson, and surveyed and laid off for the former and himself some large plantations in Bedford County, Va. He died full of years, and greatly beloved, at the house of his youngest child, William, with whom he had made his home during his latter years. Gov. James Clark, of Kentucky, was one of his grandsons. The senior member of the firm, M. H. Clark, married, in 1861, Miss Elizabeth W. Kerr, daughter of Mr. M. M. Kerr, of Clarksville, Tenn., and has two children, a son and daughter. The former, Morris K. Clark, is associated with the firm in their business. M. H. Clark was chief and confidential clerk of the executive office of the Confederate States, and the last acting Confederate States treasurer and made the final disbursements of the treasury. He saw some service in the trenches around Richmond, Va., and received his "baptism of fire" in helping to repel the "Dahlgren raid" on the city. Jefferson Davis made him a staff officer with the rank of captain. He claims to have been the last Confederate officer on duty, performing his last duties in November, 1865.

The junior member, Lewis R. Clark, joined Company A, Forty-ninth Tennessee Regiment, as a private, was captured at the surrender of Fort Donelson and imprisoned at Camp Douglas. After his exchange he was elected junior captain of that hard-fighting regiment, the Tenth Tennessee, and served through the war, fighting his way up to the senior captaincy. At the bloody battle of Chickamauga the gallant Tenth carried into battle 328 muskets, and lost in killed and wounded 224 men; of the ten captains in the line eight were killed or wounded. Capt. Clark, who was in command of the skirmish line during the severest portion of the engagement, brought out only six men of the twenty-eight he carried in. Though his clothes were cut with bullets in many places, he was one of the fortunate two captains of the regiment who escaped unhurt. He was afterward wounded at the battle of Jonesboro, Ga. He gave his parole at the surrender of Johnston's army at Greensboro, N. C. In the consolidation of many Tennessee regiments in North Carolina, he was appointed lieutenant-colonel of one of these consolidated regiments, but did not accept the well-earned promotion. He returned to Clarksville after the close of the war, rejoined his brother in business and represents the house in the tobacco market of Hopkinsville, Ky.

E. M. Clark, of the firm of Smith, Clark & Co., was born in Troy, N. Y., March 14, 1814, son of Edward Clark, who was a native of Vermont, born at Bradford in 1784, and died at Schenectady, N. Y., in 1867. He was of English descent, and our subject's mother was of Scotch descent. Our subject came to Clarksville in 1840, and here has since resided. He has been in business in the city of Clarksville since 1842. After the close of the war he became a member of the above-named firm, and in this capacity now continues. He is a practical mechanic, and is one of the leading carpenters and contractors of the city. He was married, in 1843, to Miss C. A. Covington, by whom he had eight children, seven of whom survive their mother, who died February 27, 1884. Mr. Clark is a Democrat in his political views, and cast his first presidential vote for Van Buren. In 1830 he joined the Methodist Episcopal Church, and has been an official member ever since, and is a strict temperance man. He has an excellent constitution, and prides himself upon never having abused it. He is well and favorably known in this part of Tennessee, and is a first-class citizen.

Louis T. Cocke, farmer, was born in Tennessee January 28, 1831. He is the sixth of fifteen children born to John and Hester R. (Corlew) Cocke. His parents are natives of Tennessee, and were born in 1798 and 1863, respectively. Our subject was united in marriage to Miss Rebecca J. Crow, a native of Alabama, born November 26, 1831, and the second of nine children born to Isaac and Mary A. (Cocke) Crow. Her parents were born in 1803 and 1806, and died in 1852 and 1858, respectively.

Our subject and wife are the parents of nine children: James T., Susan F., Mary A., Lucy E., Isaac F., Hester J., Samuel C., Phœbe A. and William E. Mr. Cocke was educated in the common schools of the county, is a Methodist in his belief and an ardent Democrat. He has a good farm, the principal products of which are corn, tobacco and wheat. He is now building an addition to his house, which will be, when completed, a fine farm residence. In 1882 he was elected justice of the peace in his district, and this office he filled in an able and competent manner. On January 17, 1884, he had the misfortune to lose his wife.

Pleasant Cocke was born in this county and State July 30, 1833. He is the eighth of fifteen children born to John and Hester R. (Corlew) Cocke, prominent and useful citizens. Mr. Pleasant Cocke was united in marriage to Miss Mary A. S. Starkey, a native of Tennessee, born May 29, 1841, and the third of three children born to Thomas and Frances (Roberts) Starkey. Her father was a native of Tennessee, born in 1798, and died November 25, 1862. Her mother was born in North Carolina in the year 1803. Our subject and wife are the parents of six children: Susan F., Sallie S., John T., Stephen M., Annie E. and Pleasant. Our subject was educated in the common schools of the county, is a member of the Methodist Episcopal Church and a Democrat. He is a successful farmer, and is living on the farm where he was born. He takes great interest in the education of his children. He has in his possession the first dollar he ever earned; it was coined in 1798 and contains the thirteen stars.

Enoch N. Cooksey was born in Tennessee December 6, 1841. His father, Jesse Cooksey, was a Virginian, born in the year 1793. He immigrated to Tennessee when but seventeen years of age and participated in the war of 1812. Our subject's mother, Sarah Heathman, was born in North Carolina about 1803 and died in 1882. His father died in 1866. Mr. Enoch N. Cooksey was united in marriage to Miss Mary Dority, a native of Tennessee, born July 18, 1851. Her father was John Dority, a native of this State, born February 11, 1821, and her mother was Emily Toler, also a native of Tennessee. She was born May 11, 1822, and died in the year 1862. The fruits of the union of our subject and wife were seven children: William T., Virginia, Thomas E., Francis E., Sallie M., James C. and Newton. Our subject was reared on a farm. In 1861 he enlisted in Company E, Fiftieth Tennessee, and went immediately to Fort Donelson where he was taken prisoner and held for seven months. He was then taken to Vicksburg and exchanged. He was engaged in the battles at Raymond, Chattanooga and Missionary Ridge; was with Joseph E. Johnston during his retreat to Atlanta and Nashville. While at Nashville he was taken prisoner and carried to Camp Chase, where he remained two months, and was then released at Richmond, Va., and granted a furlough. He traveled through the Southern States until after the surrender in 1865, when he returned home and resumed his occupation of farming.

B. J. Corban, a native of this State, was born April 6, 1853. He is the elder of two children born to Burrell and Sarah A. (Andrews) Corban. His father was born in Tennessee in 1811 and his mother was born in Virginia in the year 1818. Our subject was wedded to Miss Maria C. Batson in the year 1874. She is a native of Tennessee and was born June 16, 1853. She is the eighth of eleven children born to Stephen C. and Maria A. Batson. Her father is a native of Tennessee and was born in the year 1811. Her mother is a native of Virginia and was born in 1824. To our subject and wife were born five children: Burrell B., born October 3, 1874; Repps L., born November 11, 1877; Esken, born and died in 1879; Sidney W., born December 2, 1880, and Joanna M., born November 27, 1883. Our subject was a telegraph operator in early life. In 1876 he began merchandising and is now in business at Corbandale, a station on the Louisville & Nashville Railroad, that takes its name from our subject's father. In 1882 he was elected justice of the peace in the Nineteenth District.

John B. Coulter, of the firm of Coulter Bros., dealers in dry goods in Clarksville, Tenn., was born in Elktown, Todd Co., Ky., April 18, 1846, son of Robert S. and Fannie (Bradley) Coulter, and of English lineage. His father was born in North Carolina in 1802 and his mother in Virginia in 1810. The father was a cabinet-maker and farmer and came to Kentucky at a very early period. The father died near Elktown in 1858 and the mother in California in 1880. John B. is the youngest of five children. One of his brothers, Capt. R. T. Coulter, was killed at the battle of Franklin. B. F. Coulter is in California, as is also the sister, Sarah. John was educated in the Elkton schools and at the age of fifteen began clerking in a store in that place. He came to Clarksville in 1865, and from that time to 1874 was salesman for B. F. Coulter. In 1877 he began the dry goods business in Clarksville and has continued ever since, meeting with good success. In November, 1871, he was united in marriage to Susie A. Stratton, born in Virginia in 1846, daughter of R. H. Stratton. They have five children: Fannie Bell, Richard S., Susie J., Sarah W. and Hettie A. Mr. Coulter is a Democrat and a member of the K. of H., and he and wife belong to the Christian Church. He is one of the leading dry goods men of the city and is doing well financially.

Robert F. Crabtree, a native of Tennessee, was born October 7, 1852. His father, James M. Crabtree, was born in Kentucky, about 1825, and was wedded to Laurena Trice, a native of Tennessee, born about 1829. To this union three children were born, of whom our subject was the second. Mr. Robert F. Crabtree spent his boyhood days on a farm and was educated in the best schools of the county. His first business experience was with J. W. Howell, dealers in tobacco; afterward he engaged in the same business with G. J. Davie, remaining with him until the spring of 1869. In the fall of the same year he engaged in the grocery business with Pettus & Bros. In 1875 he went into the general merchandising business for himself, and soon afterward ran, in addition to this, a wholesale liquor house until 1881 when he discontinued the liquor business. In 1883 he began retailing liquor in connection with his other business. He is a member of the Masonic Lodge and a stanch Democrat.

William H. Crouch is a son of Hardin and Dorothea (Murray) Crouch, who were of English lineage and natives of "the Old Dominion." The father was a farmer, and he and wife immigrated to this county, where they resided the remainder of their lives. The father died in 1845, and the mother in 1859. To them were born three children, our subject being the youngest. He was born in Tennessee, December 12, 1813, and received his education in the country schools. He has always been a tiller of the soil, and since 1837 has been extensively engaged in the tobacco trade, not only selling it but raising it himself. He was married, in 1846, to Miss Margaret Rudolph, born in the immediate neighborhood of her present residence. To their union the following children were born: Dorothea A., Jack and Charles R., all living. Mr. Crouch, up to the dissolution of that party and since then, has been a stanch supporter of Democratic principles. He and wife are members of the Cumberland Presbyterian Church. Mr. Crouch has a commodious and beautifully located residence about eight miles from Clarksville, where he and sons are tilling a large farm.

William H. Crouch, M. D., is a native of Montgomery County, Tenn., and was born September 17, 1854. He is the second of eight children born to John S. and Mary B. (Combs) Crouch. John S. Crouch was a native of Tennessee, born in 1810 and died in 1873; his wife was a native of Kentucky, and was born about 1828 and died in 1871. The subject of this sketch was united in marriage to Miss Margaret H. Hunter, a native of Tennessee, and born May 20, 1857. She is the daughter of Henry and Margaret Hunter, natives of Tennessee, and born in 1823 and 1829. To our subject and wife were born one child, viz.: John H., born June 20, 1882. Mr. Crouch was reared on a farm, and began reading medicine in 1878. In 1883 he entered the University of Tennessee, at

Nashville, and graduated in 1885. In March of the same year he moved to the place where he now resides, in Collinsville, and began the practice of medicine. He has been extremely successful, his practice extending into Dickson and Cheatham Counties.

Capt James Joseph Crusman, wholesale and retail grocer, of the firm of Crusman & Howard, is a native of Clarksville, born July 3, 1837, son of Cornelius and Margaret E. (Allen) Crusman, and is of Scotch-Welsh descent on the father's side. The father was born in Charlottsville, Va., in 1800, and came to Clarksville in his youth. He was elected sheriff of the county when about twenty-one years of age, and served again by reelection. During the gold fever in California he and a company of men went there. He died November 11, 1851, being assistant surveyor of customs at San Francisco at the time of his death. The mother was a daughter of Gen. J. J. Allen, of Scotch-Irish descent, a soldier in the war of 1812, and was born in Kentucky in 1810 and died in Clarksville. Our subject was educated at private schools and Stewart College, and began clerking in a store in 1855. In 1860 he began business for himself in partnership with Samuel Johnson, who transferred his interest to Charles Mitchell in a few months. In 1861 both partners enlisted in Company H, Fourteenth Tennessee Infantry, our subject being made second lieutenant in 1861, and in 1862 was made captain, which position he held until the close of the war. He was wounded at the battle of West Point in 1862, and was taken prisoner at Petersburg, Va., in 1864, but made his escape two months afterward. He was a good and brave soldier, and in the summer of 1865 returned to Clarksville, and in the fall of that year began the business in which he has since continued. In 1883 he formed a partnership with E. M. Howard, one of the representative men of this city. They carry an excellent line of goods, and are doing a large and paying business. Clarksville is largely indebted to Mr. Crusman for the flourishing grocery trade that has been built up here. Mr. Crusman was formerly a Whig, but is now a Democrat. In 1881 he was elected mayor of the city, filling the position very creditably. He is a Mason and a Knight Templar.

John T. Cunningham, senior member of the firm of Cunningham Bros., grocers of Clarksville, Tenn., was born in Dickson County, Tenn., October 23, 1850, and is the eldest son of eight children of Dr. E. W. and Harriet N. (Talley) Cunningham, who were natives of North Carolina, born in 1829 and 1831, respectively. The father at the age of twenty-three entered the Philadelphia Medical College, from which he graduated, and later located in Dickson County, Tenn., and there resided and practiced until his death, in 1869. He was a leading physician of that county for twenty-five years. Two of our subject's brothers came to Clarksville in 1881, and established a grocery store, and since 1883 John T. has also been a resident of the city and a member of the firm. They rank among the leading grocery merchants of the town, and besides carrying a large stock of staple and fancy groceries, also deal in coal. John T.'s early days were spent in laboring on the farm, and in attending the country schools. September 7, 1871, he wedded Miss M. Weems, of Columbia, Tenn., born December 14, 1849. They have four children: Elijah C, Sallie N., John T. and Lady G. Mr. Cunningham is a Democrat and a Royal Arch Mason and K. of H. His wife died April 14, 1884.

Hon. William M. Daniel, one of the first lawyers of the State, is a native of Tennessee, having been born in Henderson County, February 4, 1838. He is the second of six surviving children of C. S. and Martha A. (Foster) Daniel. Both his father and mother were natives of Virginia, the former being born in Brunswick County in 1806, and the latter in Charlotte County in 1809. They removed to Tennessee in 1833, and settled in Henderson County, where they remained till 1840, when they came to Montgomery County, where the father died in 1866, and the mother in 1884. Mr. Daniel's parents being in very moderate circumstances he determined to have a better education than was in their means to give him, and after leaving the public schools, by his own exertions he was enabled to take a course of study at Stewart College, now Southwestern Presbyterian University. Having completed his college education in 1859, he began the study of law in Clarksville, under the direction of Gen. William A. Quarles. He was just entering upon the practice when the war came on, and early in the spring of 1861 he enlisted in Company A, of the Fourteenth Tennessee Infantry, Confederate States Army, as a private. In 1862 he was detailed for service in the signal department, and had charge of Lookout Station for Gen. A. P. Hill's division. In 1863 he took charge of the signal department for Gen. Anderson's division. In 1864 he again united with his regiment, but was subsequently trans- ferred to the Thirteenth Virginia Cavalry, and with it remained until the surrender at Appomattox. He returned home at the close of the war, as many other gallant soldiers did, penniless. Resuming at once the practice of the law, he formed a partnership with the late Judge R. W. Hum- phries, which continued until 1869, when he was admitted to a partner- ship with his old preceptor, Gen. Quarles, and this relation continues between them. Although he came home from the war without a cent, he soon manifested great energy and business capacity. He was both con- servative and enterprising, and when the people along the line deter- mined to build the Clarksville & Princeton Railroad, they recognized his financial ability by selecting him as its president Mr. Daniel has never sought political preferment, though he is a man of strong convictions. When the financial troubles of the State seemed to be most embarrass- ing in 1880, it was thought that his financial ability would be much needed in the State Legislature, and he was nominated by the Democrat- ic convention for the State Senate. Though much against his inclination, he accepted the nomination and was elected. In the Senate, as elsewhere, he was equal to all emergencies, and even filled the delicate position of chairman of the celebrated investigating committee with much satisfac- tion. In 1882 he was again elected to the Senate, and was chairman of the Judiciary Committee. In 1877 Mr. Daniel removed to his present place of residence, where he has some 200 acres one mile and a half from Clarksville, on the Nashville Pike. This place was very poor and worn when he bought it, and he has taken great pains in reclaiming it. At great expense he has brought it up to a high state of cultivation, and now has it stocked with thoroughbred Jersey cattle. He has one of the finest herds of Jerseys in this part of the State, and has taken much pleasure in them. He was united in marriage, January 31, 1867, to Miss Minor De Graffenreid, of Williamson County, Tenn. By this union he has the following children: Fontaine D., Margaret M., Susie Bell, William M., Jr., Thomas M. and Robert H.

Jesse A. Davidson was born and reared in the county where he now lives January 31, 1851. His father, Absalom Davidson, was of English descent, and died in the county of his birth (Montgomery) in 1854. He was first married to Martha Whitworth, by whom he had three children: John W., Elijah F. and William H. After his first wife's death, which occurred about 1846, he married Margaret Stephens, a native of Sumner County, Tenn., and of English descent. To his last marriage were born these children: James T., Elizabeth, Jesse A. (our subject), Rufus M. and Alice E. Jesse A. was educated in the common schools of his native county, and has always followed the life of an agriculturist. On October 16, 1881, he wedded Margaret Walls, who was born in Montgomery County, June 21, 1862, daughter of Esquire Walls, a resident of the same county. To Mr. and Mrs. Davidson have been born two sons: Jesse H., born June 5, 1883, and George W., born March 21, 1885. Mr. Davidson is a Democrat, and he and wife are members of the Methodist Episcopal Church.

Thomas G. Davie, was born in Montgomery County, Tenn., September 24, 1847, and is the fourth of five children born to William and Mary (Poole) Davie, natives of North Carolina. His father was born in the year 1796, and died in the year 1866. His mother was born in 1812, and died in 1852. His father immigrated to this State in the early part of the present century, and located on a portion of the farm on which our subject now lives. Mr. Thomas Davie is a life-long farmer and a stanch Democrat. In 1878 he moved to the farm on which he now lives on Little West Fork of Red River, the principal products of which are corn, wheat and tobacco. He was educated in the common schools of the county, and is an intelligent and enterprising farmer.

Clay E. Dean was born in Clarksville, Montgomery Co., Tenn., January 7, 1848, and is the youngest of seven children born to Elijah H. and Jane B. (McCarroll) Dean. His father is a native of South Carolina, and came to Tennessee with our subject's grandfather when quite young. Our Subject's mother is a native of Tennessee, and passed from his world to the better one January 23, 1853. His father then married Miss Jane Baily, a native of Pennsylvania. There were three children born to this union. On January 13, 1878, Mr. Elijah Dean quietly departed this life. Our subject was united in wedlock with Miss Felicia A. Channell, who was born in Montgomery County, Tenn., April 24, 1856. She is the second of twelve children born to Mathew W. and Allethia (Smith) Channell, both natives of Tennessee. To Mr. Clay Dean and wife were born five children: Ruth, Kate E., Edith A., Clayra and Finis M. Our subject is now farming and is an extensive tobacco grower; he also runs a blacksmith shop on his farm, and is a building contractor. His dwelling presents a beautiful appearance to the passer-by.

James D. Duboise, farmer, of Montgomery County, is the son of Joel Duboise, who came from South Carolina to Dickson County, Tenn., in the year 1818. He bought a tract of land in Stewart County, living here ten years. He departed this life at Natchez, Miss., of cholera. He was the father of five children, viz.: J. D., Joel, William, Nancy and Mandy. After the demise of Mr. Duboise, Mrs. Duboise married a Mr. Milan and went to Illinois. Our subject was born January 11, 1823, in this State. Mr. Duboise is the owner of a tract of valuable land in Montgomery County. In the year 1841 he was united in marriage to Miss Milia Milam. After her death, which occurred in 1843, Mr. Duboise was again married to Miss Rena Kennedy in the year 1848. At the breaking out of the war between the North and the South, Mr. Duboise entered the army as a private under Gen. Forrest. He participated in the battles of Fort Donelson and Shiloh. In politics he is a Democrat, adhering to the Whig party until its death. He is also a member of the Methodist Episcopal Church. He is a good man and an honor to any community.

William B. Dunlop was born November 23, 1852, in Clarksville, Montgomery Co., Tenn. His father, Hugh Dunlop, was a native of Scotland, born in the early part of the present century, and immigrated to Kentucky, where he engaged as a dealer in tobacco. He then moved to this county, and there continued the same business. He was married to Miss Rebecca Talley, a native of this county, and to this union one child, our subject, was born. Mrs. Rebecca Dunlop died in 1861, and in 1863 Mr. Hugh Dunlop married Miss Mattie Williams, a native of Arkansas, who is yet living, but Mr. Dunlop died in 1879. Our subject was educated at Stewart College, in Clarksville, and, upon reaching his majority, he commenced the business of farming, which he has continued ever since. He has an excellent farm, well improved, and situated on the Louisville & Nashville Railroad. His staple crops are tobacco and wheat. In 1880 he married Miss Lizzie Williams, a native of Clarksville, Tenn., and daughter of Joseph and Sarah Williams. To this union one child has been born, William B. Our subject is a Democrat and a member of K. of P. at Clarksville.

John Edmonson, farmer, was born in the State of Tennessee, June 3, 1823, a son of Samuel and Nancy (Jones) Edmonson, and is of Scotch-English origin; the father was born in Mechlenburg County, Va., in 1787, and the mother in Lunenburg County in 1797. The family came to

Tennessee about 1816; here the father died in 1865, and the mother in 1873. The family consisted of eight children, John being the fourth. He spent the free and healthy life of a farmer's boy, and obtained his education in the country schools. At the age of nineteen he began farming for himself, and now owns 136 acres of good land. He was married, December 2, 1846, to Miss Bedee H. Roberts, a native of Montgomery County. To their union were born nine children, two of whom are living: Laura V. and John R. Mrs. Edmonson died in 1869, and in 1874 Mr. Edmonson took for his second wife Mrs. Louisa Matlock, nee Moore, of Wilson County, Tenn. Mr. Edmonson was formerly a Whig in politics, but is now a Democrat. In 1854 he was elected magistrate and served six years, giving good satisfaction.

Aristotle Eldridge, M. D., a native of Virginia, was born April 12, 1832, and is the son of William H. and Elizabeth (Scarbrough) Eldridge, natives of Virginia, who were born in the years 1800 and 1803, respectively. Our subject's father lost his first wife in 1850; he then married Miss Pollie Laird in 1858. She was born in Virginia in 1806, and died in 1862. He was again married in 1862 to Miss Martha Crowder, a native of Virginia, born in 1806. Mr. William Eldridge died in 1865. Our subject was united in marriage to Mrs. Bettie W. Eldridge, his deceased brother's wife, a native of this State and born September 30, 1836. She is the daughter of William and Nancy Haynes, natives of North Carolina. To our subject and wife were born seven children, viz.: Pattie, born June 15, 1860; Edwin, born November 3, 1861; Mary A. W., born July 11, 1862; Sallie B., born June 14, 1866; William H., born January 17, 1867; Lena A., born December 7, 1869; and Pocahontas, born March 8, 1874. Our subject is a descendant of the celebrated English planter, Rolfe, and the Indian princess, Pocahontas. He entered the university at Nashville in 1856, where he took one course of lectures. He then went to Arkansas and began the practice of medicine, remaining two years; he then returned to the university at Nashville, where he graduated February 25,

1858, and received his diploma March 1 of the same year. He then began merchandising at Palmyra, this county, and was very successful until 1862, when his property was set on fire and destroyed by the Federal soldiers. Since that time he has been engaged in the practice of his profession.

John S. Elder, dealer in hardware and agricultural implements, was born near Clarksville, Tenn., December 24, 1852, son of Joshua and Malissa (Martin) Elder, and is of Scotch-English origin. He is a member of one of the first families of this section of Tennessee and has long been identified with the business interests of Clarksville. For several years Mr. Elder's father was president of the Branch Bank of Tennessee at this place, and was holding that position at the breaking out of the late war. He died in Clarksville in 1874, at sixty-nine years of age. Our subject came to Clarksville when about ten years of age and was educated at Stewart College and at Bryant and Stratton's Business College in Cincinnati, Ohio, and graduated from that school in 1874. In 1874 he engaged in the hardware business in this city, buying a one-third interest in the firm of E. S. Moore & Co., and this union continued one year, when he, in partnership with E. Turnley, bought the business of Moore & Co. In 1877 Mr. Elder purchased his partner's interest and conducted the business until January, 1886, when he associated with him his brothers, M. W. and J. E. Elder, and the firm is now known as Elder Bros. In 1878-79 he erected Elder's Opera House. Mr. Elder is a Democrat and a K. of P. and a member of the Presbyterian Church.

J. P. Eleazer was born in this State in 1838. He is the fifth of seven children born to Levi and Susan (Weakley) Eleazer. His parents are natives of this State and were born in 1808 and 1805, respectively. Our subject was united in marriage to Miss Martha M. Weakley in 1868. She is the fifth of seven children born to John C. and Nancy Weakley; her parents are natives of Tennessee. Her father was born in 1797 and her mother in 1805. Our subject and wife have two children born to their union, Thomas H. and Robert B. Mr. Eleazer's occupation in early life was merchandising. In 1885 he moved to Montgomery County, Tenn., and located on one of the finest tracts of land on the South Side. It lies on Cumberland River, contains good bottom land, and the Louisville & Nashville Railroad runs through it. His elegant residence is well located, and is within about 300 yards of the railroad.

William J. Ely is a member of the firm of Hancock, Fraser & Ragsdale, and was born in Clarksville, Tenn., October 5, 1835. He is the third in a family of eight children, and is of English lineage. His father, Jesse Ely, was born in Logan County, Ky., February 12, 1803, and died in Clarksville January 19, 1847. He was a resident of this county many years, and was a hatter by trade, following that business for many years in this city. The mother was Charlotte Jamison, born in Montgomery County, Tenn., March 28, 1809. She attended school in a log schoolhouse that stood where the city market house now stands. She died in this city August 17, 1875. William Ely was educated at private schools and the Clarksville Male Academy, and when fourteen years of age began the printer's trade in the Chronicle office, remaining four years. He then served as deputy postmaster for several years, and in 1854 removed to Peaches Mills, where he engaged in general merchandising, continuing until 1861, when he returned to this city and continued merchandising until the breaking out of the war. During that time he was in the ordnance department. In 1865 he accepted a position with B. O. Keesee, hardware merchant, with whom he remained one year. For eighteen years he has been in the tobacco business, doing business from September 1, 1869, to November 1, 1876, under the firm name of Turnley, Ely & Co., and from November 1, 1876, to November 1, 1884, under firm names of Turnley, Ely & Kennedy, and Ely & Kennedy. The partnership expiring by limitation in 1884, he took the position of book-keeper with his present firm, becoming an equal partner in the business in 1885. He was married in 1858 to Fannie Galbreath, of Kentucky. She died in 1860, and nine years later he wedded Miss Johnie Brown, born in Kentucky in 1845. They have one child, Edith, born September 28, 1874. Mr. Ely is a Democrat, and a member of the K. of H. and Masonic fraternities, and a man who has been identified with the interests of the city for many years. He and wife are members of the Baptist Church.

Edward B. Ely, director of the First National Bank, was born in Clarksville, Tenn., February 12, 1842, son of Jesse and Charlotte (Jamison) Ely, and is of Scotch lineage. He is the sixth in a family of eight children, and was educated in the common schools and at Stewart College. In 1858 he began baking in the confectionery store of G. A. Ligan & Co., and a year later commenced the business for himself and has since continued. In 1861 he removed to his present place of business. He was burned out April 4, 1878, but erected his present business house the same year, and has been very successful, carrying the largest stock in the city. He was married, August 21, 1867, to Maria L. Council, a native of Memphis, born in 1850, daughter of H. D. and Ann E. Connell. Her father died of yellow fever in 1874. They have six children: Edward L., born 1870; Huelin D., born 1872; Jesse L., born 1874; Wharton C., born 1876; Warren, born 1880, and Laura Lee, born in 1885. Mr. Ely is a Democrat, and in 1882 was elected a director of the First National Bank of Clarksville, and has since served by re-election. He is a member of the K. of H., and he and his wife belong to the Baptist Church. Mr. Ely is a leading man of the city, and a representative of one of the oldest families in the county.

W. L. Evans is the son of Hugh and Sallie (Chisnan) Evans. Hugh Evans came to this county in 1826 and purchased a farm in the Eighth District. The grandfather of our subject came to this State from Virginia in the year 1810 and was killed in the war of 1812. To Hugh and Sallie Evans were born eight children, viz.: William L., L. W., W. L., Mary F.,

Sallie A., Caroline, Ross and Amos. Our subject was born October 15, 1832, in Montgomery County, Tenn. He received his education in the public schools of the county, which, at this early day, were limited. Mr. Evans was a farmer, and never pursued any other occupation. He began work on his own responsibility in 1853, and has been married twice. His first wife was Miss Hardin Cherry. To this union were born four children, viz.: James, Jennie, Lila and Sallie. Mrs. (Cherry) Evans died in 1874. In the year 1875 Mr. Evans was again married to Miss Jane Seay. Our subject owns 250 acres of land in Montgomery County, and is an honorable and upright man in every respect.

Mr. L. W. Evans was the son of Hugh Evans, and was born in 1834, in this State. Mr. Evans was a farmer, and was married to Miss Frances Shepherd, of this county. To this union were born four children: William, Emerson, Sarah and Arthur. Mr. Evans departed this life in the year 1871, leaving Mrs. Evans to rear her children unaided, and to look after the interests of the farm. Mrs. Evans is the daughter of Ludwick Shepherd, who came from North Carolina to this State in the early part of the present century. Mrs. Frances Evans was born in the year 1840, December 19. She possesses 150 acres of finely cultivated land in this county, and is a consistent Christian and a member of the Cumberland Presbyterian Church, joining this body in the early part of her life. She is highly respected as a good, conscientious woman.

John W. Faxon, banker, of Clarksville, traces his ancestry back in a direct line to Thomas Faxon, who was born in England in 1601, and who immigrated to America previous to 1647 with his wife, Joane, and three children. Charles Faxon, son of Ebenezer Faxon, who was a captain in the Colonial Army, is the ancestor of those bearing the name now living in Clarksville. He was born in 1799; wedded Lucy Ann, daughter of Oliver Steele in 1823, and made his home for many years in New York State, where he won renown as an editor at Catskill and at

Buffalo. In 1843 he removed with his family to Clarksville, Tenn., where he began the publication of the Primitive Standard, an Episcopal journal, with Rev. James Heber Otey, afterward bishop of the diocese of Tennessee, as editor. At the same time he started the Clarksville Jeffersonian, which, under the editorship of himself and sons, Charles O., Leonard G. and Henry W., became one of the foremost Democratic journals of the State. Gifted with all the superior and ennobling qualities of man, he not only occupied a high position in State affairs but was loved and respected in private life for his social qualities. He died July 18, 1867. Mrs. Lucy A. Faxon, his wife, was in every respect a most suitable companion. Highly educated, a great reader, she aided him in his labors and made his home a happy one. She died May 21, 1874. Their descendants have evinced many of the superior talents displayed by them. The family born to them is as follows: Charles O., born February 18, 1824, died January 28, 1870. He ranked among the foremost editors of the State. Henry W., born February 7, 1826, was a journalist of note in York State, was a well known author, his master-piece being "Beautiful Snow," whose authorship was falsely claimed by others. He died September 5, 1864. Leonard G., born November 20, 1827, followed journalism in Tennessee, Illinois and Kentucky, and has one son living in the latter State. Emily L., born September 13, 1829. was happily married, and died August 2, 1883. James G., born November 26, 1831, and is now living in this county. Lucy A., born January 13, 1834, is a widow and is now living. Mary L. is married and resides at Knoxville. She was born March 19, 1836. George B., born May 13, 1838, is living at Faxon's Station on the Louisville & Nashville Railroad. John W., whose name heads this sketch, is the only one of the family living at Clarksville, and thus deserves a more extended notice. Born May 24, 1840, he was reared to manhood in Tennessee and educated at Montgomery Masonic College, Clarksville. He began life as clerk in the postoffice for his brother, but at seventeen years of age engaged as clerk in a bank at Rogersville. Two years later he was appointed assistant supervisor of banks for Tennessee, a position he resigned to enter the Confederate service as sergeant of Company A, Fourteenth Tennessee Regiment. He was detached from the regular service to act as clerk for Gen. Anderson, but in October, 1861, was discharged for disability. He was then appointed brigade-major under Gen. Gholson, of the Tennessee forces. He served in the Wilderness campaign, when by reason of the injury occasioned by the severe concussion of a shell he was discharged. After the war he was assistant cashier in the Northern Bank at Clarksville until April 13, 1883, when he resigned to become teller in the American National Bank, of Nashville. In January, 1884, he was elected cashier of the Bank of Hopkinsville, which he resigned to accept the cashiership of the Farmers and Merchants National Bank at Clarksville. Mr. Faxon edited the Charlotte (N. C.) Bulletin for a time in 1864 and for fifteen years was Clarksville's correspondent to the Louisville, (Ky.) Courier-Journal. He is one of the city's best men. February 22, 1865, Florence, eldest daughter of Owen . and Catharine (Boss) Herring, became his wife, and by him is the mother of four children: Ruth, Ross S., Reita, and Marion. Esther M., born June 11, 1842, is the next youngest to John W. Faxon. She lives in Kentucky. Sarah B., born November 17, 1844, and is a resident of Kentucky. Caroline G., is the youngest child of Charles Faxon. She was born May 18, 1848, is married and resides in this county.

John Fields is a native of Halifax County, Va., born September 18, 1805, son of David and Nancy Fields, also natives of Virginia The mother died March 18, 1818, leaving five children, our subject being the third child. The father was a blacksmith and farmer, and died in 1840. John was educated in the common schools, and settled where he now lives in 1853. He was married, in 1823, to Maria Buckley. She was born in 1804, and was the daughter of Tapley and Jennie Buckley, who were born in North Carolina. Mr. and Mrs. Field became the parents of seven children: Jane, John P., James C., Elizabeth A., Robert E., Richard F. and Emma T. They own 150 acres of well improved land, all under good cultivation. John P., James C. and Robert E. participated in the late war. John P. was killed at Sharpsburg, Md., in 1862. James G was killed at Spottsylvania Court House, Va., in 1864. Robert E. was married to Lizzie Hopkins in 1877. They have two children: Kittie H. and John T. Elizabeth A. Fields was married to W. I. Barbee in 1864, and became the parents of four children: Jennie, Emma, Ellen, Ruby T. The Fields family were among the early settlers of the county and some of them figured conspicuously in the war of 1812. They are members of the Baptist Church, and are Democratic in politics.

Joseph J. Fletcher, a native of North Carolina, was born February 2, 1813, and is the son of Thomas and Mary (Thornton) Fletcher, who were born May, 1766, and November, 1786, and died 1834 and 1859, respectively. Our subject was united in marriage to Miss Claudell Bowers, a native of Tennessee, born April 21,1816. She is the first of eight children born to Joseph and Mary Bowers, who were born in 1795 and 1800, and died in 1844 and 1869, respectively. To our subject and wife were born ten children, viz.: Mary A., born July 7, 1840; Joseph T., born April 13, 1842; Ruffin S., born September 19, 1844 Sallie E., born September 21, 1846; Martha P., born January 1,1848; Winnie A., born June 4, 1849; Joseph R., born March 26, 1851; Claudell B., born April 15, 1853; Joshua D., born June 15, 1855, and Francis O., born July 6, 1857. Mrs. Fletcher died August 15, 1861. Our subject is a shoe-maker by trade, and in early days he made all the shoes for his neighbors. Of late years he has confined himself solely to his farm.

Joshua D. Fletcher was born in this county and State June 15, 1855. His father, J. J. Fletcher, was born in North Carolina, February 2, 1813, and was married to Miss Claudell Bowers, a native of Tennessee, born April 21, 1816, and died August 15, 1861. Our subject was united in marriage March 18, 1884 to Miss Ida B. Williamson, born in Tennessee June 18, 1858. Her father was B. M. Williamson, a native of Tennessee, born in 1818. Her mother, Addie Bowers, was born in Tennessee December 26, 1835. To Joshua Fletcher and wife was born one child—Boyd W., born April 17, 1885. Our subject was reared on a farm and received his education in the best country schools until the age of seventeen, when he went to Palmyra and clerked for his uncle two years. He then returned to the farm and remained one year; at the expiration of that time he returned to Palmyra and clerked again. He then engaged in the general merchandising business at Shiloh, with W. J. Elliot as partner. This partnership existed about two years, when our subject purchased the entire stock and began business for himself. He has besides this store two shingle machines that are almost constantly running, and also a fine farm, near his business, of 150 acres. This he thinks of making a stock farm. He trades considerably in horses, mules and cattle. Mr. Fletcher is one of the leading men of the county, is full of life and energy and an ardent Democrat.

Joseph W. Foster was born in Virginia February 9, 1818, and is of English descent. About the year 1836 he moved to Henderson County, Tenn., where he lived two years, he then moved to Clarksville, this State, and began teaming. His father, John S. Foster, was born in Virginia, and moved to Tennessee in 1836. He was a farmer by occupation and married a lady who was a native of Virginia. Our subject married Miss Mary Averit, also a native of Virginia and of English descent, born in the year 1823, and is a daughter of Henry and Sallie Averit. To Joseph W. Foster and wife were born seven children: Lucy, Sarah, Lettie T., William H., Mary L., Lena and Edward L. In 1848 our subject had taken many contracts on street work in Clarksville, and also did a large portion of the work on the Nashville, Russellville & Hopkinsville Pikes leading out from Clarksville. He was also contractor on the Louisville & Nashville Railroad when they were first building it. He moved to his farm where he is now living in 1874. He has a good farm and has it well stocked; he is also a very extensive tobacco raiser.

Finis E. Foust is a son of Jacob and Eliza (Morrow) Foust, natives of Tennessee, born in 1815 and 1819 respectively; the former of German and the latter of Irish descent. To them were born seven children, only three of whom are now living. Finis E. was the youngest in the family, and was born in Tennessee September 11, 1851. He was educated in the common schools of Montgomery County, and has always been a tiller of the soil on the homestead which now belongs to him and Ms mother. On the 19th of December, 1876, he was married to Mary A. Horsley, a native of the county, born September 17, 1853. They became the parents of the following children: Rufus E., born in 1879; Emmet L., born in 1880, Elizabeth E., born in 1883, and Nannie P., born in 1885. Mr. Foust is a supporter of Democratic principles, and he and wife are members of the Cumberland Presbyterian Church, his parents being members of the same. Mr. Foust is a member of the Fredonia Lodge of F. & A. M., in which he has held several offices. He is one of the enterprising citizens of the county and takes an active interest in educational matters.

J. M. Fowlkes was born in Virginia July 2, 1846, the eldest son of Henry A. and Emma M. (Chilton) Fowlkes. The father was born in Virginia in 1812, and the mother in the same State in 1819. In 1836 the father went to Alabama, and later came to Tennesse, but returned to Virginia in 1839. In 1849 they came to Montgomery County, Tenn., and have ever since resided in that county. Our subject was educated at Stewart College, of Clarksville, and in 1862 began clerking at a store in this city, and continued as a clerk for several years. In 1870 he engaged in the sewing machine business and for ten years was general agent for the Wheeler & Wilson Company and had the contract for an extensive territory. In 1881 he began dealing in sewing machines for himself, and buys direct from the manufacturers. He was married, July 2, 1873, to Miss Rebecca L. Davis, daughter of Jefferson Davis. She was born in

1848. Mr. Fowlkes is a Democrat in his political views. He is a member of the Christian Church and his wife belongs to the Baptist Church.

Henry Freeh, wholesale and retail grocer and one of the proprietors of the Sewanee Planing-mills, born in Cincinnati, Ohio, January 15, 1838, son of Conrad and Margaret (Walker) Freeh, and of German ancestry. The parents were natives of Germany, born in 1800 and 1810 respectively, and came to America in 1832, locating in the Queen City, and removed to Montgomery County, Tenn., in 1856. The father died in 1874 and the mother in 1884. Mr. Freeh received a liberal education in the Cincinnati public schools, and afterward learned the cabinet-maker's trade. He came to Clarksville in 1849, but after a year's residence returned home, where he remained until 1861, when he again came to Clarksville and has here resided. He engaged in the grocery trade, and now does a large business. In 1872 he became one of the proprietors of the above named planing-mills. He is a member of the Clarksville Lumber Company. In 1869 he was elected mayor of the city, and served two years. During his administration he raised enough money by subscription to erect the city hall and market house, both credits to the city and to the push, enterprise and public spirit of Mr. Freeh. In 1875 he was chosen alderman, and was school commissioner in 1878-79. He was married in 1870 to Amanda G. Byrne, a native of Kentucky. Of six children born to them only one survives, Mary B. Mr. Freeh is a Democrat, and is one of the most shrewd and successful business men of the city. He and wife are members of the Presbyterian Church.

Wesley H. Frey is a son of Thomas Frey, who was a native of Robertson County, Tenn., born in 1821, and of German descent. He married Jane Farthing, a native of Virginia, and to them were born nine children, our subject being the eldest. Both parents are still living. Wesley H. Frey was educated in the district schools, and in October, 1861, enlisted in the Fiftieth Regiment Tennessee Infantry, and was captured with his regiment at Fort Donelson, but escaped from his captors and afterward joined Capt. Tyler's company in Col. Woodard's cavalry, and served with them until his regiment was exchanged, when be again joined it. At Missionary Ridge he was again captured and held a prisoner of war at Rock Island, Ill., until the close of the war. He then returned home, and in 1866 married Matilda E. Jones, a native of Robertson County, Tenn., and daughter of Richard and Elizabeth Jones, of that county. To Mr. Frey and wife were born Ida E., Walter L., Emily E., Mary J., Rosa L., Annie P., Alice, Wesley B., Charles E. and Nellie T. Our subject has resided on his present well improved farm since his marriage. He is a supporter of Democratic principles, and is at present secretary of the F. & A. M. at Port Royal. He is also a member of the Cumberland Presbyterian Church.

A. G. Goodlett. In the days of the "reformation" a family of Protestants, by the name of Gotlieb, moved from Germany to Scotland, where they could enjoy that religious liberty peculiar to their views. The Scotish accent changed "Got" into "Gude" and "lieb" into "leet," and in the course of time Gudeleet became Goodlett. In 1757 Adam Goodlett, of Edinburgh, a young man who had just finished his education in the best schools of Europe, came on a visit of pleasure to this country. While in the colony of Virginia he met and fell in love with Miss Rebecca Balderson, and, seeking her hand in marriage, gained her consent, under a pledge that he should make his permanent home in this country and not return to Europe. By this union the following children were born: John, James, Ebenezer, Erskin, Adam G., Robert, Margaret, Francis, Ellen, Nancy and Eliza. Shortly after the war of 1776 Adam Goodlett moved with his family to Bardstown, Ky. After a few years' residence at this place he moved to Nashville, Tenn., where he died in 1822. His remains, with those of his wife, repose at Mount Olivet Cemetery. Ebenezer E., third son of Adam and Rebecca Goodlett, married Eliza Hammond and located in the town of Princeton, Ky., to practice medicine; to them the following children were born: Adam G., Job H., William, Robert D., Margaret, Francis, Eliza and Sarah. The eldest son, Adam G., was born January 1, 1810. In 1833 he married Eliza T. Turner, daughter of John and Martha Turner, nee Gleaves, and in 1846 moved to the locality near Nashville, now the town of Goodlettsville. In 1853 he moved to Nashville and took charge of the Cumberland Presbyterian Church, dying September 14, 1866, as pastor of the Second Cumberland Presbyterian Church of Nashville; his widow survived him a few years, dying January 21, 1871. To the Rev. Dr. A. G. Goodlett and Eliza T. were born the following children: Rebecca A., Ebenezer E., Martha, Eliza T., Adam G., William A., John A., Jennie and Finis E. Rebecca A. married J. W. Grisham in 1855; he died in 1861, leaving surviving him his widow and three children. Ebenezer E. has been a druggist in Nashville for many years, and is a graduate of one of the Nashville schools of medicine. In 1859 he married Josephine Brown; no issue. Eliza T. married Maj. W. H. Joyner in 1865. They reside at Gallatin, Tenn. They have one child, James Joyner, a young man of refined manners, temperate and industrious. William A. Goodlett married Mary Grooms in 1864. In 1868 he died, leaving a daughter, Jessie, who yet survives and lives in Nashville. John A. died in 1855. Jennie and Finis died in 1860 and 1861. The second son, Adam G., the subject of this sketch, was born June 22, 1842, near Nashville, Tenn. He was educated in the schools of Nashville, having spent the years from 1857 to 1860 at the Western Military Institute, then under the management of the late Lieut.-Gen. Bushrod Johnson. In 1863 he married Sallie D. Hooper, daughter of John J. and Mildred Hooper, nee Wadlington. In March, 1865 Sallie D. died, leaving a son who survived her a few years, dying in his sixth year. Shortly after the death of his wife he moved to Charlotte, Dickson County, and commenced the practice of law. June 10, 1866, he married Florence Gold, daughter of William and Mary Gold, nee Brigham. To them have been born the following children now living: Adam Gold, born October 31, 1870; Florrie May, born June 17, 1873; Earl Gordon, born February 24,

1875; William V., born April 15, 1881; Herbert De Leon, born August 15, 1883. In 1871 our subject moved to Clarksville, where he continued in the practice of his profession up to 1883, when he purchased a fine stock-farm of over 1,000 acres, located within three miles of the court house of Clarksville. Upon this farm he now resides, surrounded by his herds of fine cattle, horses, sheep, etc. His herd of A. J. C. C. Jersey cattle number over sixty head, while his stud of trotting horses contains animals of high breeding as well as individual excellence. He has a very large Norman stallion and Jack, and also breeds Jack stock and large draft horses. He and wife are members of the Episcopal Church. In politics he is a Democrat, belonging to the small band of "Sky Blues" who wanted to pay the debt of the State dollar for dollar. He is a Knight Templar Mason, K. of P., K. of H., and favors prohibition.

S. E. Garrard is the son of S. L. and Mary (Young) Garrard. The family came from North Carolina, but Mr. S. L. Garrard was born and reared in Tennessee, in the year 1840 or 1843. He was married to Miss Mary Young, of Virginia, and six children have blessed them: J. H., W. M., S. E., E. E., C. S., E. L. January 22, 1874, Mr. S. L. Garrard died in this county. He was a member of the F. & A. M. Our subject, Mr. S. E. Garrard, was born July 30, 1853, in this county and received his education in the country schools until 1873, when he went to Mississippi and attended school there six months; he then returned and went to farming. In 1876 he went into the dry goods business at Seg, Tenn., which place takes its name from him. He was married to Miss Annie Riggins of this county in the year 1881, and their family relations are rendered lappy by the addition of two children: Mattie and Bascomb. Mr. Garrard possesses a fine tract of land in this county and is a good man.

J. J. Garrott, son of Jacob and Ann C. (Going) Garrott, was born in Montgomery County, near Clarksville, Tenn., December 30, 1833, and is of Scotch-Irish origin. The father was by birth a Virginian, born in

1796, and his mother was born in South Carolina in 1802. The family came to Tennessee about 1816 and became prominent citizens of this and Christian County, Ky. Both parents died in Illinois. Mr. Garrott grew to manhood on the farm and received the advantages the common schools afforded. In June, 1861, he enlisted in Company F, Seventh Kentucky C. S. Volunteers, and was commissioned captain in 1862. He was wounded five times and was at Shiloh, Vicksburg, Port Hudson, Baton Rouge, and the last year of the war was in the cavalry service under Gen. Forrest. He came home in 1865 and in the fall of the same year began the merchandise business in New Providence, continuing eight years and then for two years was engaged in the tobacco commercial business in New York City. His present vocation is farming his 800 acres of land. He removed to his present place of residence in 1873. He was married January 4, 1870, to Nannie P. Grinstead, of Kentucky, Mr. Garrott is a Democrat and Mason, and he and wife are members of the Baptist Church and he is a leading citizen. November 19, 1883, he killed one of several burglars who were breaking into his house and received a shot in return.

Nathaniel V. Gerhart, general merchant, was born in Dauphin County, Penn., February 7, 1827, son of Rev. Isaac and Sarah (Vogel) Gerhart, of German descent, and the youngest of five children. His father was born in Bucks County, Penn., about 1788, and was a leading clergyman in the German Reformed Church and was a minister of the gospel for fifty years. He died in Lancaster, Penn., in 1866. The mother was also a Pennsylvanian, born near Philadelphia in 1794 and died at Lancaster in 1862. Nathaniel V. was educated in the schools of Gettysburg, Penn., and came West in 1849, and in 1853 located in Louisville, Ky., and there remained until 1873, when he removed to Clarksville where he has since been engaged in merchandising. He is one of the prosperous merchants of the city and four of his sons are associated with him in business. He was married in Louisville in 1853 to Miss Analiza Piemont, who was born in Norfolk, Va., in 1827, daughter of John Piemont To Mr. and Mrs. Gerhart were born the following family: Virginia, Isaac P., Charles C., Joseph H., Ludia, Harry C. and Bayles W. During the war Mr. Gerhart was a Union man. He is now a Democrat and belongs to the Presbyterian Church. His wife and children are Episcopalians.

John A. Gholson, M. D., was born in the city of Clarksville, Tenn., December 26, 1838. He is the son of M. G. and Louisa (Rogers) Gholson. His father is a native of Kentucky and was born in the year 1814. His mother was born in Tennessee in the year 1816. Our subject was united in marriage to Miss Lyle in 1860. She was born in this State in the year 1840, and is the daughter of Thomas and Margaret M. Lyle, both of whom are natives of Tennessee and both born in the year 1807. Mr. John Gholson and wife have eight children born to their union: Alexander R., John A., Hugh P., Louisa, Milton G., Lillian A., Lottie E. and Dora I. Our subject was educated in the best schools of the county, having attended Stewart's College in Clarksville. In 1859 he entered the Medical University at Nashville, where he graduated in 1861. He at once returned home and enlisted in the Fourteenth Tennessee Regiment under Col. Forbes, where he served as hospital steward. He surrendered with Lee at Appomattox Court House in 1865, after which he returned home and began the practice of medicine. He lives but a few miles from Orgain Cross Roads, and the country being thickly settled gives him all the practice he can possibly attend to. He is a very successful physician.

A. B. Gholson, attorney at law and notary public, is a native of Montgomery County, Tenn., born February 26, 1861, son of Dr. John A., and Mrs. Gholson, formerly a Miss Lyle, who were natives of the county, born in 1838 and 1841, respectively. At the beginning of the war the paternal grandfather, Col. Milton Gholson, enlisted in the Fourteenth Tennessee Regiment, Confederate States Army, and was at once made lieutenant-colonel. His health soon failed and he returned home and was subsequently commissioned brigadier-general of militia by Gov. Harris. He assisted in raising two or three regiments of troops in Tennessee, and died in this county in 1883. Our subject's early days were spent on a farm and in attending the country schools. In 1881 he began the study of law, and in 1884 entered the law office of Judges Smith and Lurton. From 1881 to 1884 he was deputy county trustee and was licensed to practice law, in September, 1884. In August, 1885, he was appointed deputy clerk and master under Polk G. Johnson, and still fills the position. In 1885 he was elected notary public for four years, and is a leading attorney and prominent young man of Montgomery County. He is a Democrat, a K. of P. and a member of the Methodist Episcopal Church.

James P. Gill, dealer in fine horses, was born in Logan County, Ky., August 21, 1850, son of J. F. and Mary E. (Gunn) Gill, born in Virginia and Kentucky, in 1816 and 1828, respectively. The Gill family removed to Kentucky in 1831, and settled in Logan County. There the father died in 1884. The mother yet resides on the old homestead James P. Gill was educated in the country schools and the Kentucky Wesleyan University at Millersburg, graduating in 1871, entering the institution in 1868. He then taught school in Bell's Chapel, Ky., for three years, and in 1874 removed to Cadiz, Ky., and for one year was engaged in the tobacco business. From 1876 to 1881 he kept a livery stable in Cadiz, and at the latter date came to Clarksville, where he has since resided engaged in the livery business. For the last ten years he has given much attention to the purchase and sale of fine horses and mules. In 1886 he erected a fine brick livery barn, the cost amounting to about $7,000. Mr. Gill owns 174 acres of fine land near the city, and is well to do financially. He was married, in 1878, to Lizzie Chappell, a daughter of J. W. Chappell, a prominent resident of Cadiz, Ky. They have two children: Joseph C. and Mary E. Mr. Gill is a Democrat and Mrs. Gill is a member of the Methodist Episcopal Church.

Benjamin K. Gold, leaf tobacco broker, is a native of Montgomery County, Tenn., born December 21, 1837, son of John and Sarah (Collins) Gold, both of whom were born in the Old Dominion and came to this State in early days and settled in Montgomery County, where they spent the remainder of their lives. Our subject's early days were spent on the farm and in attending the country schools; later he became a student in Stewart College, at Clarksville, where he received a good practical business education. For two years after leaving school he acted as head clerk in a large wholesale and retail grocery store at New Providence, after which he bought the proprietors out and conducted the business on his own account, dealing also in tobacco. On account of the war he was compelled to quit the grocery business, but continued to deal in tobacco. He moved to Louisville, Ky., in 1862, where he remained four years buying tobacco largely for shipment, and also running a large re-handling establishment, after which he returned to New Providence and erected a large tobacco factory, which he operated for a number of years and then sold out and offered his services to the trade as a broker in leaf tobacco, in which business he is now engaged. He has been an active member of the tobacco trade for twenty-five years and is one of the most extensive and successful buyers on the Clarksville Tobacco Board of Trade. In 1860 he married Mary J. Oldham, born in this county in 1841. They have this family: Clarence O., Ora L., Mamie, James K., and Benjamin H. Mr. Gold is a Democrat in politics, and is one of the successful business men of the city of Clarksville, his annual dealings in tobacco reaching into the hundreds of thousands of dollars. He comes of one of the best known families in the county and ranks high as a citizen.

Lewis T. Gold, tobacco broker and dealer in leaf tobacco, was born in this county December 15, 1841, son of John and Sallie (Collins) Gold I for parents' history see sketch of Benjamin Gold). Our subject's early days were spent on the farm and in attendance at the country schools. At the age of sixteen he went to New Providence and for about two years was engaged as a salesman in the grocery house of Gold & Co. In April, 1861, he enlisted in Company L, Fourteenth Tennessee Volunteers, and in the early part of 1862 was taken ill and sent to the hospital, and being disabled and unfit for active service was sent home on furlough. There he remained until the latter part of 1862, when he was transferred to Company A, Forty-ninth Tennessee, and in this capacity served until the close of the war. He then returned home and remained only a short time and then went to Louisville, Ky., and for more than a year was engaged in the tobacco business in that city. He then returned to Tennessee and began business in New Providence, and for two years devoted his attention to the tobacco trade. Later he carried on the warehouse business for four years, and in 1874 began dealing in leaf tobacco, and two years later began the commission business, and is now one of the most extensive buyers of the Tobacco Exchange. He is a thorough and practical business man, and his wide experience in the business places him among the best posted men in the place. He has made his own way in life. November 5, 1873, he was married to Sallie G. Pettus, born in New Providence July 6, 1854, daughter of Thomas F. and Martha Pettus. They have two children: Mattie P. and Stephen. Mrs. Gold is a member of the Presbyterian Church, and he is a Democrat, and a member of the F. & A. M.

Rufus J. Goostree was born in Sumner County, Ten a., March 4, 1833. His father, James W. Goostree, was born in Virginia in 1803, and came to Tennessee when a small boy. He was a farmer and a member of the Cumberland Presbyterian Church. He died in Nashville in February, 1881. His father, James W. Goostree, emigrated from Ireland. The mother's maiden name was Catharine Taylor. She was of Scotch descent, born in Virginia in 1805. She and the father were married in 1823, and became the parents of nine children, of whom our subject is the sixth. He received a common education, and at the age of twenty-two left home and began doing for himself. He was engaged in the livery business for some time, and in 1859 came to Montgomery County, and the same year was married to Mary Wylie, who died the following year. In 1867 he wedded Rachel A. Hinton, who was born September 30, 1835, in Davidson County, Tenn. She was a daughter of John J. Hinton, a prominent citizen of Davidson County. During the building of the Louisville & Nashville Railroad Mr. Goostree was a contractor thereon, and during the late war he served over four years in the Fourteenth Tennessee Regiment. He was wounded at Petersburg, Va., and surrendered with Gen. Lee at Appomattox Court House. He has resided on his present farm for eighteen years. He is a Democrat, and he and wife are members of the Presbyterian Church.

James A. Gordon, Jr., is a native Virginian, born September 18, 1809, son of James and Elizabeth Gordon, who were born in Scotland and settled in Virginia in the middle part of the eighteenth century, and were engaged in farming. To them were born six children: James A., Mary A., Daniel, Elizabeth E., Virginia A. and Fioneis M. Our subject was the first of their children. In 1849 he was married to Josephine Thomas, born June 11, 1833, daughter of Dr. B. W. and Mary (Brumfield) Thomas, who were married in 1831. James A., Jr., was educated in the common schools, and settled in Montgomery County, Tenn., in 1850, where he purchased 150 acres of land near Spring Creek. He and wife became the parents of eight children: Alonzo A., Laura E., James A. (deceased), Lillie C. (deceased), Nannie B., Ora C., Minnie C. and Elmer B. Mr. Gordon died January 20, 1878. Since that time the wife has been living on the old homestead, and has the farm well improved and in a good state of cultivation. The family are Democrats in politics, and are among the pioneer families of this county. They are comfortably situated, and are doing well financially.

Matthew Gracey, of the firm of F. P. Gracey, is a native of Eddyville, Ky., where he was born March 4, 1847, son of Matthew and Maria (Tilford) Gracey, and is of Irish-German descent. He is the youngest of nine children, and received a fair education in the schools of his native town. In February, 1866, he came to Clarksville, and since that time has been engaged in the wharf-boat, coal and grain business. He was married, November 30, 1876, to Miss Marian C. Castner, a native of Clarksville, born October 21, 1851, daughter of Dr. W. J. Castner and Mary (Beaumont) Castner. They have three children: Lucy C., Frank P. and May B. Mr. Gracey is a Democrat, and cast his first presidential vote for McClellan. In 1874 Mr. Gracey joined the K. of P. order. He is one of the first business men of the city, and a thoroughly practical man. He and wife are members of the Episcopal Church.

Capt. Frank P. Gracey was born in Lyon County of the blue-grass State, June 30, 1834, his birth occurring in Eddyville. He was commander of a Kentucky battery during the late war between the North and South, and proved a tried and true soldier. Julian Gracey is the only child born to his marriage with Miss Irene Cobb, which took place in Clarksville, Tenn., November 10, 1857. She is a daughter of Dr. Joshua Cobb, a prominent physician of that city. Julian is connected with the legal department of the Louisville & Nashville Railroad at Montgomery, Ala. Mr. Gracey is a prominent business man of Clarksville, Tenn., where by industry and economy he has amassed a moderate fortune.

William H Green, deceased, was born in this State and county November 7, 1840. His father, Henry J. Green, was born in 1804, and his mother, Sarah Browder, in the year 1816. Both were natives of Virginia. They were united in marriage November 11, 1835. In the year 1869 our subject was united in marriage to Miss Cynthia Monroe, a native of Kentucky, born December 26, 1851. Her father, James, was born in 1823, and her mother, Elizabeth (Pendleton) Monroe, in 1828; both natives of Kentucky. To our subject and wife were born three children, viz: Mary M., born December 16, 1871; William H., born April 6, 1873, and Louisa M., born November 10, 1877. Mr. William Green was educated at Stuart College, in Clarksville, and Russellville College, at Russellville, Ky. Politically he was a Democrat. In 1861 he enlisted in Company A, Fourteenth Tennessee Volunteers, Confederate States Army, as a private. He was in all the principal battles fought in Virginia, and although he was always at the front he escaped without a wound. He surrendered with Gen. Lee at Appomattox Court House, and returned home to his life-long occupation of farming, which was brought to a close by death January 15, 1883. He was a noble soldier, and a man who always contended for the right. He was a prosperous farmer, and no man in this county was more public-spirited than he. By his death the county lost one of its truest and best men. His wife, since his death, has assumed full control of the farm. The elegant residence is situated in a beautiful place, and is about two miles from the Hopkinsville & Clarksville Pike.

Dr. C. W. Greenfield was born February 23, 1830, in Todd County, Ky., and is of Scotch-French extraction. His father, William Greenfield, was a native of North Carolina, born April 3, 1794, and took for his wife Miss Ruth W. Thompson, who became the mother of two children, and who died August 26, 1817. In 1819 the father married Miss Jane Bourne, who bore him five children, and who died May 6, 1827. In 1828 he was again married to Mrs. Piety H. Yancy, a native of Tennessee, and a daughter of Whitmil and Dorathy W. Fort. By her he became the father of two children: Cyrus W. (our subject) and Whitmil F. The father of Dr. Greenfield died July 2, 1835, and after his death his widow married Col. T. M. Ewing, of Todd County, Ky., and there she died, August 11, 1840. Our subject, when a child, moved with his parents to Montgomery County, Tenn., and was educated in private schools here and in the Jefferson Medical College in Philadelphia, from which he graduated in 1853. He then returned home and began the practice of his profession in

the neighborhood where he now resides, and where he has since continued the practice and the superintending of his farm. In 1856 he married Miss Nancy A. Barker, a native of Kentucky, and to this union the
following children have been born: Maria N., William B., (deceased),
Eugenia W., Thomas L., Cyrus and Sarah Y. Dr. C. W. Greenfield has
traveled extensively over the United States, Mexico, Central America,
the northern part of South America and the West India Islands. His
farm and residence is about fifteen miles from Clarksville, and near the
northeast corner of Montgomery County.

Mrs. M. D. Griffey is the daughter of L. H. and C. B. (Davis) Smith,
both natives of Kentucky. After marriage they moved to Indiana, where
they remained eight or nine years, and then returned to Kentucky. Their
married life was made happy by the addition of seven children, five of
whom are yet living, viz.: William H., M. D., Georgia, Nannie and
Leonard H. Mrs. M. D. Griffey was born March 15, 1835, in Indiana,
and received a good education at Elkton, Ky., after which she taught
school for several years in Kentucky and Tennessee. In 1858 she was
married to Mr. W. Griffey, of Kentucky, to whom were born two children, viz.: Ella and Katie C. Ella was married to Mr. Otis P. Ellett in
1877. In 1885 Mr. Ellett died, leaving two children, viz.: William and
Katie. William Griffey died in 1878, leaving four children, he being
twice married. Mrs. Griffey owns a fine tract of land in the Fourth District, and is highly esteemed by all who know her.

Benjamin B. Hackney, a prominent citizen and farmer of Montgomery County, was born in Christian County, Ky., November 21, 1825. He
is the son of Fielding and Elizabeth Hackney, natives of Virginia. In
1829 the Hackney family settled in Montgomery County, Tenn., where
they engaged in farming. In 1855 Benjamin was united in matrimony to
Drusilla Hackney, daughter of David Hackney, a native of Spottsylvania
County, Va. The subject of our sketch and lady had one child born to

them, viz.: Alice Hackney. Mr. B. B. Hackney is a strong Democrat, and he and family are members of the Oakland Christian Church. He has a well improved farm of 107 acres, and is in very comfortable circumstances and is respected by all who know him.

John L. Hail was born in Halifax County, N. C., May 5, 1813. His father, John H. Hail, was born in North Carolina about the year 1783. He was educated in the country schools, and was a Methodist in belief. He was a farmer and an old time Whig. He was united in marriage to Miss Sallie Green about the year 1805. She was born in North Carolina in the year 1784 and received her education at the country schools; she was also a Methodist in belief. To them were born twelve children, viz.: Alexander, William, Drury, Eliza, John L., Mary, Elizabeth, Nancy, Benjamin N., Benjamin W., Martha A. and Wilson. Alexander died about the year 1809; William died December 7, 1832; Elizabeth died in March, 1833; Drury died in August, 1833; Eliza died in June, 1834; Benjamin W. died about the year 1858; Mary died March 21, 1869, and Martha A. died April 1, 1878. Mr. John H. Hail moved to Montgomery County, Tenn., December 15, 1821; here he died in June, 1833; his wife died May 15,1864 The subject of this sketch came to Montgomery County, Tenn., with his father in the year 1821, and was educated in the common schools of the county. He is a Democrat and a Methodist in belief. He was engaged in early life in the business of shoe-making and merchandising. In 1859 he began farming and has been very successful.

William P. Hambaugh, a native of this county wad State, was born July 16, 1854. He was educated at Stewart College at Clarksville and began clerking in a grocery at New Providence, where he remained six months and bought an interest with Herndon, Gold & Co., at Trice's Landing. Here he remained only twelve months, sold out and purchased an interest in a grocery with J. H. Pettis & Co., in New Providence. In 1874 he and Mr. Pettis rented the Ringgold Water-mill and did business under the firm name of W. P. Hambaugh & Co. The mill was purchased by W. P. Hambaugh in the year 1875, and in this year it was destroyed by fire and was a total loss. They immediately rebuilt the mill, having it running again the latter part of the year. In 1878 our subject sold his interest in the grocery and purchased his partner's interest in the mill and became sole owner. This mill has always flourished and competes in quality of flour with the best mills in Montgomery County. It is on the Little West Pork at Red River and near the Clarksville & Hopkinsville Pike. Our subject is the eldest of four children born to P. C. and Virginia (Burgess) Hambaugh who are natives of Virginia and Kentucky respectively. In 1875 Mr. Hambaugh was united in marriage to Miss Nina DeL. Nisbet. She is of French descent and a native of Georgia, born April 13, 1854. Mr. and Mrs. Hambaugh are the parents of three children, viz.: Catlett N., Virginia B. and William P., Jr.

Herbert O. Hambaugh was born in Ringgold, Montgomery Co., Tenn., June 4, 1858, and is the son of P. C. and V. B. Hambaugh, who were born in Virginia. The father came to Montgomery County, Tenn., in 1842, and was engaged as clerk in a tobacco house in New Providence, and afterward owned an interest in the same and was also engaged in the grocery business and pork packing until 1858, when he sold out and moved to Ringgold, Tenn., and was engaged in the milling business until 1865. Since that time he has been successfully engaged in the tobacco business. He is president of the Franklin Bank at Clarksville. He was married to Virginia Burgess in 1855 and became the father of four children, our subject being the second. He was educated in the university of Clarksville and Vanderbilt University of Nashville. He was in business with his father for some time but in 1884 moved to where he now lives and purchased the woolen and flour-mills known as Peacher's Mills. The products of the mills are very famous throughout the State and are regarded superior to any in the market. He is also engaged in the grocery and general merchandise business and is considered one of the county's best business men and citizens. March 28, 1882, he was married to Nellie Cabaniss, born March 28, 1860, daughter of L. D. Cabaniss, who was at one time a very prominent dentist in Clarksville. They have one child, Lucy Bell, born March 9, 1883. Mr. Hambaugh is a member of the F. & A. M. and K. of P. and is a Democrat in politics.

A. Scott Hammon, a native of Georgia, was born September 20, 1857. His father, J. E. Hammon, was born October 16, 1825, and his mother May 1, of the same year. They were both natives of Georgia, and immigrated to southern Kentucky in 1866, bringing him with them. After arriving at the age of twenty-one our subject immigrated to Montgomery County, Tenn., and engaged in farming. February, 22, 1881, he was united in marriage to Mrs. Carrie Mason, a native of Kentucky, born about the year 1848. In 1880 he moved to the farm on which he now lives; it is located in the northwestern portion of District No. 3, and is on the Clarksville and Garrettsburg road. The principal products of his farm are corn, wheat, tobacco, and he has very recently directed his attention considerably to the raising of stock. Mr. and Mrs. Hammon are the parents of one child, a girl viz.: Carrie L., born April 23, 1885. They are respected and esteemed by all who know them.

Thomas R. Hancock, tobacconist, is a native of Charlotte County, Va., born July 17, 1842, son of N. H. and Palina G. (Rudd) Hancock, and is of English descent. Both parents were born in 1807. His grandfather, Martin Hancock, was a Virginian. The mother of our subject died in 1847, and his father still lives in his native country, and is seventy-eight years of age. Our subject attended the common schools, though on account of the war he was unable to prosecute his studies very extensively, and the major part of his education has been gained by active business life. In 1861 he enlisted as one of the Brook Neal Rifles, of Campbell County, Va., which was called out by the State, and he was made its second lieutenant. After its disbandment Thomas enlisted in Company A,

Twenty-first Virginia, Second Brigade of Jackson's division, and served until the close of the war. He was wounded at the battle of Cedar Creek, Va. In 1866 he removed to Trigg County, Ky., and for two years was engaged in the dry goods business. He then moved to New Providence, Tenn., and for two years was book-keeper for Thomas Herndon. In 1871 he went to Hopkinsville, Ky., and was engaged in the tobacco business until 1879. He was then tobacco inspector in New York City four years. He returned to Kentucky and opened a commission tobacco house, and still continues in the business. He has three partners. In 1884 he came to Clarksville, Tenn., where he carries on the same business. January 26, 1875, he was married to Rebecca E. Ragsdale, born in Kentucky in 1853. They have four children, as follows: William M., James W., Douglas B. and Thomas R., Jr. Mr. Hancock is a Democrat He has made his own way in life, and, although not wealthy, is a very successful business man. His wife is a member of the Methodist Episcopal Church.

John Hargrove, farmer, was born in Montgomery County, Tenn., September 7, 1826. He is the third of five children born to John D. and Martha (Green) Hargrove. His father was born in North Carolina, in the year 1788, and his mother was born in the same State in 1794. In 1857 our subject joined his fortune with that of Miss Fredonia Allen, a native of Tennessee, born October 7, 1836. She is the eighth of nine children born to James and Mary Allen. Her father was a native of Virginia, and was born in the year 1776. Her mother was born in North Carolina in the year 1800. Our subject and wife are strict members of the Methodist Church. They have no children. He is a successful farmer, and directs his attention principally to the raising of corn and tobacco. He has a good farm and residence. In his early days he accumulated enough of this world's goods to make himself and wife comfortable for the remainder of their days.

Thomas T. Harper, farmer, was born in Montgomery County, Tenn., July 12, 1832. He is the son of David and Ailsey (Lee) Harper. Mr. David Harper, father of our subject, was born in Virginia in the year of 1800 and died in 1848. His wife was born in Virginia, in 1798, and died in 1870. Our subject was united in the holy bonds of matrimony to Miss Mary E. Collins, a native of this State, born in 1838. She is the daughter of David and Eliza (Bowe) Collins. Her father was a native of Ohio, and her mother a native of Tennessee. To Thomas Harper and wife were born seven children: Stacker D., William D., Eliza A., Thomas M., Julia L., Minnie L. and Samuel R. In 1876 Mr. Harper had the misfortune to lose his wife. He then married for his second wife, Miss Catharine Collins, a sister to his first wife. She was born in 1853. Our subject is a successful farmer and lives about half a mile from the place of his birth. In 1858 he was elected constable in this district and held this office for nine years; in 1873 he was elected magistrate of this district and held this office also for nine successive years. In 1872 he moved to the farm on which he now lives; it lies on Hurricane Creek and contains good, fertile land. His neat cottage residence is situated in the suburbs of Collinsville and on the main road leading to Clarksville.

William C. Harris, farmer, was born in this State September 27, 1850. He is the only child born to Sampson C. and Jane (Mathews) Harris, who were born in this State in the early part of the present century. Our subject was united in marriage to Miss Lucy Swift, a native of this State, born September 30, 1854. Her parents are natives of this State. To Mr. Harris and wife were born five children: John W., Edgar, Sampson C., Sidney B. and Thomas C. Our subject moved to the farm, on which he now lives, in 1875. It lies on Barton's Creek, and about half a mile from Collinsville. The principal productions of this farm are corn and tobacco. He has a good, substantial residence, well located and about a quarter of a mile from the public road leading from Clarksville into

Dickson County. Mr. Harris is a man who will make friends wherever he goes.

Marcellus A. Harris was married to Martha A. Jones, in 1872; they have four children, viz.: Lena B., Margery N., Charles H. and Willis G. Sarah M. Harris was married to James L. Kennedy in 1866. By this union seven children were born: Mary J., Willie H., James R., Pattie F., Thomas F., John T. and George M. Lavina B. Harris was married to William W. Redmon in 1874; they have four children: Mary E. (deceased), Jessie B., Collie L. and Zylphia (deceased). Mr. Redman is deputy sheriff of Davidson County, Tenn. George J. Harris was married to Katharine Hancock in 1875; they have three children: Irene M., Walter and Anna May. The Harris family was one among the early settlers of Montgomery County, and at the time they settled here deer and bears were very plenty. They are all good church-going people and members of the Methodist Church. Mr. Harris was in politics a Democrat, and was respected by all. The family figured largely in the war of 1812.

John Harris was born October 1, 1808, son of Austin and Nonnie Harris, natives of Virginia. Austin Harris was the son of one of the members of the old Harris family and a farmer by occupation. He settled in Todd County, Ky., in the early part of this century, afterward settled in Montgomery County, Tenn., where he died in 1848. His wife, Nonnie (Almon) Harris, was the daughter of a very prominent Methodist minister of Virginia; her death occurred in 1873 in this county. Our subject was united in marriage with Mary E. Johnson, a daughter of Aquilla and Martha Johnson, natives of Virginia, the former born in 1785 and the latter in 1789. To them were born nine children: Thomas H., William M., Elizabeth A., Aquilla J., Martha L., Marcellus A., Sarah M., Lavenia B. and George J. Thomas Harris was in the war and was killed at the battle of Shiloh in 1862. William M. Harris was also in the late war and participated in the battles of Henry and Donelson. His company surrendered at Donelson, he escaped and reorganized with Sidney Johnston; was in the battle of Shiloh. Aquilla J. Harris was another son who was in the war, and was in the battles of Shiloh, Henry and Donelson; was captured at the battle of Manassas Gap, and held until the close of the war. He then returned home and was married to Laura T. Gordon, by whom he had seven children: Edgar A., Bay G., Hilder J., Ressa G., Mary S., Inez, John R. and Birdie B. Elizabeth. A. Harris was married to J. K. Muir in 1861; they have four children: John T., Mattie F., James H., Bessie M. Martha F. Harris was married in 1876 to W. P. Kennedy, who is farming on the old Harris homestead.

J. M. Harris was born in this State September 25, 1846, and is the son of William S. and Eliza W. (Jones) Harris, who were married in 1830. His father was a native of Virginia, born in 1806, and immigrated to Tennessee in 1828. His mother was also a native of Virginia and was born in 1815, immigrating to Tennessee with her father when but a child. Our subject was the youngest of seven children and was united in marriage, November 19, 1884, to Miss Etta Ragsdale, a native of Virginia, born September 20, 1862. Her father, I. S. Ragsdale, and her mother, Miss Seroggin, were both natives of Virginia. Our subject received his education in the best schools of Christian County, Ky., and Montgomery County, Tenn. In early life he began farming and has very successfully followed that occupation. He now lives at the home of his birth. At the early age of sixteen he enlisted in Company A, Second Kentucky Cavalry, and was engaged in several of the principal battles fought in the latter part of the war. He surrendered and was paroled at Washington. Ga., in 1865, and arrived home May 17 of this year. He is a useful citizen.

Thomas L. Harvie, stemmer and dealer in leaf tobacco, is a native of Scotland, born December 31, 1842, son of Thomas and Janet (Longwill) Harvie. Both parents were born in 1822 and in the same State. They both died in 1852. Thomas is of pure Scotch descent and was educated in his native country. He first served an apprenticeship at the dry goods business and afterward worked in groceries. He immigrated to America in 1867 and located in Marshall County, Ky., where he engaged in the tobacco business. He resided in that county seven years and then moved to Paducah, Ky. In 1877 he came to Clarksville and for four years was in the employ of T. D. Luckett & Co. In 1881 he engaged in the business for himself and has since continued. His building is 64×144 feet and three stories high and has a hanging capacity of 180 hogsheads. Mr. Harvie has prospered in his business enterprises and is a worthy citizen of the county. He was married, in 1880, to Marie Harvey, of Elkton, Ky. They have one son, Roy L. He is a member of the Presbyterian Church and his wife of tie Christian Church.

Arch Heggie, a native of this county and State, was born February 17, 1836. His father, John Heggie, was born in 1779, and married for his first wife Miss Pollie Hunt. To this union were born six children. In 1833 Mrs. Heggie died. Our subject is the second of five children born to John and Betsey (Powell) Heggie. John Heggie was born in North Carolina and died in the year 1827; his wife, Betsey, was born in Tennessee and died in 1842. November 20, 1860, our subject was united in marriage to Miss Jane Rose, a native of Tennessee and a daughter of Isaac and Elizabeth (Suiter) Rose. Isaac Rose was born in North Carolina in the year 1806 and Mrs. Rose was born in Tennessee in 1810 and died in 1883. To our subject and wife were born seven children, Laura, Lydia A., Wiley F., Levi S. H., Beadie W., John I. and Sallie W. Mr. Arch Heggie was educated in the common schools of the county, and is a member of the Methodist Church. He is a railroad carpenter by trade. In 1860 he began farming, the principal exports being corn and tobacco. He was also a speculator in tobacco until recently.

Hon. Gustavus A. Henry, the leading Whig orator and politician of his day, was born of Virginia ancestry, in Scott County, Ky., October 8,

1804. He resided in that county until fourteen years of age, when he removed to Christian County, Ky. Early in life he manifested superior in-
tellectual qualifications, and was given all the advantages of a thorough
classical education, graduating from Transylvania University, then the
leading institution of the entire South. So well fitted was Mr. Henry for
public life that in early manhood he represented Christian County in the
Legislature of Kentucky, serving through the sessions of 1831 and 1832.
About this time he formed the acquaintance of Miss Marion McClure, at
that time the belle of Clarksville, Tenn. The acquaintance ripened into
affection and they were married February 17, 1833. Never perhaps did a
marriage have a more decisive effect upon a man's destiny than had this
upon that of Mr. Henry. While it brought him a life full of domestic love
and happiness it excluded him from that brilliant political career then
opening up to his vision and possession in his native State. That State,
the home of the great Clay, and thoroughly Whig in its politics, was fast
finding out and coming to appreciate his ability. Being a great favorite of
the people and of Mr. Clay he would have been the next member of
Congress from the district in which he lived; but coming to Tennessee,
then as fully Democratic as Kentucky was Whig, and as fully under the
domination of Jackson as Kentucky was under that of Mr. Clay, his op-
portunities were cut off, yet he was always in the fore front of the battle
and, though in a hopeless minority, always labored for the success of the
Whig party. He was the Whig elector for his district in 1840, and ran
unsuccessfully for Congress in 1842 against Hon. Cave Johnson. He was
elector at large for the State in 1844, 1848 and 1852. In 1851-52 he was
in the Legislature of Tennessee and in 1853 ran for governor against
Andrew Johnson. He had so won the esteem of the people that when the
time came for men to be chosen without regard to politics, but upon
their merits, he was elected the first senator from Tennessee to the Confederate Congress. With regard to the Rebellion of 1861, he bore the
same relation to it that his great ancestor, Patrick Henry, sustained to
the Revolution of 1776. He was the peer of most of the great men of the

South, and his services were more than once gratefully acknowledged by his old school-mate and friend, the President of the Confederate States. After the fall of Vicksburg and Port Hudson, President Davis called upon Hon. G. A. Henry to make a speech to the people of the South to inspire them with his own sublime courage. At its close all crowded around him, President, senators and members of Congress. The President considered its reasonings as powerful as the thundering cataract and its eloquence as inspiring as the bugle's blast, sounding the charge for the hosts of the army to engage in battle. As a lawyer Mr. Henry was greatly distinguished, more especially as the advocate. His mind could not bear the toil necessary to become familiar with the minutiae of technical details. He could not scratch and pick, like the barn yard fowl; the eagle's flight suited best his nature and his genius, and the peculiar grandeur of the flights of his oratory won for him the proud sobriquet of the "Eagle Orator of Tennessee." His great speech in the Senate closed his public career. On March 4, 1854, Mr. Henry was confirmed by Bishop Otey in the communion of the Episcopal Church, and he was indefatigable in the performance of the duties devolving upon him as vestryman and as senior warden of the Episcopal Church at Clarksville for many years. His death occurred September 10, 1880.

Samuel A. Hinton was born January 26, 1848, in Dickson County, Tenn., and is the son of John H. and Frances S. (Lines) Hinton. John H. Hinton was born in the State of Virginia May 27, 1816. In 1833 he immigrated to this State and settled in the town of Clarksville. In 1840 he was joined in marriage to Miss Frances S. Lines, who was born in Clarksville, Tenn., August 26, 1821. To this union eleven children were born: John L., Catharine A., Sarah A., Samuel A., Mary L., James H., William E., Martha H., Richard W., Fannie L. and John O. William Lines, the father of Mrs. Hinton, built one of the first houses of the town of Clarksville, and was the first jailor of the place. John H. Hinton was a local preacher of the Tennessee Conference, also a teacher, and died

September 26, 1864; his wife died July 20, 1877. Samuel A. Hinton, subject of our sketch, is a farmer by occupation, and in 1872 was married to Miss Julia M. Mills, born in Montgomery County, Tenn., January 10, 1852, and daughter of Thomas and Caroline Mills. To Mr. and Mrs. Hinton, six children were born: Ruth, Carrie, Burr, Mills, Eugene and Edgar. Mr. Hinton is a successful farmer, owns a good tract of land in the Seventeenth District, Montgomery County, and he and wife are members of the Methodist Episcopal Church, and are highly respected by all who know them.

Samuel Hodgson, marble dealer, was born in England and came to America in 1842, and after residing in Illinois and Indiana fen years, came to Clarksville, Tenn., which State has been his residence. He is a prominent business man of Clarksville, and in early life served an apprenticeship in the marble business. He began business for himself on a limited scale and with a small capital, but by his many sterling business qualities is one of the most extensive marble dealers in the South. He imports his marble statuary and fine monumental work direct from Carrara, Italy, and deals in all the native granites, and imports his Scotch granite from Glasgow and Aberdeen, Scotland. Besides this work he is a prominent real estate owner at Clarksville, having built and owns some of the best business houses in the city, the last being the Farmers & Merchants National Bank. By his marriage with Miss Julia Kearney he had two daughters who died in infancy, and five sons now living: Charles W., Samuel J., Frank T., Jesse F., and Lee M. The history of the business part of the city would be incomplete without mentioning Mr. Hodgson's name as among the most worthy and upright business men of the city.

William I. Holmes, M. D., was born in Cumberland County, Penn., July 21, 1810, and is the second of four children and of Scotch-Irish descent. The father of Dr. Holmes was Andrew Holmes, who was born in the "Keystone State" in 1770. Our subject's grandfather was born in Ireland in 1730, and came to America in 1756. He commanded a company of partisan rangers during the Revolutionary war, and died in Cumberland County, Penn., in 1810. The father died in Carlisle, Penn., in 1855. The mother's maiden name was Ann Irvine, born in Pennsylvania in 1771, and died in 1850. Our subject was educated at Dickinson College, at Carlisle, Penn., graduated in 1829, and the same year began the study of medicine in the office of Dr. J. K. Finley. He attended lectures at the University of Pennsylvania and graduated in 1834, and the same year came to Montgomery County, Tenn., where he practiced his profession thirty-five years. He came to Clarksville in 1869, and since that time has lived a retired life. For some time he was the only physician between Clarksville and Charlotte, in Dixon County, and did a very extensive practice. October 22, 1846, he wedded Agnes A. Allen, born December 26, 1824, daughter of Nathaniel H. Allen, a lawyer, farmer and State senator. Of six children born to Dr. and Mrs. Holmes five are living: John A., born in 1847; Mary, born in 1853; Lucy, born in 1857; Sarah H., born in 1863, and Alfred, born in 1865. Mrs. Holmes died October 13, 1865. Politically the Doctor has always been a lifelong Democrat. Since 1831 he has been a leading member of the Presbyterian Church, and for many years has been a prominent man of the county. He is exceptionally well educated, and owns more than 2,000 acres of land.

James O. R. Hooper is a son of James B. and Eliza (Hodge) Hooper, born respectively in Tennessee and North Carolina in 1809 and 1811. The father was a son of William A. Hooper, who was born in North Carolina, and came to Tennessee when the settlers were obliged to take refuge in forts to protect themselves from the Indians. The Hooper family are of Irish extraction. The father, James Hooper, died January 10, 1881, and his wife December 5, 1879. Our subject attended the district schools and worked on his father's farm until he reached his majority, and then worked as clerk in the store of James Alley, in Turnersville, Tenn. In November, 1861, he enlisted in the Forty-ninth Regiment

Tennessee Confederate Infantry, and served until its surrender at Fort Donelson. He was not captured, as he was sick at that time and detached from his regiment He returned home and after his recovery reported to the Confederate authorities at Port Hudson, where his regiment was reorganized after its exchange in 1862. He served with this and other regiments, and finally surrendered with the Fourth Tennessee Regiment at Greensboro, N. C. After his return in 1866, he married Ann J. Rogers, a daughter of Callum and Nancy Rogers. Mr. and Mrs. Hooper became the parents of these children: Viola, Charles A., Thuanice (deceased) and Annie M. Mr. Hooper is a Democrat, and his wife is a member of the Methodist Episcopal Church. In 1870 he purchased the farm where he now lives. He has been industrious, and his farm is in a good state of cultivation.

Edward M. Howard, wholesale and retail grocer, and junior member of the firm of Crusman & Howard, is a native of Clarksville, born August 8, 1853, son of Edward and Mary (Crusman) Howard, and is of English descent His father was born in Sumner County, Tenn., about 1798, and his mother in Clarksville in 1802. The former died in 1853 and the latter in 1854. Our subject was reared by his mother's relatives. He first attended private schools, and in 1867 he began clerking in the store of J. J. Crusman. Here he remained three years, and then entered Stewart College, graduating in 1874. In the fall of this year he accepted a position with his old employer, and until 1880 was book-keeper and confidential clerk. In 1880 he went to New Orleans, La., and there for some time represented the interests of a prominent Cincinnati firm. In 1881 he returned to Clarksville, and in 1882 formed a partnership with J. J. Crusman. He is a prominent young business man of the city, and a true gentleman in every respect. He is a Democrat, and a member of the Presbyterian Church.

Louis C. Huffman is a native of Virginia, and was born April 22, 1853. He immigrated to Tennessee with his father when quite young, and located in Montgomery County. His parents are natives of Virginia, and were born in 1804 and 1812, respectively. Our subject was united in marriage to Miss Mattie J. Mason in 1880, who was born in this State in the year 1866. Her parents are natives of Tennessee and Kentucky, and were born in the early part of this century. Mr. and Mrs. Huffman have three children: Thomas H., Fannie M. and Mattie L. Our subject was educated in New Providence, this county, and is a stanch Democrat He entered into business at New Providence, remaining there for three years, and then in 1878 located and began business where he now is. He carries a general stock of goods, and is an upright and honorable man. The place is known as Ringgold postoffice, and is situated about six miles from Clarksville on the Hopkinsville Pike. Mr. Huffman is Postmaster there also.

B. W. Humber is a son of Edward and Lucy (Wisdom) Humber. Mr. Edward Humber came to this country from Virginia about the year 1832, and first settled in Todd County, Ky., where he engaged in farming. Leaving Todd County he went to Hopkinsville, Ky., and afterward to Trenton, Ky. After living here for some time he moved to Montgomery County, Tenn., in the year 1854, where he died in 1875. He was the father of three children, two of whom are now living: Mary E. and B. W. The subject of this sketch was born March 3, 1833, in Todd County, Ky., came to this county in 1854, and went into business in 1855. He taught school in this county until the breaking out of the war, when he joined the army of his country, enlisting in the Forty-ninth Tennessee, C. S. A., under Col. Bailey. He was disbanded at Greensboro, N. C. After the war he came back to Montgomery County, and took school-teaching as his profession. He is now teaching at Woodlawn, Tenn., and is considered one of the best educators of the time. He is a member of the Christian Church, and in politics is a Democrat, being a Whig until the death of that party, and cast his first vote for Millard Fillmore. Our subject is a member of the F. & A. M., and in the year 1866 was wedded to M. R. Greenhill, of this county. To this union have been born six children: W. H., M. J., A. L., M. F., C. M. and Lizzie L. Mr. Humber is a man who commands the respect of all his fellow-men.

John Hurst, wholesale grocer, is a native of Montgomery County. Tenn., where he was born March 29, 1841, son of Frank and Eliza (Flack) Hurst, and is of Scotch origin. His father was born in Tennessee in 1810, and by occupation was a farmer. He died in Texas in 1873. The mother was born in Todd County, Ky., in 1818. The family came from North Carolina in pioneer days and have since been residents of Tennessee, Our subject was the eldest of six children and was educated in the country schools. In 1859 he began clerking for S. F. Beaumont in a hardware store, continuing until April, 1861, when he enlisted in Company H, Fourteenth Tennessee Volunteers, and served four years. He was captured in 1863 as the army was falling back from Gettysburg and was a prisoner seven months. In 1865 he began clerking in the grocery house of Capt. J. J. Crusman and in this capacity continued eleven years. In 1876 he engaged in the grocery business for himself, and since 1883 has kept a strictly wholesale establishment. He employs seven salesmen and keeps the largest house of the kind in his section of the county. He was married, in 1872, to Amaryllis Smith, a native of Louisa County, Va. They have three children: Ethel, Walton and Sallie. Mr. Hurst is a Democrat and he and wife are members of the Baptist Church.

Thomas H. Hyman, tobacco auctioneer, is a native of Louisville, Ky., born December 28, 1837, son of Samuel and Henrietta B. (Oliver) Hyman, and is of English-Irish origin. His father was born in England in 1812, and his mother in Missouri in 1817. The father came to America when quite a small lad and the family settled in New York, but subsequently removed to Louisville, Ky., where the father died in 1882. The mother is still a resident of that city. Our subject attended private schools and was a pupil of William Butler at the time he was killed by Mat Ward. He attended a Catholic college of his native city for some time and afterward spent one year at Boyd's Commercial College, acquiring a good business education. In 1856 he came to Clarksville, Tenn., and with the exception of two years has made that city his residence. He has been a tobacco auctioneer for twenty years and is one of the best at the Clarksville Tobacco Exchange. He is a Democrat, and was city marshal in 1862 and eleven years chief of the fire department. He has been a member of the city council for ten years, and was one of the leaders in the establishment of the public schools in the city. He was married in 1860 to Eva H. Cooper, of New Orleans, La., born in 1842. They have three children: Samuel A., Emma M. and Edward J. Mr. Hyman is a Royal Arch Mason, being a member of that lodge twenty years. In the Blue Lodge he has been Senior Deacon for many years. He and his wife are members of the Methodist Episcopal Church Martin Van Buren Ingram was born in Montgomery County, Tenn., June 20, 1832, son of Moses and Cytha (Halsell) Ingram. The father was born in North Carolina in 1780 and died in 1852. He was a descended of an English family that came to North Carolina over 200 years ago, and came to Tennessee with his parents when quite young. He was twice married, his first wife being Nancy Darnell, by whom he had four children. He was a hatter by trade and a Democrat of unyielding views. At the age of seventeen our subject took charge of his father's farm and negroes, and at the death of the latter became guardian for his younger brothers and sisters, and managed his mother's affairs up to her death in August, 1856. He then became owner of the homestead by purchase, but two years later sold his farm and engaged in the manufacture of wagons and buggies in Clarksville with J. B. Miller, which connection, however, was soon dissolved. February 8, 1860, he wedded Annie L., daughter of Dr. Willis H. Farmer, of Springfield, and to them were born seven children: Emmett, Willis, Lannie, Warren, Emma, Georgie and Talbert. Mr. Ingram was in the Confederate service and was a member of Hawkins' battalion, which was attached to Manney's brigade. Soon after the battle of Shiloh, on the 27th of April, he was honorably discharged for disability. He followed in his father's footsteps in regard to politics, and supported Douglas in the campaign of 1860. At the close of the war he engaged with Archie Thomas in the publication of the Robertson Register at Springfield, and soon became sole proprietor. The paper was suspended to begin the Clarksville Tobaoco Leaf, which is spoken of elsewhere in this work He joined the Masonic fraternity in 1856, and posted himself thoroughly in the ritual and read the best works on Masonry, which led him to embrace Christianity, and he united with the Baptist Church at Graysville, Ky., in 1857. Later he was included as one of the deacons in the organization of the Baptist Church in Springfield. In 1869 his membership was transferred to Clarksville, and soon after he was elected clerk of Bethel Baptist Association, in which position he served three terms.

Nathaniel P. Irby, farmer, was born in Tennessee, November 22, 1826. He is the youngest of six children born to Geral T. and Martha (Woodfin) Irby, natives of Virginia, and both born in 1784. Our subject was united in marriage in 1852, to Miss Mary N. Waller, a native of this State, born September 13, 1832, and the fourth of twelve children born to Daniel and Sallie O. Waller. Her parents are natives of North Carolina and Virginia, and were born in 1803 and 1804, respectively. Our subject and wife's wedded life was rendered happy by the addition of ten children born to them, viz.: Mary E., Geral T., Ben D., George E., Charley T., Martha E., John R., William W., Sallie A. E. and Nancy F. Our subject is an industrious and stirring farmer, has a neat residence well located, and is respected by all who know him.

George S. Irwin, junior member of the firm of Kendall, Pettus &. Co., was born in Todd County, Ky., August 23, 1854, and is a son of F. G. and Mary L. (Snadon) Irwin. The father was a Kentuckian, born in

1826, and his mother in 1834. His paternal grandfather was William Irwin, a Virginian. Our subject came to Clarksville with his parents in 1867, and was educated at Stewart College, and in the fall of 1874 entered Poughkeepsie Business College, where he obtained a good practical education. In the fall of 1875 he went to Louisville, Ky., and for one year was shipping clerk for Wheat & Chesney. He then returned to Clarksville and took a position with Kendrick, Hamburgh & Co., and in the fall of 1879 was admitted as a member of the firm. In 1879 the firm was changed to Kendrick, Pettus & Co., and as such now continues. Mr. Irwin has charge of the office work and correspondence. He is a Democrat and a member of the Methodist Episcopal Church, and a successful business man.

James Hickman Johnson, deceased, the eldest son of Cave Johnson, was born October 8, 1840. He received many educational advantages in school and colleges, and was a student in the law department of the Cumberland University at the breaking out of the war. He then joined Capt W. A. Forbes' company, which afterward was a part of Company A, Fourteenth Tennessee Regiment, and was elected lieutenant of Company G of the same regiment, and was afterward promoted to captain, and then to major of the regiment. He surrendered to Gen. Grant at Appomattox Court House, April 9, 1865. He was severely wounded at Cedar Run., Va., August 9. He was among the bravest of brave soldiers, and was with the Fourteenth Tennessee Regiment, C. S. A., in all skirmishes and battles from the beginning until the close of the war; and owing to Col, Forbes' death, he was the one to surrender the regiment at the command of Gen. Lee, at Appomattox Court House, Va. Maj. Johnson died at Clarksville, October 28, 1880, and was buried by the side of his father in Greenwood Cemetery. He was married October 15, 1867, to Mary Boyd, who was born October 1, 1843, and daughter of George C. and Virginia C. Boyd. To Mr. and Mrs. Johnson were born two sons:

Cave, born July 24, 1868, and died August 1, 1869, and George Boyd, who was born May 12, 1870.

Dr. T. D. Johnson may be mentioned as among the first of the medical profession in Clarksville, He was born in Robertson County, Tenn., January 21, 1842, and is the second son of Hon. Cave and Elizabeth (Dortch) Johnson. The early life of Dr. Johnson was spent in schools and colleges. He was a student at the military school in Nashville, and also attended the University of North Carolina. Subsequently he began the study of law, but continued it only a brief period. In 1861 he enlisted in Company A, Fourteenth Tennessee of Confederate States Army. In 1862 was wounded at Gaines Mill, Va., and the next year was wounded at Fredericksburg, Va., and at Chancellorsville received a third wound. He was a brave and faithful soldier, and continued in the service until the close of the war, having surrendered with Gen. Lee's army. In 1865 he began the study of medicine in Clarksville, and later attended the medical department of the University of Virginia and the College of Physicians and Surgeons, at Baltimore, Md., graduating from the latter institution in 1869. He was for some time resident physician at Bayview Hospital, but in 1869 located in Clarksville, where he continued to practice his profession until 1875, when he received an appointment by the Egyptian Government as staff surgeon, with the rank of major in the Egyptian Army. He was sent with that army on its campaign into Abyssinia, and March 7, 1876, was wounded with a spear at the battle of Goura, and was a captive for forty-eight days, and suffered great hardships at the hands of his captors. The Doctor owes his life to the noted chief, Bass Walda Celessie, who controlled the provinces of Ambrara and Semaine. For the valuable services rendered by the Doctor, and the high estimate of his ability as a surgeon and gentleman, he was decorated by the khedive with the order of Medjedieh, and is perhaps the only Tennesseean who was ever decorated by a foreign government. Foreseeing the failure of Egyptian finances he resigned and came home, and since 1877 has been in active practice in Clarksville, and is one of the leading physicians in Tennessee. He was married, in 1880, to Miss Carrie Lurton, daughter of Dr. L. L. Lurton. They have three children: Sarah, Thomas Dickson, Jr., and Polk Gundy, Jr.

Polk G. Johnson is the youngest son of Cave Johnson, and was born in Clarksville, Tenn., November 2, 1844, a namesake of James K. Polk and Felix Grundy. He entered school at five years of age, and continued under private tutorage until 1858, when he entered Stewart College. At the breaking out of the war he joined Company A, Capt. J. E. Bailey Forty-ninth Tennessee Regiment, C. S. A., Nov. 29, 1861. He was at the battle of Fort Donelson, and surrendered with his company February 16, 1862 He remained a prisoner at Camp Douglas, Ill, until exchanged at Vicksburg September 5, 1862. He served as a private soldier in the Forty-ninth Tennessee Regiment until September, 1863, when he was detailed for duty at the headquarters of Brig.-Gen. Quarles, and September 4, 1864, was appointed first lieutenant and aid-de-camp, and his commission bears date September 4, 1864, signed John C. Breckinridge. Secretary of War. He served on Gen. Quarles' staff until that general was disabled, when he was assigned duty as assistant inspector-general on Gen. McComb's staff, and was his only personal staff officer at the surrender of Gen. Lee, at Appomattox Court House, the others having been wounded or captured. He was in fifteen battles, and after receiving his parole, returned home, and in 1865 went to Canada and entered McGill College, Montreal. He afterward attended the law department of the Cumberland University, at Lebanon, Tenn., and received the degree of B. L. in January, 1868. He was associated with Gen. W. A. Quarles in law practice until his appointment as clerk and master of the chancery court in July, 1870. He married Emma V. Robb, daughter of Col. Alfred Robb (who was killed at Fort Donelson in 1862), October 1. 1868. She died in 1872, and in 1875 he wedded Nannie W. Tyler, daughter of Hon. John D. Tyler, of this county. They have two children: Cave and Mildred; In 1871 Mr. Johnson was reappointed clerk and master of the chancery court for a term of six years, and August 6. 1877, was re-elected, and again in 1883, and is now holding that office, his term not expiring until February 21, 1889. He has been active in advancing the interests of the city and county, and with several other gentlemen was instrumental in building up the beautiful cemetery at Clarksville. He was treasurer for the building of the Trinity Church, and boasts that it does not owe 1 cent. Mr. Johnson has taken part in all the enterprises of the city, and has been much interested in its history in the hope of thereby inducing others to feel a pride in its advancement.

William P. Johnson was born on the farm where he now resides September 25, 1848, and is of Scotch-Irish descent. The father, James C. Johnson, was born in 1811; in 1847 he married Frances E. Coleman, and to them were born four children, all dead except our subject. The father was a farmer, and died in 1873; the mother is yet living, and resides with William P. on the old homestead. William was educated in the common schools, and attended the Washington Lee University at Lexington, Va., and at Bryant & Stratton's Commercial College at Louisville, Ky. He aided his father on the farm until the latter's death, and then assumed complete control, and has given his attention to farming and stock raising ever since. His farm, "Lake View," consists of 700 acres, and lies about ten miles from Clarksville, and our subject owns all except his mother's interest. He raises large quantities of tobacco, wheat, corn and hay, and makes a specialty of raising fine stock, such as Jersey cattle, South Down sheep and Berkshire hogs in immense numbers. November 14, 1871, he wedded Bettie W. Marshall, of Green County, Ky., born February 7, 1855, daughter of W. B. and Martha A. Marshall. Mr. and Mrs. Johnson have two children: Mary B., born July 22, 1873, and James T., born June 28, 1875. Mr. Johnson is a supporter of Democratic principles, and is a stockholder and a director of the Farmers and Merchants National Bank at Clarksville.

M. Clark Johnson is a son of Alexander L. and Diana C. W. (Terry) Johnson, natives of Virginia and Tennessee, respectively. The father came to Tennessee about 1819, and worked at different callings, and after his marriage he purchased a farm adjoining our subject's. The mother died in 1871. She was the mother of nine children, our subject being the fourth. He was born September 1, 1841, and was educated in the schools of John D. Tyler and James Ross. In 1861 he enlisted in the Fiftieth Tennessee Infantry, C. S. A., and served with it until the surrender of Fort Donelson, when he made his escape and joined the Thirteenth Tennessee Infantry, and served with that regiment until the battle of Shiloh, when he was transferred to the First Kentucky Cavalry, and was in that command until August 1, 1862. He then joined the Second Kentucky Cavalry, which belonged to Gen. Morgan's brigade, and served with him until the close of the war. He was with Morgan north of the Ohio, but before the latter's surrender he crossed the river as advance guard, made his escape, and joined a portion of Morgan's command in West Virginia. In 1866 Mr. Johnson was married to Mary J. Wilcox, a native of St. Louis, Mo., daughter of Dr. C. L. and Amanda Wilcox, who came to Tennessee at an early period. The Doctor died July 21, 1880. Mr. and Mrs. Johnson are the parents of these children: Emmarene, Sadie, Lizzie, Ewing and Edward T. Mr. Johnson owns a large farm, called the "Pine Grove Farm," and has given his attention to farming and raising thorough-bred cattle, sheep and hogs. He is a member of the Guthrie Grange, P. of H.

Robert L. Johnson was born in the State of Tennessee May 25, 1829. He is the grandson of the old Revolutionary war veteran, Teresha Johnson. Robert Johnson's father was Len H. Johnson, a native of Virginia, born September 3, 1797. He immigrated to Tennessee at an early day, and located on the same farm that our subject is living on at the present time. He was appointed postmaster under Jackson's administration, and kept the office in his dwelling. Game, at this time, was abundant in this portion of the country, and he and Hon. Cave Johnson spent many days together hunting and fishing. Our subject's mother was Mary W. Kendrick, born in Virginia March 16, 1803. His parents were married March 22, 1820, and to this union were born seven children. Robert L. Johnson was united in marriage to Miss Victoria Greenwood, a native of Tennessee, born August 17, 1838. Her parents are William M. and Jane C. Greenwood. To our subject and wife were born five children, viz.: Carrie A., Minnie L., Greenwood, Robert O. and one not named. On February 26, 1883, he had the misfortune to lose his wife, and on August 22, 1883, he was married to Miss Eliza J. Hinton, who was born February 29, 1837, in Virginia, and is the daughter of Benjamin J. and Elvira Hinton. Our subject is a stanch Democrat, and is now living in the house of his birth. His large residence is situated on an elevation near the West Fork of Red River, and affords a splendid view for a considerable distance around. He has fine clover fields, but his principal products are corn, wheat and tobacco. He is esteemed and respected far and near as a good man.

J. G. Joseph is identified with the business interest of Clarksville and is known in that city as the "Star Clothier." He was born in Cincinnati, Ohio, January 2, 1842. His parents, Joseph and Rachel (Wolf) Joseph were natives of England, the former born in Exeter in 1801 and the latter in Plymouth in 1814. The father came to America in 1837 and located in the Queen City. He was a jeweler and died in Cincinnati in 1873. The mother yet resides in Hamilton, Ohio. The early boyhood of our subject was spent in Cincinnati. At the age of ten years he went to live with an uncle in Indianapolis, Ind., and was educated in the Northwestern Christian University and the Commercial College of that city. He then clerked for a number of years in his uncle's clothing establishment, and in 1860 began business for himself in that city and from 1864 to 1869 acted in the capacity of traveling salesman. At the latter date he came to Clarksville and engaged in the clothing and gents' furnishing

business and the same now continues. He is one of the organizers of the
Franklin Bank and is one of its stockholders. He was made a Mason in
1868 at Center Lodge, No. 23, Indianapolis, and is a member of the Royal Arch Chapter of this city, and elected secretary of the same in 1882.
He is the first charter member of the K. of P. lodge and in 1874 was
elected Past Chancellor. He is the author of the degree of "Wise Men."
Also first charter member of Abraham Lodge, No. 58, I. O. B. B., at Indianapolis, Ind., and was elected its president in 1866. After living in
Clarksville six months District Grand Lodge, No. 2, I. O. B. B. consisting
of the States of Ohio, Indiana, Illinois, Missouri, Michigan, Kentucky
and Tennessee met in Memphis, Tenn., and he was elected as representative to the Grand Lodge from Abraham Lodge, No. 58; it was the
last Grand Lodge that Tennessee met with District No. 2; he still belongs
to District No. 2, and is an active member of all endowments to I. O. B.
B. Is one of the charter members of Clarksville Division No. 7, Uniform
Rank, K. of P., lately organized. He was married, in 1872, to Carrie Rexinger, a sister of Samuel Rexinger, who for eighteen years was postmaster in this city. They have three children: Joseph, Ruby and Edith. In
politics Mr. Joseph is a Democrat and cast his first presidential vote for
Seymour. He has been a delegate to every Democratic State Convention
of Tennessee since 1870. By inheritance he is a member of the Hebrew
Church, but is now more liberal in his religious views.

M. L. Joslin, harness dealer, was born in Dickson County, Tenn., December 29, 1836, son of Henderson and Martha (Lee) Joslin, and is of
English descent. Both parents were born in Tennessee in 1809, the former in Dickson County and the latter in Williamson County. The father
died in 1840. Our subject was raised on a farm, and in 1854 began learning the harness-maker's trade, at which he has since worked, save four
years spent in the Confederate Army. In 1867 he came to Clarksville and
has since been engaged in his present business. In 1861 he lead to the
hymeneal altar Miss M. V. Walter, of Dover, Stewart Co., Tenn. Their

children's names are Mattie V., William W., Fonnie, Minnie, John, Edward and Charles. Mr. Joslin has been identified with the Democratic party since the war. He belongs to the Masonic fraternity and is a member of the Christian Church. He has an extensive harness store in Clarksville and is doing well from a financial standpoint.

John W. Keesee. The Keesee family may be traced to John Keesee, who was born in Virginia in 1783. He was a soldier in the war of 1812 and came to Tennessee in 1816 and settled in Montgomery County near Clarksville. He was one of the early pioneer settlers and by occupation was a "tiller of the soil." He was the father of the following children: Mary, Ann R., G. S., Reuben, John A., William P., B. O., P. H. and R. J., who was a Confederate soldier and died in 1865, before returning home. The father died in 1867. Bellfield O. Keesee came to Clarksville in 1846 and for many years was a leading business man of this city. He organized what was known as the Montgomery Savings Institution, now the Clarksville National Bank. He died December 26, 1875. The father of our subject was G. S. Keesee, who was born in 1817 in this county. His mother was Mary (Bourne) Keesee, who was a native of Port Royal, Tenn., born in 1831 and died in 1854. The father was a farmer, but now resides with his son in the city. Our subject, John W., was reared on the farm where he remained until 1868, when he came to Clarksville. He first attended the country schools and later was a student in Stewart College. For a number of years he was in the employ of his uncle, B. O. Keesee, but in 1873 he engaged in business for himself in partnership with M. C. Northington. They were in the tobacco business two years and then began keeping a wholesale and retail grocery store and are now one of the leading firms in this part of Tennessee. Mr. Keesee's marriage to Eva Simpson was solemnized in 1877. She was born in Alabama in 1855, daughter of W. T. Simpson. They have two children: Lulu S. and John W. Mr. Keesee is a Democrat and is a member of the K. of P. He and wife are members of the Methodist Episcopal Church. He is a leading business man and a representative of one of the oldest families.

J. D. Kendrick, an extensive farmer and stock raiser of the Fourth District, is the son of Dennis L. and Nancy H. (Duncan) Kendrick, D. L. Kendrick was a native of North Carolina, and died there. Mrs. Kendrick immigrated to Tennessee in 1826, and settled in the Fourth District, where she died December 3, 1868, and where her body was laid to rest in the Kendrick burying-ground. She was the mother of three children: Lucy A., J. H. and J. D. J. H. Kendrick died in 1885, and was buried beside his mother. J. D. Kendrick was born January 17, 1822, in North Carolina, and came to Tennessee with his mother. In the year 1864 he was married to Miss Frances J. Johnson, who was a native of North Carolina. Their wedded life was made happy by five children: Carrie, Morris D., Laudie, J. D. and Ione, all of whom are living, with the exception of Ione, who died in 1876. J. D. Kendrick owns one of the finest tracts of land in the county, and is one of the influential citizens.

James C. Kendrick was born in Montgomery County, Tenn., near La Fayette, Ky., January 17, 1845, son of James and Sarah L. (Smith) Kendrick, natives of Virginia and North Carolina, respectively. About 1820 the Kendrick family came to Tennessee and settled in Montgomery County, where the father died in 1847. Mr. Kendrick attended the common schools and Center College in Boyd County, Ky. He then followed the occupation of farming until 1872 and still owns the old homestead. Since 1872 he has been engaged in the tobacco warehouse business, and is a member of the firm of Kendrick, Pettus & Co., one of the leading tobacco firms of the South, doing business in 1885 of over $1,250,000. In 1869 he wedded Nettie Donahue, daughter of T. J. Donahue, who for many years was an eminent physician of this county. They have five children; Charles B., Harriet B., Maud B., James and Sarah. Mr. Kendrick is a Democrat and one of the prosperous business men of the city. His wife is a member of the Presbyterian Church.

William H. Killebrew was born in Christian County, Ky., May 13, 1838. He is the son of George W. and Mary A. Killebrew. George Killebrew was born in Montgomery County, Tenn., February 13, 1814, and died February 20, 1871. His wife, Mary Ann Moore, was born in Kentucky, March 31, 1819, and is still living in Montgomery County, Tenn. In 1861 William H. Killebrew settled on 522 acres of good land where he now lives. On the 3d of November, 1864, he was united in marriage to Nora Johnson, of Montgomery County, Tenn. By this union twelve children were born, viz.: George G., Emma L., Fannie, George H., Samuel, J. F. J., Mary M., Nora, Lizzie, Nora, William H. and Meek, the last three, are deceased. William H. Killebrew was educated at Bethel College, Ky., and is a very prominent Democrat; is also a member of the Oakland Christian Church. Mr. Killebrew is one of many men who started out in life with very little means, but with energy and perseverance he has become a very successful farmer.

David Kincannon, wholesale and retail dealer in hardware, queensware, etc., was born in McMinn County, Tenn., December 2, 1827, son of Frank and Elizabeth (McCroskey) Kincannon, and of Irish lineage. His parents were born in Sevier County, Tenn., the father in 1800 and the mother in 1802. The paternal grandfather was George Kincannon, born in Virginia in 1765. He came to Tennessee in very early times, and died in this State. Frank Kincannon was the first registrar of Bradley County, Tenn., and held that office till his death in 1844. The mother of our subject died in 1866. Although our subject was born in McMinn County the greater part of his early life was spent in Bradley County. He attended the country schools, and in 1847 he began learning the tinner's trade and served as an apprentice two years. He then began business for himself, and continued the manufacture and sale of his goods until the breaking out of the war. He came to Clarksville in 1865 and the same year opened a tin shop, and for ten years worked at his bench in that city. In 1868 he added a full line of crockery and in 1879 a complete stock of hardware, and now has one of the most extensive establishments of the kind in the State. In the fire of 1878 he lost $10,000. In 1852 he wedded Lucretia F. Britton, a native of McMinn County, born February 18, 1828, daughter of William and Mary Britton. Mr. and Mrs. Kincannon became the parents of this family: Fannie A., Walter B., Mary E. and James C. Our subject is a Democrat, and one of the leading Masons in this part of the State. He became a Knight Templar in 1867. He is a Presbyterian and his wife is a Methodist.

William Kleeman, butcher, was born in Bavaria, Germany, May 6, 1835, son of S. W. and Fannie (Meyer) Kleeman, and is of German. lineage. His parents were both born in Bavaria, the father in 1783 and the mother in 1804, and they died in 1849 and 1852, respectively. Our subject was educated in the schools of Bavaria, and when ten years old began learning the butcher's trade. At the age of fifteen he left home, and for two years worked as a journeyman butcher. He came to the United States in 1852, locating in New York City, where he plied his trade for ten years in the Union and Washington Markets. In 1802 he went to Shelbyville, Ill., and there resided until 1865, when he came to Clarksville and engaged in the mercantile business, continuing until 1878, when he began the butchering business, and opened the first daily market the city ever had, and is now the leading butcher in this section. In politics he is a Democrat. In 1882 he was elected to the council of Clarksville and re-elected in 1885, and again in 1886, and is now chairman of that committee. He was married, in 1858, to Amelia Rothschild, born in Bavaria in 1839, and came to the United States in 1852. They have six children: Seward, Isaac, Daisy, Arthur, Violet and Edward C. Mr. Kleeman belongs to the Masons, I. O. O. F. and K. of P. fraternities, and is a leading citizen of the city. He is a member of the city school board, being elected in March, 1886. He is also chief of the fire department.

Hon. Richard Ledbetter, farmer, was born in Rutherford County, Tenn., January 25, 1835. The father, William Ledbetter, was a Virginian, born in 1800. He was president of the State Bank at Nashville for a number of years, and at the breaking out of the war was cashier of a branch of the Planter's Bank at Murfreesboro. He represented Rutherford County in the lower house of the Tennessee General Assembly for two terms. He died at Murfreesboro in 1862. Our subject's mother was Eliza A. (Welborn) Ledbetter. She was born in North Carolina in 1810. Our subject, Richard Ledbetter, grew to manhood on the farm, and in 1850 entered Union University at Murfreesboro, and graduated from that school four years later. Subsequent to his graduation he farmed for some time, and at the breaking out of the war was engaged in the grocery business at Murfreesboro. In 1862 he removed to Stewart County to protect the Iron Mountain Furnace property, of which his father was the proprietor for several years. Later he engaged in farming in that county, where he still owns a farm. He is a Democrat, and in 1879 was elected to represent Montgomery and Stewart Counties as joint representative in the lower house of the Tennessee General Assembly. In December, 1883, he removed to Clarksville, Montgomery County, locating at the Capt. Valliant place, on Greenwood Avenue, and here now resides, engaged in the lumber and building material trade. He was married, in 1868, to Maggie Chilton, a native of Clarksville, and daughter of Robert S. Chilton. He is a Mason, made such in 1862. He belongs to the A. L. of H., and he and wife are members of the Christian Church. He is a leading politician, and is considered by all one of the county's first and best citizens.

Col. J. W. Lockert was born June 11, 1828, in Montgomery County, Tenn., and is of Scotch-Irish descent. He is the son of William and Elizabeth (McFadden) Lockert, natives respectively of South Carolina and Tennessee. The father of Col. Lockert purchased a farm on the south side of Red River, six miles from Clarksville, and here all his children were born and raised. Our subject was educated in the common schools of the county, and at the age of eighteen went to Clarksville, where he learned the trade of blacksmithing. In 1852 he married Miss Sarepta Wilson, a native of this county and State, and daughter of Samuel and Polly Wilson. To him and his wife were born the following children: William S., Charles C., Hamilton E. and Clayton, all living but Charles. To 1864 Mrs. Sarepta Lockert died, and in 1867 the Colonel married Miss Sarah Miles, a native of Robertson County, Tenn., and daughter of Andrew and Kittie Miles. To this union one child, Rebel Lee, was born. Early in the year 1861 the Colonel raised a company of soldiers for the Confederate service, and was commissioned captain of the same. The company joined the Fourteenth Regiment Tennessee Infantry, and was designated Company K. He was elected first as captain of his company, and soon after the first year's service was promoted to the office of major of his regiment, and a few months later was promoted to the office of lieutenant-colonel, and in that capacity he served till the close of the war. He was in all the battles in which his regiment was engaged, up to and including the battle of Gettysburg, where he received a severe gunshot wound. Here he was captured, and held as a prisoner of war until the end of the conflict. The principal business of the Colonel has been that of farming. He has, however, been engaged for a few years since the war in running a saw-mill in this and Robertson Counties. His farm lies on the north bank of Red River, and is exceedingly fertile and well cultivated.

Thomas Dade Luckett was born in Jefferson County, Ky., November 4, 1843, and is the tenth of a family of thirteen children, and is of English descent. His father was A. P. Luckett, of Virginia, and came to Kentucky in early days. He was magistrate, and died in Missouri. The mother died in Texas in 1882. Our subject spent his boyhood days in Missouri, and at the age of fifteen returned to Kentucky. In 1860 he began clerking in a drug store in Owensboro, Ky., and in 1862 he enlisted in Company C, Third Kentucky Cavalry. He was in Morgan's command, and was taken prisoner in 1863, and was kept at Camp Douglas, Illinois, for eighteen months, when he was released and again joined his command. After the close of the war he returned home and entered the employ of Kerr, Clark & Co., and was stationed at Eddyville, Ky., and remained in their employ eight years. In 1875 he came to Clarksville, and formed a partnership with M. H. and L. B. Clark in the general tobacco business, and has met with good success. In 1869 he wedded Maria Gracey, a native of Kentucky, born in December, 1843. They have three children: Mary S., Gracey H. and Bobbie. Mr. Luckett is a Democrat, and had at one time seven brothers in the late war. His brother Robert was killed at Stone River, and William was wounded at Vicksburg, and afterward died in the hospital, and L. D. Luckett was killed at Perryville in 1862. Our subject and wife are members of the Episcopal Church. He is one of the leading men of the city, and has been a member of the city council.

Horace H. Lurton, president of the Farmers and Merchants National Bank, and one of the first lawyers of the State, was born in Campbell County, Ky., February 26, 1844, son of Dr. L. and Sarah (Harman) Lurton, who were born in Scott County in 1820 and 1824, and died in Tennessee in 1877 and 1881, respectively. The paternal grandfather was a native and a leading physician of Kentucky, and the maternal grandfather, Zebulon Harman, was a Virginian and a Methodist minister. He organized the first Sabbath-school and church in Kentucky, and was one of the early pioneers of that State. In 1861 our subject joined Col. Ben Hill's regiment, and became sergeant-major, but was discharged in February, 1862, owing to ill health. In the latter part of the same year he joined the Second Kentucky Regiment, and at the surrender of Fort Donelson was sent as a prisoner of war to Camp Chase, Ohio, where he succeeded in making his escape the following April, and two months later joined Dortch's Cavalry (afterward Company G, Third Kentucky Cavalry of Morgan's Brigade), and in July, 1863, was again taken prisoner, and remained such until the close of the war. In September, 1865, he entered the law department of the Cumberland University, and graduated from that school two years later. He was licensed to practice in 1867, and the year following became the law partner of Hon. G. A. Henry. Ten years later he became associated with Hon. James E. Bailey in law practice, and upon the resignation of Hon. C. G. Smith, as chancellor, he was appointed to fill that vacancy, and at the election in 1876 he was chosen without opposition. Since 1878 he has been the law partner of C. G. Smith, and has gained a wide-spread reputation. Fannie Owen, who was born in 1845, became his wife September 17, 1867, and the mother of his three children: Leon O., Mary and Horace H., Jr. Mr. Lurton is a Democrat and a member of the Episcopal Church. He became president of the Farmers and Merchants Bank in 1884, and belongs to the I. O. O. F. and K. of P. fraternities.

Hon. Berry Lyle, a native of Montgomery County, Tenn., was born January 29, 1831, and when eight years of age hired out on a farm for $3 per month. He worked a great deal at iron furnaces, and often put in extra time by working late at night. His greatest desire, even in youth, was to get a good education, and while attending school he made the best possible use of his time. In 1849 he received a recommendation from his last teacher that he was fully competent to teach school. He soon procured a school, which he taught for six months, afterward clerking one year at the Yellow Creek Furnace. He then taught school and clerked in stores for a few years. In 1854 he and his brother went to Missouri, where, after a short time, his brother was taken sick, and our subject had to return home with him. In March, 1855, Mr. Lyle was wedded to Miss Alley N. Trice, a native of Tennessee, born February 12,

1839, daughter of John and Harriet Trice. To their union were born seven children: Emily C. (deceased), Henry J. (deceased), Ida E., Margaret E., Lulie A., James T. and Sarepta (deceased). Mrs. Lyle died June 14, 1866. For his second wife Mr. Lyle married Mrs. Eliza A. (Trice) Alsup, September 30, 1872. This lady was born in Tennessee November 17, 1841, and died April 29, 1881, after bearing two children: Berry H. and Beulah A. In 1860 he was elected justice of the peace in District No. 8, and filled the office until he sold his farm and moved to New Providence, where he entered into the livery and tobacco business. In 1865 he was elected sheriff, and in 1867 was elected to the State Senate. In 1870 he was appointed postmaster at New Providence, which office he held for seven years. During the last few years he has farmed and dealt in tobacco, the latter occupation yet engaging his attention.

Henry Lyle was born in Montgomery County, Tenn., December 12, 1813, and is the son of Jordan and Annie (Bumpass) Lyle, natives of North Carolina, who moved to Tennessee about the year 1807, where they died in the years 1845 and 1861, respectively. Our subject was united in marriage to Miss Jane B. McCorkle, a native of Tennessee, born January 26, 1816, and the daughter of Abraham and Sallie (Lytle) McCorkle, natives of South Carolina. To our subject and wife were born thirteen children, viz.: Albert P., Sallie A., Louisa J., Mary D., Henry T., Sarepta A., Martha E., Edward, Lucy A., an infant not named, and Robert L., Samuel F. and Laura B. Mr. Lyle is of English-Scotch-Welsh descent, and was educated in the common schools of the county, is a member of the Methodist Church, a Democrat, and in 1848 was elected tax collector of Montgomery County, which office he filled creditably for thirteen years. In 1872 he moved to the farm on which he now lives. It is said to be as fine a farm as is to be found in Montgomery County; besides this he owns three others in this county and one in Houston. He is an enterprising farmer and a good citizen.

William J. Lyle, a native of this county and State, was born July 21, 1836. He is the second of twelve children born to James and Sallie A. (McCorkle) Lyle. His parents were natives of this State, and were born in 1809 and 1814, respectively. Mr. Lyle, Sr., died in 1855. Our subject was united in marriage to Miss Elizabeth Batson, a native of this State, born September 6, 1842. She is the second of twelve children born to Carney and Maria (Williams) Batson. Mr. Carney Batson was born in Tennessee in the year 1811; his wife was born in Virginia in 1820. To our subject and wife have been born eleven children: Sallie M., Clay, Carney B., Annie, Lizzie, Martha G., Robert, John A., Louis L., James R. and Kate. The seventh child died in 1876. Our subject is a farmer by occupation. In 1875 he moved to Collinsville, and has been engaged in merchandising ever since. He is also postmaster at that place, where he is respected by all.

William J. MacCormac, photographer, was born July 5, 1838, and is the elder of two children born to John MacCormac (merchant of Edinburgh, Scotland) and Lydia (Brett) MacCormac of Newry, Ireland. Our subject left his home in Edinburgh, before completing his education, to seek his fortune in the New World, and after much wandering came to Clarksville, Tenn., in 1855, which year dates the beginning of his work and study as a photographer. After the surrender of Fort Donel son he sold his business interests in this city, and, during the remainder of the war, served as photographer in the topographical engineer corps of Sherman's army. In 1866 he visited Scotland for the third time since coming to America and returned the same year. He then located in Louisville, Ky., in the grocery and commission business, and later under the firm name of MacCormac & Cull en, engaged in the wholesale manufacture of boots and shoes. In 1870 he returned to Clarksville and resumed his trade. His study in Europe and the large cities of America made him one of the best artists in the State. He is a member of the Photographers Association of America and was vice-president of that body one year.

During the war Mr. MacCormac was a Union man, since that time he has been a strong Democrat. He is a Mason and an active member of Clarksville Commander of Knights Templar. In 1871 he wedded Mary Leonard, daughter of Col. T. D. Leonard, who was born in Onondaga County, N. T., and came to Tennessee in 1840 and traveled throughout the Southern States as agent and dealer in patent rights. In 1845 the colonel began keeping livery stable in Clarksville and conducted that business successfully for three years. In 1849 he married Mrs. Tredonia Dalney, daughter of Hon. John H. Marable. The colonel organized a company of adventurous spirits and started overland to California the morning after his wedding. On reaching New Mexico he was taken sick and compelled to return home. He settled on a farm and since that time has been engaged in the real estate and auctioneer business. A few years ago he received a stroke of paralysis and although retaining much of his good humor and spirits is a helpless invalid. Mrs. MacCormac is a member of the Methodist Episcopal Church.

James McDowell Massie, M. D., is a native of Lexington, Rockbridge Co., Va., born November 3, 1854, and is of Scotch-Irish lineage. His father was Col. James W. Massie, a lawyer and later a professor in the Military Institute of Virginia. He was born in Augusta County, 1826, and was lieutenant-colonel of the Fifty-first Virginia; he died in the Old Dominion in 1872. The mother of our subject was Sophonista B. McDowell, a native of Virginia, born in 1827 and died 1870. James McDowell attended the Washington College at Lexington, Va., and in 1874 began the study of medicine at the University of Virginia, and graduated from the medical department in 1876, and the same year went to New York and for some time was assistant surgeon in the University of New York. From July 1877 to 1880 he practiced medicine at Richmond, Va., and came to Clarksville in December, 1880, and here has continued the practice of medicine and surgery. April 7, 1880, he was married to Miss Lizzie Copland, who died May 4 of the same year. In

1881 the Doctor married Miss Kate L. Johnson, daughter of Robert W. and Jennie E. (Drane) Johnson. They have two children: Robert J. and Sophy McDowell. Dr. Massie is a Democrat and a member of the Presbyterian Church.

A. B. Maxey was born in Robertson County, Tenn., February 28, 1838, son of Charles C. and Eunice (McCormac) Maxey, natives of Virginia, who came to Tennessee many years ago and settled in Robertson County and there remained until 1840, when they came to Clarksville, about eight years after the father died. The mother died in 1866. At ten years of age our subject began supporting himself. He first worked on a farm at 10 cents per day and later learned the carpenter's trade, and this continued until the breaking out of the late war. In April, 1861, he enlisted in Company A, Fourteenth Tennessee Volunteers, and served until the close of the war. He then returned to Clarksville and resumed his work at his trade. In February, 1878, he was elected city bridge-keeper of Clarksville and was re-elected every year until 1886. He is now engaged in the manufacture and sale of the Collins, Elder and Maxey's Patent Tobacco Curer. He was married January 17, 1866, to Mary V. Bailey of Clarksville. They have four children: Lizzie, Bailey, Allie and Egbert. Mr. Maxey is a Democrat and a member of the K. of P. He and wife belong to the Christian Church.

Robert H. McFall, one of the pioneers of Montgomery County, was born here December 8, 1816. His father, Henry McFall, was a native of Prince Edward County, Va., born there in the latter part of the last century. The McFall family is of Scotch-Irish origin. The father of our subject was educated at Hamilton City College, Va. He immigrated to Tennessee in 1809 with his parents, and settled in Davidson County, where they remained two years; from there they moved to Montgomery County. His wife was Zaney Nolen, born in Davidson County, this State, in 1787. To this union were born five children: Eliza, Robert H., Mary

J., Sallie A. F. and Samuel J., whose death took place April 24, 1850. The subject of this sketch was educated at the first schools of the South Side, and is one of the best informed men in this section of the county. He was reared on the farm, where he assisted his father until he reached the age of twenty-one, when he began life for himself. He is an extensive land-owner, and is now giving considerable attention to stock. Politically he has been a life-long Democrat, and for twenty-seven years has been justice of the peace in this county, and has faithfully discharged the duties of that office. For some time, in his early manhood, he was employed as foreman of one of the extensive iron furnaces. In the year 1861 he was united in marriage with Miss Malinda Gallaher, who was born July 17, 1824. To this union four children were born: James H., born April 27, 1862; William A., born January 29, 1864; Robert J., born December 31,1866, and Marable, born November 24, 1868.

William W. McMurry was born February 26, 1823, in Dixon County, Tenn., and is of Scotch-Irish extraction. His father, William McMurry, was a native of North Carolina, born in 1793. About the year 1819 he married Miss Mary Reed, of Dickson County, and to this union eight children were born, of whom our subject is the second. William McMurry, Sr., died in the year 1849, and his wife in 1840. Our subject was educated as the average country boy, and assisted his father on the farm until he reached the age of nineteen, when he went to Clarksville and learned the trade of brick-mason and plasterer, working at his trade about fifteen years, when he bought the farm where he now resides. In 1856 he took for his wife Miss Susan Collins, a native of this county, and daughter of Edward C. and Sallie A. Collins. To this union the following children have been born: Charles R., George B., Henry J., Robert Lee, Sarah E., Franklin and Emo. Mr. W. McMurry owns a fine, large farm, and also a general store at Ross View, which is the name of his place. In politics he is a stanch Democrat, and at present is postmaster at Ross View. He and wife are members of the Episcopalian Church.

J. W. Meacham, M. D., is the son of J. H. Meacham, of Woodlawn, Tenn. J. W. Meacham was born January 30, 1857, in Montgomery County, getting his education in the country schools until the year 1881, when he attended the medical university at Louisville, Ky., where he graduated in 1884 with great honor. He has now in his office a certificate of honor, signed by the faculty of the above-named school. In 1884 he began the practice of medicine at Woodlawn, Tenn., and at present is a resident of that place. He has control of $1,200 stock of drugs. He is a good physician, and is so considered by all who know him. His practice brings him in about $2,500 per year. He is a man of integrity, and has the confidence of all.

Henry Clay Merritt, president of the Clarksville National Bank and a member of the Clarksville bar, is a native of Todd County, Ky., born April 12, 1839, son of Dr. D. E. and Penelope (Hamum) Merritt, and is of Scotch-Irish ancestry. The father was born in Tennessee in 1800, and the mother in Kentucky in 1810. The grandfather, Samuel Merritt, was born in North Carolina in 1773. In 1790 the Merritt family came to Tennessee and settled in Williamson County. In 1826 the father of our subject went to Kentucky, where he practiced medicine for many years and was a leading citizen. There he died July 20, 1883. The mother died September 10, 1885. Our subject's boyhood days were spent on a farm in the blue-grass State. He attended the common schools in the neighborhood, and in 1858 entered the Cumberland University at Lebanon, Tenn., and there remained until the breaking out of the war. He graduated from the law department of that school in 1861, and the same year enlisted in Company K, First Kentucky Infantry, and served in that capacity one year. He then joined the cavalry service of Gen. Morgan, and was captured July 19, 1863, at Buffington's Island, Ohio, and was a prisoner of war two years and one month. In 1865 he came to Clarksville and was admitted to the bar, and has since been engaged in the practice of his profession. In 1874 he formed a law partnership with Hon. John F. House, with whom he is yet connected. In 1876 he was elected president of the Clarksville National Bank. In 1869 Mr. Merritt was elected mayor of Clarksville, and re-elected in 1870. He is a Democrat and a leading politician, and was married October 30, 1866, to Mary C. La Prade. To them was born one child, Mary Fisher, a much-beloved daughter, who died September 29, 1880. Mrs. Merritt died August 4, 1881. In 1882 Mr. Merritt married Maude Bailey, daughter of Hon. James E. and Elizabeth Bailey. They have one child, Elizabeth Lusk. Mr. Merritt is a gentleman of good business and social standing, and commands universal respect.

John Minor was born in this county and State March 26, 1837. He is the elder of two children born to Charles and Mary H. E. (West) Minor. Our subject's father was a native of Virginia, and was born in 1802. His mother was a native of Tennessee, and born in 1813. In 1873 the subject of this sketch was united in marriage to Miss Bettie J. Smoot, a native of Christian County, Ky., born January 7, 1856. Her parents are William G. and Susan C. Smoot, natives of Virginia and Kentucky, respectively. To our subject and wife five children have been born: John, born March 22, 1874; William S., born September 6, 1876; Joseph W., born April 6, 1879; Gentry, born September 11, 1881, and died September 17, 1883, and Mary W., born October 10, 1885. Our subject was in the late war, and organized a company of cavalry inside the Federal lines; was mustered into the Confederate Army in August, 1862, as captain of the Tenth Tennessee Cavalry, and served in this capacity until April, 1863, when he was promoted to major. In June, 1864, all the other field officers being killed or captured, he was left in command of the regiment until the spring of 1865, just before the surrender of the army, when the Tenth and Eleventh Regiments consolidated Our subject was left an orphan at the early age of three years, and was reared by his mother's relatives. He is merchanizing and farming at Sailor's Best and owns a fine farm in a high state of cultivation. He intends directing his attention to stock raising in the future. His dwelling presents a beautiful view from the Cumberland River, being situated but a short distance from it.

Henry H. Mockbee was born in Montgomery County, Tenn., April 30, 1832, and is of Welsh descent. He is the son of Risdon and Margaret (Howard) Mockbee, natives of Tennessee and Kentucky respectively. The father died in 1848 and the mother in 1865. Our subject was married to Miss Caroline Duke, a native of Tennessee, born in 1837. She is the daughter of Robert and Elizabeth (Boone) Duke. Mr. Henry Mockbee and wife were the parents of seven children: Darnicia, Lennie, Margaret A., Emma, Charlie E., Robert E. and Martha E. In April, 1875, Mrs. Mockbee was called from her earthly home to find a better one in heaven. Our subject took for his second wife Miss Martha Woodard, a native of Tennessee, born July 7, 1831, and the daughter of John and Susan (Henry) Woodard. At the breaking out of the civil war Mr. Mockbee enlisted in Company A, First Arkansas Regiment, under command of Col. Thedford. They were soon called to re-enforce Gen. Price for the purpose of making an attack on Seigel and Lyons at Springfield, Mo. After the battle of Springfield the troops of Arksansas disbanded, and our subject came to Tennessee and enlisted in Company B, Third Tennessee Cavalry. He was engaged in the battles of Murfreesboro, Cross Roads, Franklin, Chickamauga, Atlanta and others. Mr. Mockbee is living in the home of his birth, which is situated on the road leading from Palmyra to Clarksville. He was educated in the country schools, and is a Missionary Baptist, a Democrat, and was elected justice of the peace, which office he filled in an able and creditable manner.

Dr. Benjamin F. Moody was born September 10, 1856, near his present residence. He was named after his father, who was also a physician, and was born in Cheatham County, Tenn., in 1822, where he was reared and educated. He attended the University of Louisville, Ky., where he graduated. He was also a farmer and died on his farm about nine miles from Clarksville July 3, 1885. He was an excellent and much respected physician, and was married in 1848 to Elizabeth Gardner, daughter of Cullen Gardner. To them were born two sons, both practicing physicians, our subject being the younger. The mother is still living on the old home place. Our subject was educated in the common schools and at Neophogen College in Robertson County, Tenn. He studied medicine under his father and finished his course at the Vanderbilt University at Nashville, graduating in 1879. Since that time he has practiced his profession on his father's place and also superintends the farming of the old home place. In 1882 he wedded Fannie Mason, a native of Logan County, Ky., born August 9, 1857, daughter of Col. R. C. Mason. To them have been born two children: Lawrie M. and Sarah E. The Doctor has a beautiful residence, and by his energy and thorough knowledge of his profession has obtained an extensive practice. He is a Democrat

J. Aden Morrison was born in Paris, Tenn., August 17, 1851. His father, John Morrison, was born in Kentucky in the year 1823, and is a self-made man. At the early age of fifteen years he left home and by constant study gradually climbed the ladder of fame, and is now one of the leading physicians of this county. His mother was Martha T. Anderson, daughter of Rev. R. T. Anderson, the well-known Baptist minister; she is a native of Kentucky and was born in 1828. There were three children born to this union, our subject being the second. He was united in matrimony, May 1, 1871, to Miss Emma J. Wilson, a native of this State, born December 12, 1853. She is the first of two children born to John W. and Martha W. Wilson, both natives of Tennessee. To Mr. J. Aden Morrison and wife were born three children: Arthur, Ermina and Addie. Our subject was reared in New Providence of this State, and was given a fair education at the best schools of that place. By occupation he is a carpenter and mill-wright and has studied medicine for a number of years; altogether he is a good honest man and is respected by all.

Robert D. Moseley, county clerk, was born in what is now Cheatham County, Tenn., November 18, 1835, and is of English lineage. His parents were John and Elizabeth (Frazier) Moseley, born in North Carolina in 1787 and 1797, and died in 1847 and 1866, respectively. The paternal grandfather, John S. Moseley, was a North Carolinian and came to Tennessee at a very early period. Our subject's boyhood days were passed on a farm. He came to Montgomery County in 1863, of which county he has since been a resident. He has lived in Clarksville since 1874, and the year previous was elected revenue collector for Montgomery County. In 1876 he was elected county trustee and in 1878 was chosen clerk of the county court and re-elected in 1882. In 1858 he wedded Miss Bettie Major, who died in 1859, and he then married Bettie G. McCauley, who died in 1883, having borne these four children: Lizzie B., Lena M., Edward and Corinne. In 1885 Mr. Moseley married Mrs. Rosa Young, who lived only two months. Mr. Moseley was a soldier in the Forty-ninth Tennessee Infantry, Confederate States Army, but was discharged at Port Hudson, owing to physical disability. He is a member of the I. O. O. F. and K. of P. fraternities.

R. M. Moss is the son of William and Sallie (Rivers) Moss. William Moss was born and reared in Granville County, N. C., and in 1853 immigrated to Kentucky, settling near Garettsburg where he followed the occupation of farming. He was united in marriage to Miss Sallie Rivers, of North Carolina, and by this union had these children: Richard, W. D., Franklin, George, John, Joe, Thomas, R. M., Elizabeth, Emily J., Eliza, Martha and Sarah. William Moss died in Kentucky in the year 1872, and was a member of the Methodist Episcopal Church the greater part of his life. R. M. Moss, the subject of this sketch, was born January 9, 1825, in North Carolina. He immigrated to this State in the year 1840 or 1841 and settled in this county. In 1843 he was married to Miss Henrietta Clardy, of this county, and to them have been born four children: Herschel, Eudora, Ella B. and Robert Lee. Mr. Moss possesses a fine piece of

214 | GOODSPEED'S HISTORIES

fertile land and is a member of the Methodist Episcopal Church and is respected by all.

Hon. Arthur H. Munford, attorney at law and native of Montgomery County, Tenn., was born June 2, 1849, and is one of ten children born to William B. and Amanda G. (Johnson) Munford, and is of English-Irish descent. His father was born in Kentucky in 1810, and his mother in Tennessee in 1818. The grandfather, William Munford, a Virginian, was one of three brothers who went to Kentucky during the early settlement of that State. Mr. Munford's father came to Clarksville in 1839, and was a man of great public spirit. He was at one time president of what was then known as the Memphis, Clarksville & Louisville Railroad, now the Louisville & Nashville, and was president of the Branch Bank of Tennessee at Clarksville. He was a Whig, and in 1845 represented Montgomery County in the General Assembly of Tennessee. He was trustee of Stewart College many years and was a leading member of the Presbyterian Church. He died July 9, 1859. The subject of this sketch was educated at Stewart College, and in 1868 began studying law in the office of Gen. Quarles, and was admitted to the bar in 1872. In 1876 he and his brother, Louis G., became partners, continuing thus until 1881. During 1873-74-75, he was city attorney of Clarksville, and in November, 1884, was elected to represent Montgomery County in the State Legislature, being chairman of the judiciary committee of the House, also a member of the committee to redistrict the State, and the conference committee from the House. April 29, 1880, he married Miss Lillie May Underwood, a native of Warren County, Ky., born May 17, 1854, daughter of the late Hon. Joseph R. Underwood, who for many years was prominently connected with the history of the blue-grass State. He was a member of Congress, of the court of appeals, of the United States Senate, an eminent jurist and an ideal man. Mrs. Munford's mother's maiden name was Elizabeth Cox. To Mr. and Mrs. Munford were born two children: Elizabeth U. and Josephine U. Mrs. Munford died March

16, 1885. She was a member of the Presbyterian Church. Our subject is a member of the F. & A. M. and K. of P.

Louis Green Munford, attorney at law, a native of Montgomery County, Tenn., was born in the city of Clarksville, February 13, 1854, son of Hon. William B. and brother of Hon. Arthur H. Munford, and is of Anglo-Irish descent; was educated at Stewart College; began reading law in 1874 at nights, while filling the position of book-keeper in the Northern Bank; licensed to practice law January 1, 1876, and in Febuary following was elected city attorney of Clarksville and re-elected in 1877. In 1880 he was an independent candidate for the Legislature, a representative of the "doctrine of submission to the people," and, although not elected, ran nearly 200 votes ahead of his ticket. July, 1881, went to New York City; for two years was associated in the practice of law with Hon. Benjamin H. Bristoe, ex-secretary of the United States Treasury, and a member of Grant's cabinet. During his life in the Empire State he gained prominence by writing an article for the New York Nation, defending Tennessee against the charge of repudiation. While in that city he was chairman of the Seventh Assembly District Committee of the City Reform Club. January, 1884, he located in Louisville, Ky., and while in that city was engaged as one of the council for the defendant in the celebrated murder case of the Commonwealth vs. Frank Rankin. He returned to Clarksville in July, 1884, and here has since continued the practice of his profession. He is a Democrat and now president of the Montgomery County non-partisan prohibition alliance. He is one of the leading lawyers of Tennessee and a representative of one of the most extensively known families of this State.

Robert R. Neale, tobacco stemmer and dealer, was born in England and is a son of Robert Neale, who lived and died in his native land (England). Our subject received a liberal education at Clifton College and subsequent to his school life read law for some time in London, but later

abandoned that profession. He was bound in Bristol to learn the wholesale provision and grocery business. He then went to Liverpool and for
two years was stock keeper in an extensive provision house. In 1871 he
engaged in the provision business in Liverpool on his own account, and
continued the same until 1876, when he came to the United States and
located in Clarksville, Tenn., and at once engaged in the tobacco business which he has since continued. He now employs from thirty to sixty
people in his stemmery. He is a careful and wide-awake business man
and is a member of the Episcopal Church.

James Sterling Neblett, publisher, is a native of Montgomery County,
Tenn., born January 31, 1833, and of Irish extraction. Dr. Josiah Neblett,
his father, was born in this county in 1810. He was a skillful physician
and practiced his profession until his death in 1842. The mother's maid-
en name was Lucy B. Thompson. She was born in 1805 and became the
mother of nine children, these five are now living: Ann, Virginia,
Amanda, James S. and William R. The mother died in 1846. Our subject's paternal grandfather was Sterling Neblett, born in Virginia, and
came to Montgomery County, Tenn., at a very early period with his
parents. He was a member of the county court in 1818 and died in this
county at about eighty years of age. The subject of this sketch was reared
on a farm and was educated in the country schools. He came to Clarksville in 1849 and served a three years' apprenticeship as printer in the
Chronicle office. In 1857 he, in partnership with James A. Grant, purchased the Chronicle and continued as a firm until 1878. Mr. Grant then
sold his interest to W. P. Titus. From 1878 to 1885 the firm was known
as Neblett & Titus. Mr. Neblett then retired from the business. He has
spent more than a quarter of a century as a publisher, and is about the
oldest man in the newspaper business in the State. The Chronicle under
his administration was always conservative. January 31, 1867, he wedded Sue T. Orgain, born in the county in 1842, daughter of Griffin and
Sallie Orgain. To Mr. and Mrs. Neblett were born five children: D. Mac,

Fannie, Maggie, Ruth and Sallie. Our subject was a Whig before the war but since that time has been a Democrat. His wife is a member of the Methodist Episcopal Church, and he belongs to the K. of P. and the G. C., a temperance organization.

Jones Daly Neblett was born near where he now lives July 23, 1839. His father was Sterling Neblett, born in Montgomery County, Tenn. in 1810. He was a farmer and was married in 1832 to Ann Keesee, who was born 1816 and by whom he had eight children. His death took place in Humphreys County in 1859, and the mother in the same county in 1870. Our subject's grandfather was Sterling Neblett and his great-grandfather was John Neblett. The family came from Lunenburg County, Va., to Tennessee in the pioneer days of this country. Jones Daly Neblett is the second of the family and was reared on the farm and attended the country schools. In 1861 he enlisted in Company H, Fourteenth Tennessee Volunteers, as a private. He was wounded at the seven days' fight at Richmond, and in 1865 came home and for some time was engaged in the hardware business in Clarksville. In 1863 he engaged in the tobacco business, continuing until 1876 when he began farming on the old Judge Abe Martin farm, where he owned 470 acres of land—200 acres being rich bottom land. He was married February 4, 1868, to Clara Smith, a native of Logan County, Ky., born April 27, 1849, daughter of Joab and Angeline Smith. Of seven children born to them there are now living Norman S., born in 1870; Annie C., born in 1872, and Coulter, born in 1878. Mr. Neblett is a Democrat and belongs to the Masons and K. of H. He and wife belong to the Christian Church and he is a representative of one of the first families of the county and an honorable, upright citizen, being one of the best and most successful farmers in the county.

John. S. Neblett, farmer, was born in Montgomery County, Tenn., March 18, 1850, and is of Scotch origin. He is the sixth of eight children and was reared on a farm and educated in the country schools. However, the principal part of his education has been obtained by contact with business life. At the age of sixteen he came to Clarksville and began clerking in the grocery house of Capt. J. J. Crusman, with whom he remained five years. He then accepted a similar position with Keesee & Northington, remaining with them two years. In 1878 he was elected county trustee and re-elected in 1880 and again in 1882. In 1884 he again took a position with the firm of Keesee & Northington, with whom he has remained to the present time. Ruth, born in 1874 and died in 1878; Georgia A., born December 15, 1876, and Gholson, born June 30, 1878, are the children born to his marriage with Pattie E. Gholson, which occurred January 1, 1873. Mrs. Neblett died December 17, 1883; and December 13, 1884, Mr. Neblett married Lillian S. Lyle, daughter of Hon. W. J. Lyla Our subject is a Democrat and is an Odd Fellow and K. of P. He and wife are members of the Episcopal Church and he is a leading citizen and a representative of one of the old families of the county.

Robert O. Neblett, a native of this State, was born November 25, 1846, and is the son of James H. and Mary (Thompson) Neblett, natives of Tennessee and Virginia, respectively; the father born in 1808 and the mother in 1815, Our subject was united in marriage to Miss Marietta Minor, a native of Tennessee, born September 22, 1858. Her parents, William H. and Sarah E. (Wyatt) Minor, are natives of Virginia and Tennessee, respectively. Mr. Robert O. Neblett and wife's wedded life was rendered happier by the addition of two children, viz.: Minor E. and Homer E. Our subject is of Welsh and French descent, and received his education in the common schools of the county. He is a member of the Methodist Episcopal Church, and a Democrat. In 1879 he moved to the farm on which he now lives; it lies on Cumberland River near Hurricane Creek, and is considered as fine a tract of land as there is on the south side; the principal products are corn and tobacco. Mr. Neblett is a good neighbor and an influential man.

Edward M. Nolen is a native of Montgomery County, Tenn., where he was born December 9, 1840, in the house where he now lives. He is a son of John M. and Priscilla (Cage) Nolen, born in Tennessee, the father in 1812. The father was a Methodist minister and self educated. He began preaching about 1834, and located in Montgomery County where he married the mother, who was of German and Scotch-Irish descent. In connection with his ministerial work the father followed farming. He died in 1875 and the mother in 1879. Edward M. was reared by his Grandfather Cage. He was one of twelve children and was educated in the common schools of the county and commenced farming at the age of seventeen. In February, 1861, he wedded Laura A. Dye, daughter of Joseph and Elizabeth A. Dye. To them were born this family: George E., Clarence A., Ernest M., Richard M., Hardin H., Virgil I., Joseph M., Elizabeth E. and James C., the last two deceased. All except George E. are attending the high school at Pleasant View. Mr. Nolen was a soldier in the late war, enlisting in the Forty-second Regiment Tennessee Confederate Infantry, and with his regiment surrendered at Fort Donelson. He, however, made his escape and found his cousin, J. E. Cage, then his captain, in a hospital. He succeeded in effecting his rescue and earned him to the river, which he crossed in a skiff, and finally succeeded in bringing his captain safely home. He then joined Col. Woodard's command and served until 1862, when his own regiment was exchanged and he immediately rejoined it and served as orderly until after the battle of Franklin, when he was sent home on furlough and never rejoined, as the war soon closed. He has always been a farmer and has held several positions of trust and is now magistrate of his district. He is a Democrat and of the Christian faith. His wife and two elder children are members of the Methodist Episcopal Church.

J. S. Norfleet, a farmer, was born January 29, 1834, in this county; he is the son of James and Caroline (Higgs) Norfleet. James Norfleet was born in Montgomery County, Tenn., and at an early age was wedded to

Miss Caroline Higgs, to whom were born nine children: R. H., Thomas, James, Coudy, J. S., Knox B. Lilburn, Lucy G. and Lenora. In the year 1825 Mr. James Norfleet immigrated to North Carolina, where he remained for a period of five years and then moved back to this county in the neighborhood of Port Royal, where he lived about thirty years, then going to the Ninth District, and there died the 30th of December, 1880. Our subject, J. S. Norfleet, has a highly cultivated tract of land in the Ninth District. In the year 1867 he was married to Miss Mildred J. Perkins, of Stewart County, Tenn., and by her is the father of seven children: Lemmons, Susan C., Mattie C., Joseph F., Eddie T., Lucius S. and Chilton. In the year 1879 Mrs. Mildred Norfleet died, and in 1883 Mr. Norfleet was married to Miss Laura Tanner, and by her has had one child, Reuben M., At the breaking out of the war Mr. Norfleet enlisted in the Forty-ninth Tennessee Regiment under Col. Bailey, and at the battle of Fort Donelson was taken prisoner and carried to Camp Douglas, where he was held seven months and then exchanged at Vicksburg, Miss., going in the same regiment until the close of the war. He was at the battle of Atlanta, Ga., and the bombardment at Port Hudson, receiving a wound at Atlanta; he was taken to several different places and at last reached his home in this county. Mr. Norfleet has property in the Ninth District and is liked by all. Francis M. Norris was born in Tennessee August 11, 1837, and is the son of John and Rebecca (Upchurch) Norris, natives of Tennessee, and born respectively in 1806 and 1811. Our subject is of English descent, and the education he has received was mostly by his own exertions, having attended the common schools but very little. He was united in marriage to Miss Sallie Channell, a native of Tennessee, and born January 30, 1838, daughter of Henry and Polly (King) Channell. To this union were born seven children, viz.: Miranda, born October 1, 1864; Mary F., born September 27, 1866; Ida, born April 9, 1869; Sarah A., born August 22, 1871; Lon, born November 11, 1873; Robert S., born January 15, 1876, and Fannie, born March 27, 1878. Our subject is a member of the Methodist Church and a Democrat. In early life he worked at the carpenter's trade, and in 1871 he moved to his farm, situated in the forks of Budd's Creek, which is as fine a piece of land as can be found on the south side. He is an energetic and industrious man.

Michael C. Northington, wholesale and retail grocer, is a son of Samuel and Mary E. (Carr) Northington, born April 16, 1850, and of Welsh-English extraction. Both parents were born in Montgomery County, the father in 1814 and the mother in 1825. The paternal grandfather of our subject was born in North Carolina, and came to this county in 1808 and located at Port Royal and afterward in Kentucky, where he died in 1820. Our subject's father was a farmer. In 1871 he removed to Clarksville, where he now resides. Michael C. is the second of three children and was reared on a farm, attending the country schools. He came to Clarksville in 1870 and for four years was salesman in the dry goods store of B. F. Coulter. In 1874 he formed a partnership in the warehouse business with J. W. Keesee, but in 1875 engaged in his present business, and has proved one of the successful business men of the city. October 21, 1873, he wedded Nannie V. Neblett, daughter of Mack and Ann Neblett, and became the father of five children: Corinne, Ora Belle, Samuel H., Sterling N. and Mary E. Mr. Northington is a Democrat and a member of the I. O. O. F., K. of P. and K. of H. He and wife are members of the Baptist Church. In 1884 he was elected a director of the Clarksville National Bank, and re-elected in 1885-80. He is a prominent business man and represents one of the first families of Tennessee.

W. L. Oneal was born August 1, 1864, and is the son of Peter and Mildred J. (Radford) Oneal. Peter Oneal was born and raised in this State, and in 1855 was joined in matrimony to Miss Mildred J. Radford, to whom were born five children, who are now living. They are Thomas, Mary, Reuben, Nannie and W. L. Peter Oneal lived a long and honest life and at last died at the advanced age of ninety-three years, in the year

1886. He was an active member of the Methodist Episcopal Church for a period of thirty or forty years, and in the year 1868 was elected clerk of the County Court of Montgomery County, which office he held for eleven years. He was also a member of the F. & A. M. Our subject, W. L. Oneal, was educated at Clarksville, Tenn., and is a good and upright man. His mother is now living on their farm, where they are all enjoying a comfortable and happy life.

J. F. Outlaw, M. D., is the son of John C. and Cynthia (Redit) Outlaw. John C. Outlaw was reared in Bertee County, N. C. and was united in marriage to Miss Cynthia Redit, of North Carolina, in 1808, immigrated to Sumner County, Tenn., in 1812. They became the parents of thirteen children: M. R. T., Emily E., H. H., Julia A., Almeria, Nathaniel S., J. C., Drew A., J. F., Sallie, Cynthia, Lycurgus and John J., who died August 5, 1845; he was a member of the Baptist Church for a number of years and followed the carpenter business. In 1832 he left Sumner County and went to Obion County, where he died. Mrs. Cynthia Outlaw died in Obion County in 1845, being a strict member of the Methodist Episcopal Church for forty years. J. F. Outlaw was born June 24, 1821, in Sumner County, Tenn., and received a fair education in the country schools. He then went to Mississippi to study medicine under Dr. Cocke, graduating from the Medical University of Louisville, Ky., in 1848, and began the practice of medicine in Montgomery County. On the 21st of September, 1848, he was married to Miss Agnes H. Smith, of this county, and to them were born three children, two of whom died in infancy. Dr. Outlaw is a member of the Methodist Episcopal Church, which he joined in 1845. Mrs. Outlaw is also a member of this church, joining when quite young. Our subject owns a fine tract of land and is one of the leading citizens.

Burrell W. Owens, a native of Montgomery County, Tenn., was born March 26, 1856. He is the fifth of ten children born to James and

Martha A. (Proctor) Owens. His parents are natives of Virginia and North Carolina, respectively. His father was born in 1819 and died December 31, 1885, and his mother was born in 1826. Our subject was united in marriage in 1880 to Miss Lucy B. Shurdon, a native of Ohio, born November 1, 1861. She is the last of five children born to David B. and Jane E. Shurdon. Her parents are natives of Pennsylvania and Ohio, and were born in 1823 and 1830, respectively. To the subject of this sketch and wife were born two children: Lillian M., born February 19, 1881, and Adaline H., born January 1, 1883. Our subject spent his youth on a farm. In 1878 he moved to Palmyra and began merchandising. He is postmaster and agent for the Southren Express Company, and has the confidence of all his fellow-men. Our subject has one of the most beautifully located and one of the best improved farms in the county. In politics he is a Democrat.

Capt. George M. Pardue was born July 19, 1839, in Cheatham County, Tenn., and is of French lineage. His father, Littleton J. Pardue, was born in North Carolina in 1804, and took for his wife Miss Martha A. Williams, a native of Cheatham County, and daughter of Thomas Williams. In 1869 Mr. Littleton J. Pardue died, and his widow is still living. George M. Pardue was educated in the common schools of Cheatham County, Stewart College, Clarksville, and at Cumberland University, at Lebanon. In June, 1861, he enlisted in Company G, Forty-second Regiment Tennessee Infantry, and was elected and commissioned as second lieutenant, C. S. A. He was captured with his regiment at the fall of Fort Donelson, and was held as a prisoner of war until 1862, when he was exchanged. Upon the reorganization of his regiment he was commissioned captain of his company, and served as such until the close of the war. He was in all the principal campaigns and battles in which his command was engaged until in 1864, when his health failed, and he served the balance of the time on detached service. On returning home he engaged in merchandising and farming, but after a few years discontinued merchandising and devoted his attention to farming and buying and selling timber. In 1862 he was elected representative of Cheatham, Houston and Montgomery Counties, which counties he represented for two years. After this he moved to the farm where he now resides and has been farming ever since. In 1872 he was married to Miss Charlie D. Parham, a native of this county, and daughter of Charles L. and Mary A. Parham. To this union the following children have been born: Littleton J., deceased; Charles P., Annie M., Jennie E., George M., deceased, and Lizzie M., the latter two being twins.

R. S. Payne is the son of William and Margarette (Brown) Payne, and was born October 12, 1823, in Davidson County, Tenn. The Payne family figured conspicuously in the early history of the United States. William Payne was in all the Indian wars, and also the war of 1812. The family is related to Robert Treet Payne, one of the signers of the Declaration of Independence. William Payne was born in North Carolina and immigrated to Tennessee when quite young. In 1821 or 1822 he was married to Miss Margarette Brown, of North Carolina, and to them were born six children: Greenwood, William, R. S., Melvina, Pattie and Priscilla. Mr. W. Payne was a farmer, devoting most of his time to this calling. He died at his residence in Sumner County in 1861, and his wife in the same county in the year 1850. R. S. Payne, our subject, is a farmer of Montgomery County, and, in the year 1853, was wedded to Miss Susan Gold, of this county, and to this union were born nine children, three of whom died; those living are Eugene, Earnest, Maud, Blanche, Ida and Anna. Mrs. Payne was a member of the Methodist Episcopal Church, and died January 30, 1871. When the war broke out with Mexico in 1846, he enlisted in Campbell's First Tennessee Regiment; was under Gen. Taylor, and participated in all the engagements of the war. During the late civil war he was appointed captain of the Home Guards, and was in the battles of Shiloh, Vicksburg and Baton Rouge. After the war he returned home and turned his attention to farming, which occupation he still follows. After the death of his first wife he was married again to Miss Narcissie Bryant, in the year 1876. To them were born two children, one of whom died in infancy, the other is named Robert. In 1882 Mr. Payne was elected justice of the peace, and this office he still holds. He has been school commissioner since the passage of the act. He and family are members of the Methodist Episcopal Church and are well respected.

John A. Pettus was born in Montgomery County, Tenn., at what was formerly known as the "Old Kentucky Landing," December 3, 1843, son of Thomas F. Pettus, who was born in this county in 1818. He was a clerk in New Providence a number of years, and then removed to Kentucky Landing and engaged in the tobacco business until 1844, when he returned to New Providence and resided in that place until 1875. He was founder and president of the New Providence Savings Institution, and was also engaged in the milling business, and erected a number of the best mills in the county. He was married in 1839 to Martha Cowherd, a native of Virginia. At the time of his death in 1875 he was vice-president of the Clarksville Tobacco Board of Trade. Our subject was educated in the county schools. In the fall of 1866 he engaged in the grocery business in New Providence, and in 1874 began dealing in tobacco. In 1875 he became a member of the firm of Kendrick, Pettus & Co., and the same year built the central warehouse in New Providence. In 1876 the firm located in Clarksville and purchased the central warehouse, and have been quite prosperous. Mr. Pettus was married in 1867 to Mattie Campbell, of Florence, Ala., born in 1845. They have three children: Thomas F., Anna C. and Mildred S. Our subject is a Democrat, and his wife is a member of the Methodist Episcopal Church.

Guthridge L. Pitt was born in Montgomery County, Tenn., July 15, 1860, son of O. G. and Elizabeth E. (Randall) Pitt, and is of English origin. The parents of Mr. Pitt are both natives of the blue-grass State, but now have been residents of Montgomery County, Tenn., for over forty years. Our subject's boyhood days were spent on a farm, where he assisted his father in the duties attendant on farm life until nineteen years of age. He attended the private school, Hickory Wild Academy, and Guthrie (Ky.) High School. The most of his education has been gained, however, through his own exertions at home after the day's work was done. In 1881 he began reading law under the guidance of Gen. W. A. Quarles, and in 1883 was licensed to practice his profession. In 1884 he was local editor of the Clarksville Democrat He is a young man of ability, and bids fair to succeed in his chosen calling.

William S. Poindexter, cashier of the Franklin Bank, is a native of Russellville, Logan County, Ky., a place that he claims has turned out more successful men than any town in the Union. He was born February 1, 1830, and is the third of six children. His father, Samuel Poindexter, was born in Lexington, Ky., in 1796. He was a farmer and in 1820 came to Logan County, Ky., and resided until 1875, when his death occurred. The grandfather, Peter Poindexter, was a Virginian who came to Kentucky in early times and died in that State in 1840. The mother was Elizabeth Curd, born in Kentucky in 1806 and died in 1870. Mr. Poindexter was educated at private schools in Russellville, and when thirteen years of age began clerking in a dry goods store, continuing until 1853, when he came to Clarksville and occupied the position of book-keeper for W. S. McClure, retaining his position until 1857 when he engaged in business for himself at what was then known as the Bed River Landing Warehouse, continuing one year. He then engaged in the tobacco business and from 1865 to 1868 was engaged in the dry goods business in New Providence. He did an extensive business and from 1868 to 1876 was cashier of the New Providence Saving Institution which afterward became the Franklin Bank and was removed to Clarksville, and since that time he has been its cashier. The many years he has been in the banking business has given Mr. Poindexter an extensive knowledge of banking systems, and he now ranks as one of the best financiers of his part of the State. He was married, in 1859, to Emily Everett, by whom he had one daughter, Lulu. Mrs. Poindexter died in 1864, and a year later our subject married Mrs. Mary Gee, who died in 1873. In 1875 Mr. Poindexter wedded Miss Kate Carney, of Murfreesboro, born in 1840. They have two children: William S. and Rosa K. Mr. Poindexter is a Democrat, and he and wife are members of the Methodist Episcopal Church South. Step by step he has climbed the ladder of prosperity and well deserves the success which has attended his efforts. Samuel B. Powers, a native of this county and State, was born September 23, 1838. He is the second of four children born to James S. and Elizabeth (McFall) Powers. His father was born in North Carolina, September 25,1807, and died in 1870. His mother was born August 9, 1803, and died in 1882. Our subject was united in marriage to Miss Mary E. Williams December 2, 1866, a native of this State, born June 29, 1849. She is the daughter of Perry B. and Sallie A. Williams, both natives of this State. Her father was born September 29, 1814, and her mother June 3, 1829. Her father took for his first wife Miss Sallie A. Neblett, who was born July 28, 1819, and died May 14, 1843. Mr. and Mrs. Williams died July 26, 1876, and November 13, 1875, respectively. To our subject and his wife were born nine children: Sallie A., born August 28, 1867; Joseph P., born January 16, 1869; Lizzie W., born July 6, 1872; James H., born January 27, 1874; Maggie J. born February 10, 1876; Sue M., born March 28, 1878; Addie B., born October 17, 1880; Ora M., July 27, 1883, and Freddie M., December 23,1885. Our subject is by occupation a farmer. At the beginning of the late war he enlisted in Company B, Fourteenth Tennessee Regiment, under Capt. Russell; after being there two years he was taken sick and returned home; he never recovered sufficiently to return to his command. He directs his attention principally to raising corn and tobacco.

Gen. William A. Quarles is a Virginian by birth, born near Louisa Court House July 4, 1825. His parents were born in Virginia and his ancestors were settlers of Jamestown in the early colonial history of Virginia. His maternal ancestors were Huguenots. He was taken by his parents to Christian County, Ky., in 1830, and was educated at home and in the University of Virginia, where he studied law. At the death of his father he returned home and began the management of the estate. He was admitted to the bar in 1848 and located in Clarksville, Tenn., where he was very successful in the practice of his profession and enjoyed a lucrative practice, not only occupying the first position at the bar of his county but also in the State. During the presidential election of 1852 he was elector for his district on the Democratic ticket. In 1858 he was defeated by Hon. F. K. Zollicoffer for Congress by only 250 or 275 votes in a district never less than 1,500 Whig majority. He was soon after appointed circuit court judge, during the sickness of Judge Pepper, and held the office about one year. Some time after he was appointed president of the Memphis, Chattanooga & Louisiana Railway Company, and in 1858, without solicitation, was appointed bank supervisor of the State. He was a delegate to the National Democratic Convention of Cincinnati in 1856 and at Charleston in 1860. At the breaking out of the war he immediately offered his services to the Confederate Government at Montgomery, Ala. He was soon appointed aid-de-camp upon the staff of Gen. S. R. Anderson, and his relations with the banking business enabled him to obtain for the State considerable sums of money. The second military camp organized in Montgomery County was called Camp Quarles. In Robertson County he organized the famous Forty-second Tennessee Regiment, and his military record began at Fort Donelson. He was always with his command and foremost in battle until severely wounded at Franklin, not recovering from his wounds till the end of the war. He was in the following hard fought battles: Fort Donelson, Tenn.; Port Hudson, La.; Jackson, Miss.; New Hope Church, Pine Mountain, Kennesaw Mountain, Smyrna Depot, Peach Tree Creek, Lick Skillet

Road, Atlanta, Ga., and Franklin, Tenn. In the last battle he fell, and it was supposed mortally wounded, and his command was nearly destroyed. He was always at the head of his men and did much to shield them from danger, and on this occasion his horse carried him wounded to the rear, it was supposed to die. During the battle of Lick Skillet Road Gen. Quarles made the attack, and twice his horse was shot from under him. After the close of the war and the General had recovered from his wounds he returned to Clarksville, where he has since practiced law with the same success that he had met with previous to the war. In 1875 he represented Robertson, Montgomery and Stewart Counties in the State Senate, and was a representative of Tennessee in the National Convention of 1880 and 1884 Gen. Quarles is one of the heroic figures of the Grand Army of Tennessee. He possessed that strong individuality, that charm of personality, which endeared him to his troops, and gave them the highest confidence in his personal daring and his skill and wisdom as a commander. He lead them to battle, directed them amid the fearful perils of the field with imperturbable coolness, and is known in history as one of the few capable officers, who, on many of the principal battle-fields of the civil war, swept the Federal troops back in promiscuous route. He is one of the most conspicuous figures of the most conspicuous war in history.

James K. Raimey, farmer, was born in Tennessee in 1841. His father, Solomon D. Raimey, is a native of North Carolina and born in 1811 and emigrated to Tennessee when quite young. Our subject's mother was Eliza A. McAlister, a native of Tennessee, born in 1817 and died in 1859. James K. Raimey was united in marriage, in 1873, to Miss Lou H. Hodges, a native of Tennessee, born in 1853. To our subject and wife were born two children, Eliza A., and Laura K. Mr. Raimey is living on the farm of his birth. It is on Barren Fork of Barton's Creek and about fifteen miles from Clarksville on the public road leading from Clarksville to Charlotte. The principal products of this farm are corn, tobacco and small grain. In 1882 he was elected justice of the peace in District No. 16, and has discharged the duties of this office creditably and satisfactorily and has never had an appeal taken in a single case tried before him. In politics he is a Democrat and gives his support and aid to that party.

Jacob A. Ranney is one of the prominent and wealthy farmers of Montgomery County, Tenn. He was born on the place where he now resides January 5, 1833. His parents, Samuel and Millie (Crotzer) Ranney, were born in Tennessee and North Carolina in 1806 and 1813, respectively. The father was of Scotch-Irish descent, a farmer by occupation, and died in 1855. The mother was of German-English lineage and bore her husband twelve children, six of whom are living. She is yet residing on the old homestead with our subject, Jacob A. He received the education and rearing of the average farmer's boy and in later life learned the blacksmith's trade. After his father's death he returned home, and has since resided with his mother and took charge of the farm, which he still superintends. He has purchased land almost surrounding the home place, and in 1863 erected a grist and saw-mill on his land, and in connection with farming (which is his principal business) follows milling. April 30, 1871, he married Susan A. Laughren, of English-Irish lineage. To them were born these children: Andrew, Leler, Marvin, Lizzie, Katie and Susan. Mr. Ranney is a Democrat in politics and a member of the Fredonia Lodge of F. & A. M. He has held the position of Junior Warden in his lodge for two years. He takes great interest in educational affairs and is giving his children every advantage in his power. He and wife and their eldest son are members of the Methodist Episcopal Church.

John E. Ransdell is of Irish descent, son of James P. and Margaret (Kittrell) Ransdell, born in North Carolina. They were married in 1830, and came to Montgomery County, Tenn., in 1835, and became the parents of four children. James P. Ransdell was born about 1812, and died in Tennessee in 1839. The mother died in 1838. John E., born May 22, 1834, was educated in the common schools and at home. October 17, 1866, he married Margaret Anderson, a native of the county, born February 22, 1847, and to them were born the following children: George S. (deceased), Willie H., Margaret B., John A. and Attoiley, Mrs. Ransdell is a daughter of Willie H. Anderson. Mr. Ransdell is a Democrat, and in 1861 enlisted in the Fourteenth Regiment Tennessee Infantry, and was promoted to the office of sergeant. He participated in all the battles in which his regiment was engaged up to May, 1864 He was in twenty-nine regular engagements, and was wounded at the battle of Fredericksburg in 1862, and severely shocked by the explosion of a shell at Gettysburg, which caused the loss of hearing in his right ear. He was so severely wounded at the battle of Chancellorsville that he could render no further service. In 1853 he moved to Kentucky, where he resided until 1858, when he returned home. He has worked at saw-milling, but is now farming. He has been magistrate of his district since 1876.

Benjamin R. Ramey, farmer, was born in Montgomery County, Tenn. November 11, 1828. His father, Thomas T. Ramey, was born in Granville County, N. C., about the year 1806. In the year 1816 he came to Montgomery County, Tenn., with his father and attended the country schools. He was a strict Methodist, and served the people of Montgomery County as justice of the peace for some time. He was also sheriff for eight years and chairman of the county court for several years, and was, in fact, a very useful man in the county. He was united in marriage to Miss Susan Orgain in the year 1827. She was born in Montgomery County, Tenn., in the year 1807, was educated in the country schools, and was a Methodist. Nine children were born to them. Mr. Thomas Ramey died June 19, 1879. Mrs. Ramey is still living at the ripe age of eighty years. Her father, Samuel Rogers, was born in North Carolina October 11, 1795, and was educated in the best schools of the State, was a tanner by trade and came to Montgomery County, Tenn., in the year

1823. He was united in marriage to Miss Nancy Harris, who was born in Montgomery County, Tenn., February 22, 1802; was educated in the country schools and was a Free-Will Baptist. Our subject was educated in the common schools of the country, was a member of the Methodist Episcopal Church, a Democrat, and January 11, 1860, he was united in marriage to Miss Nannie J. Rogers, who was born in Henderson County, Tenn., June 11, 1839. She is a member of the Methodist Episcopal Church. To them were born two children: Elizabeth J. and Thomas S.

Rev. J. G. Rice, Sr., was born in Lincoln County, Tenn., January 17 1830. When three years of age he moved with his parents to Lauderdale County, Ala., where he remained two years; he then moved with his widowed mother to Warren County, Tenn. Here he lived until he became twenty years of age. In October, 1850, he joined the Tennessee Conference of the Methodist Episcopal Church, and was appointed to travel the Richland Circuit in Giles County, Tenn. At the next session of conference in 1851 he was appointed to the Savannah Circuit in Hardin County. At the conference in Pulaski, in October, 1852, he was ordained deacon by Bishop Soule, and appointed to Frankfort Circuit in Alabama, a part of North Alabama being at this time embraced in the Tennessee Conference. The next year he was appointed to the Somerville Circuit in Alabama. At the next conference in 1854 he was ordained elder and sent to Winchester Station, and next he was sent to Sparta Station. While here he was married to Miss Josephine D. Plumer, of Nashville, January 24, 1856, and the following May was transferred to Kansas as a missionary, and stationed at Atchison until the meeting of the Kansas Conference in September, 1856, when he was sent to the Lecompton Station, where he remained tweve months. In the winter of 1856-57 was chaplain of the Kansas Legislature. In September, 1857, he returned to the Tennessee Conference and was appointed to the Franklin Circuit. Since then he has served in Hickory Creek, Berford, Antioch, Duck River, Chapel Hill, Spring Hill and Cedar Hill Circuits. He is now pastor of Antioch Circuit in Montgomery County, Tenn., is fifty-six years of age and has good health. He has been an acceptable member of the Tennessee Conference for thirty-six years, and has rendered valuable service in the vineyard of his Master; has a large family of children, all of whom are members of the Methodist Episcopal Church. He is a good man, and his words and deeds will remain green in the hearts of many when he has passed away.

John Bick, dealer and manufacturer of boots and shoes, was born in Germany, and is a son of Andrew and Christine (Nohrbass) Rick, who were born in Germany also. John Bick served a three-years' apprenticeship at the shoe-maker's trade, and the following four years was a journeyman shoe-maker. Being of an adventurous disposition he embarked for the United States in 1848, and landed at New Orleans, thence to Evansville, Ind., where he remained three years. He came to Clarksville in 1853, and has since resided in this city, engaged in the manufacture and sale of boots and shoes. He reached America in debt $53 for his passage money, but by industry and economy is now one of the leading merchants of Clarksville, and is the only one who deals exclusively in boots and shoes. In 1853 he was married to Christena Hekel, a native of Alsace, Germany (formerly France). They have five children: John T., Henry A., Charles B., Frank E. and Julia J. Mr. Rick is a Democrat, and for twelve years has been a member of the city council, and a member of the school board three years. Mr. Bick belongs to the I. O. O. F., and he and wife are members of the Presbyterian Church.

A. J. Riggins is the son of William and Thursa (Chisman) Riggins. The father of our subject came to this State in very early life from North Carolina, settling near Providence, Tenn. Farming was his chief occupation. He died in the year 1875. He was the father of nine children, viz.: Thomas, Charles, M. P., William, Mary, Sallie, Johnson, A. J. and G. P. Our subject was born July 17, 1834, in this county, and was reared on the farm. He started out for himself in the year 1858, and when the war broke out he hired a substitute. In the year 1856 he was married to Miss Mary Harris, and to this union have been born eight children: Annie, Ishy, Robert, Eddie, Lula, Claud, Calvin and Myrtle. In 1873 he joined the Cumberland Presbyterian Church. Mr. Biggins owns 375 acres of good land in this county, and is a man who is well respected by his fellow-men.

Richard W. Roach was born in Prince Edward County, Va., January 17, 1849, son of Capt. John I. Roach, who was born in Virginia in 1819. He was captain of a company of volunteer soldiers in the Mexican war. His death took place in Trigg County, Ky., in 1880. The mother of our subject was Miss Demaris Tuggle, who was deceased in 1859. The paternal grandfather was Bev. Elijah Roach, a Virginian, born in 1792. He was an eminent Baptist clergyman, and continued his ministerial labors until eighty-eight years of age. He died in Charlotte County, Va. (where he was born), in 1884 The family originally came from Edinburgh, Scotland, and is of Scotch-Irish descent. In 1864 our subject began clerking in a retail dry goods store at Soaring Springs, Ky., and at the end of one year accepted a position in a wholesale dry goods house in Louisville, Ky., where he remained six years. He then occupied a similar position in New York City, remaining ten years. Since 1881 he has been in the dry goods business in this city, and in March, 1885, took his brother, R. C. Roach, as partner. They are, without question, one of the leading dry goods firms in the city. They have a large and increasing patronage, and stand as firm as the rock of Gibraltar from a commercial standpoint. Mr. Roach was married in Louisville, in 1878, to Miss Hettie Dabney, of Cadiz, Ky. He is a Democrat, and was made a K. of P. in 1884 and a Mason in 1885. Mrs. Roach is a member of the Christian Church.

Ed C. Robb was born in Clarksville, Tenn., June 11, 1853, son of Col. Alfred Robb, and grandson of Joseph Robb, who emigrated from North

Carolina to Tennessee at an early day and settled in Sumner County. The family is traced to three brothers who came from Scotland to America and settled in Pennsylvania, Virginia, and Joseph in North Carolina. Alfred Robb, our subject's father, graduated from the University of Nashville in 1837, and studied and began the practice of law in Gallatin, October 9, 1844. He was married to Miss Mary E. Conrad, daughter of George C. Conrad, of Robertson County, Tenn., and in 1846 removed to Clarksville and has here continued the practice of law in partnership with Col. James E. Bailey, the firm being known as Robb & Bailey, and continued until Mr. Robb enlisted in the Forty-ninth Tennessee Regiment in the late war. He was wounded at Fort Donelson Saturday evening, February 15, and was brought home on the 16th and died on the 17th, 1862. He was a prominent lawyer and a man of sterling worth and nobility of character. His son, E. C. Robb, was educated at Stewart College. In 1875 he accepted a position with Capt J. J. Crus man, with whom he remained until 1882. He then farmed two years, and is now in the employ of S. F. Beaumont. He is a Democrat and a member of the Presbyterian Church.

John D. Robins is a native of McNairy County, Tenn., born May 17, 1843. His father, William Robins, was born in Tennessee about 1800, and died in 1850 in Mississippi. He was of English birth, and was a physician and farmer and a soldier in the Mexican war. He married Charlotte Burton, who bore him three sons and a daughter. After her death he wedded Martha B. Hornberger, who bore him six children; our subject, John D., being the third. The mother was born in 1818 and died in 1863, in Stewart County, Tenn. John D. Robins was educated in the common schools and in Stewart College at Clarksville, Tenn. He commenced business for himself by traveling for the firm of William Nolen & Co., of Paducah, Ky. From 1862 to 1865 he followed merchandising at Clarksville, and on the 4th of May, 1865, he led to Hymen's altar, Jane S. Lafland, daughter of James F. and Elizabeth Lafland. The father was

236 | GOODSPEED'S HISTORIES

born in Kentucky in 1798, and died July 23, 1855. He was in the war of 1812 and was in the battle in which the Indian chief Tecumseh was killed. He married Elizabeth Hetcher in 1830. She was born in 1807 and died in 1882. Mr. Lafland was the manager of the La Fayette Furnace Company of Montgomery County for twenty-one years. He was also a farmer and a great financier. Since our subject's marriage he has resided on a farm. He has one son, George Henry, born October 6, 1867. Mr. Robins is a Democrat and a Methodist in belief. He became a Mason in 1862 and is a member of the Clarksville lodge.

Henry R. Rogers was born March 14, 1812, in Dickson County, Tenn., and is of Scotch-Irish lineage. His father, Robert Rogers, a North Carolinian by birth, was married to Elizabeth Moore, and became the father of eight children. They came to Tennessee at an early period, and the father was a soldier in Gen. Jackson's army and was in the battle of New Orleans. He died July 15, 1815, in Tennessee. His widow afterward married Nathan Began and bore three children. She died in September, 1860. Henry R. was the seventh of the family and was educated in the common schools of Dickson County. After attaining his majority he became pilot on a river boat and served in this capacity about three years. He then returned home and followed the occupation of farming until 1863, when he moved to Montgomery County and purchased the farm where he has ever since resided. In 1835 he took for his life companion Chrissee Halliburton, a native of Dickson County, and of Scotch descent To them were born these children: Dialtha, George E., James M., Sophronia, Zora, Elizabeth, John, Stephen, Martha J., Nancy L., Robert and Henrietta. Mr. Rogers has always been a Democrat in politics and is at present magistrate of his district a position he has held for the last sixteen years. He is a member of the F. & A. M. His wife died March 30, 1884.

John A Rollon is a son of Basal and Lucy (Fleemon) Rollon, who were natives of Virginia. The mother was born in 1791, and was a daughter of Maj. John Fleemon, who participated in the Revolutionary war. Basal and Lucy Rollon moved to Coffee County, Tenn., in 1836, and there remained until 1839, when they moved to Bradford County, the same State, and in 1843 came to Montgomery County, where he purchased 175 acres of land near Spring Creek. They became the parents of four children: Ann L., Sarah E., Mary M. and John A. Our subject was the fourth child, and December 12, 1847, was married to Miss R. K. Grady, daughter of Jesse and Mary Grady, natives of Virginia, who settled in the blue-grass State in the early part of this century, and were engaged in farming. Mr. and Mrs. Rollon became the parents of nine children: William M., Basal, Mollie A., James G., Hervey W., John B., Jesse C., Stonewall J., George P. Mrs. Rollon died in 1867, and in 1876 Mr. Rollon was married to Sallie Bourne, daughter of Ambrose and Sallie Bourne, natives, respectively, of Tennessee and Kentucky. Our subject has always followed blacksmithing and farming for a livelihood. He was chosen squire in 1870, and has faithfully filled the duties of that office. He is a Democrat, and he and his family are church members. Mr. Rollon is a member of the Masonic fraternity, Royal Arch and Knight Templar degrees.

John Rosson was born in Robertson County, Tenn., December 16, 1818. His father, John Rosson, Sr., was born in Virginia, in 1772. The grandfather, Thomas Rosson, was born in 1743 and served in the Revolutionary war, and afterward moved to Kentucky and then to Tennessee, where he died in 1816. John Rosson, Sr., married Nancy Connell, of South Carolina, daughter of Giles and Elizabeth (Gibbs) Connell.

The latter was sister to Gen. Gibbs, of the English Army, who was killed at the battle of New Orleans. To Mr. and Mrs. Rosson, Sr., were born twelve children; all dead except our subject and the two youngest. The father died in 1825 and the mother in 1865. On account of the early death of his father and elder brothers our subject was almost wholly deprived of a school education. He, however, obtained a limited education by studying at home. He has always been a tiller of the soil and has done well financially. In June, 1848, he was married to Sarah Jane Morrow, born in Montgomery County, in 1827, daughter of James and Lovica Morrow. To them were born these children: James H. and Margaret. Mrs. Rosson died in 1853. Mr. Rosson came to Montgomery County in 1849 and located on his present farm, where his son and son-in-law till his farm, raising tobacco, principally. He is a Democrat, and for the last fifty years has been a member of the Baptist Church.

Joseph S. Rosson is of German and English descent, born in Robertson County, Tenn., October 10, 1842, son of Sampson Rosson, who was born in 1807. The father was married to Marinda Bobo, a native of South Carolina, and daughter of Chana and Rachel Bobo. She came to Tennessee, with her parents, when a child. She and her husband became the parents of twelve children, our subject being the seventh. The mother died September 8, 1867, and the father then came to Montgomery County, where he died October 2, 1884. Joseph S. Rosson was educated in the common schools of his native county. In May, 1861, he enlisted in the Eleventh Tennessee Infantry, C. S. A., and served with that regiment three years, being in all the battles in which it was engaged, including the battle of Murfreesboro, in which he received a gun-shot wound in the breast, which disqualified him for further active service, and from which he has never entirely recovered. He lived with his father until 1867, when he married Charlotte E. Williams, daughter of Patrick and Martha M. Williams, and two years later located in Montgomery County on his present farm. Mr. and Mrs. Rosson have these children: Edward F., John W., Clarence, Charles V., Ernest, Mary W., Joseph S., Malcolm B., Chester B. and Sampson P. Our subject's farm is one of the best and cleanest in the county. He has always been a farmer and has done well financially.

D. J. Rawlings is the son of Thomas D. Rawlings and Frances (Jolly) Rawlings. Thomas D. Rawlings was born in 1781 and reared in Brunswick County, Va. He was a farmer by occupation, and died in the year 1815. Our subject was a Virginian by birth, and immigrated to Kentucky in 1858, where he remained for five years. He then came to Tennessee and settled in Montgomery County. In 1848 he was married to Miss Mary E. Caudle, by whom he became the father of eleven children, viz.: Thomas B., died in 1879; James E., died October 6, 1879; D. W.; William A.; Etta O., died August 1, 1850; Leota, died August 13, 1861; Ida, Katy, Rosa, Orrin and Ernie. In the year 1880 Mr. Rawlings was licensed to preach the gospel by Rev. Welbourne Mooney, of the Tennessee Conference. Mrs. Rawlings is a member of the Methodist Episcopal Church, joining in early life. Our subject possesses a fine tract of land in the twenty-first district, and is a man highly respected by all.

William H. Rudolph is a tobacco dealer and a member of the firm of Shelby & Rudolph, born in District No. 11, of Montgomery County, Tenn., October 3, 1824. He is the eldest of six children, and is of German-Irish lineage. His father was Jacob Rudolph, born in North Carolina in 1803, son of John Rudolph, who was also of North Carolina, born in 1770. The family came to this county in 1805, and settled near Clarksville, on Red River. The grandfather died in 1844, and the father March 21, 1877. The mother's name was Martha Morrow. She was born in Montgomery County, February 15, 1803, and still resides in the same neighborhood where she was born. William H. was reared on a farm and acquired a common school education. He began doing for himself when twenty-two years old and purchased a farm of 106 acres. He continued tilling the soil until 1877, when he moved to Clarksville, selling his farm of 280 acres. He engaged in the grocery business, continuing three years, but on account of ill health was obliged to abandon that work. In November, 1882, he engaged in the tobacco business with Isaac Shelby, and with him has since continued. He was married, in 1846, to

Miss E. A. Lockert, who was born in the county in 1832. They have eight children: Mapheus M., Alice, Jacob W., David Xi., James T., Bettie, Mattie and Mary. Mr. Rudolph was formerly a Whig, but since the war has been a Democrat. He belongs to the Masonic fraternity, and he and wife are members of the Cumberland Presbyterian Church.

William Rudolph was born November 27, 1811, in Montgomery County, Tenn., and is the son of John Rudolph and Miss (Staley) Rudolph, natives of North Carolina, born in 1773, and both of German descent. In 1808 the parents of our subject moved to this county, and to them were born ten children, of whom our subject is the eighth. The father of our subject died May 7, 1846, and his mother died November 5, 1845. They were among the early settlers of the county, and endured the hardships of a pioneer life. Our subject was educated in the country schools, and assisted his parents on the farm until 1833, when he married Miss Mary J. Lockert, a native of this county, and a sister of Col. Lockert. To this union five children have been born: Henrietta, David (deceased), Evaline (deceased), John W. (deceased), and Fannie J. The mother of these children died June 24, 1850, and in the year 1853 their father married Miss Lucy Winn, a native of Sumner County, Tenn., and to them were born one child, Thomas B. Mrs. Lucy (Winn) Rudolph died December 6, 1862. In the year 1865 he married Miss Maggie A. Swift, a native of this county, and to the last union one child, Lola, has been born. The life business of our subject has been farming; he has, however, been engaged for a number of years in the tobacco trade in connection with farming. He owns a large farm and a commodious residence, which is pleasantly located. In politics Mr. Rudolph is a Democrat, and was a magistrate of his civil district for twelve years. He and wife are members of the Cumberland Presbyterian Church.

James R. Rudolph, a native of Montgomery County, Tenn., was born August 7, 1829. He is of German descent, and is a son of Frederick Rudolph, who was born in North Carolina in the latter part of the last century. About 1800 he came to Tennessee, and when about thirty years of age married Elizabeth Hamilton, who was of Irish descent To them were born eight children, our subject being the youngest. The father died May 28, 1860, and his wife August 9, 1857. James attended the district schools of his native county, having to go four miles to secure his education. He has always farmed on the old home place, which he now owns with other land he has since purchased. He was married to Jane Nicholson, who bore him these children: George (deceased), Marshall, Lizzie and Lena. Mrs. Rudolph died in 1875, and he then married Melissa Rhinehart, born in Tennessee October 3, 1847. They have these children: Gulema, Orville (deceased), Lester and Jesse M. Our subject was a Whig as long as that party existed, and since that time has been a Democrat. He is a good farmer, and makes a specialty of raising sweet potatoes. He is a Presbyterian, and his wife is a member of the Methodist Episcopal Church.

John N. Scott was born in Dickson County, Tenn., April 25, 1815. He is the son of Nehemiah and Christian Scott, who were natives of Sampson County, N. C. Nehemiah Scott was born December 31, 1784, and in 1837 he moved to Texas, where he died in 1878. His wife, Christian (Williams) Scott, was born March 26, 1788, and died in Dickson County, Tenn., May 8, 1826. Mr. John N. Scott settled in Robertson County, Tenn., in 1853, where he was engaged in farming, as his father had before him. He then moved to Montgomery County, where he still resides. He was married April 13, 1834, in Dickson County, Tenn., to Miss Parthena Norsworthy, who was born July 12, 1818, in Dickson County, Tenn., and was the daughter of Willis Norsworthy, of Virginia. Parthena Scott owns a fine tract of land in Montgomery County known as the Meadow Brook Farm. In politics Mr. Scott is a Democrat, and is the father of six children: Martha L., Mary C., Daniel W., John W., Robert A., Ellen L. and Fannie. Daniel W. died January 6, 1880. The whole family are members of the Methodist Episcopal Church, and are respected throughout the county. The old Scott family figured conspicuously in the war of 1812.

Archilles De Grasse Sears, pastor of the First Baptist Church at Clarksville, is a native of Fairfax County, Va., born January 1, 1804. He is the elder of two sons, and is of English lineage. Our subject's father was Charles Lee Sears, born in 1775. He was a farmer by occupation, and was an officer in the war of 1812. He died in his native State (Virginia) in 1862, and was one of three sons, as follows: William, James and Hector, of William Bernard Sears, a native of England, born in 1729. He came to America in 1755, and located in Virginia, where he died in 1816. The family date back historically to the invasion of England by William of Normandy; consequently they are descendants of the Normans. The mother of Dr. Sears was Elizabeth Worster, born in the same State and county as our subject in 1783, and died in 1807. The boyhood days of our subject were spent in Virginia. He was educated at Centerville, Va., and in 1823 came to Kentucky and located in Bourbon County, where he was for some years engaged in teaching school. He at the same time read law under Lucien J. Feimster. In 1838 he joined the Baptist Church, and the following year began his ministerial labor. He was for two years a home missionary. In 1842 he took charge of the First Baptist Church in Louisville, Ky., and in 1850 came to Hopkinsville, Ky., and had charge of the Baptist Church at that place twelve years. In 1862 he left that place and spent four years in the South, a portion of the time a missionary in the Southern Army, and the remainder supplied the Baptist Church at Columbus, Miss. In 1866 he became pastor of the same church at Clarksville, Tenn., and has here remained. He has been a minister of the gospel forty-seven years, and has baptized over 2,000 people. He is a Mason, Royal Arch, Knight Templar, Commander in Kentucky and Tennessee twelve years each, and in 1870 was elected Grand Commander. He was married, March 28, 1828, to Annie B.

Bouie, born in Virginia in 1797. They have one child, Marietta (now Mrs. Major). Dr. Sears is a Democrat, and has long been one of the most prominent and honorable men of the State.

Rev. John B. Shearer, D. D., professor of Biblical instruction of the Southwestern Presbyterian University, was born in Virginia July 19, 1832, the eldest son of John A. and Ruth A. Shearer. His father still survives (1886), but his mother died at the age of thirty-seven, leaving four sons and two daughters, four of whom still survive: Richard B. Shearer fell in battle at the head of his company at Monocacy, Md., in 1863; James W. Shearer is a Presbyterian clergyman in Florida; John Bunyan was named in faith and prayer for the pious and devoted author of the "Pilgrim's Progress," and was consecrated to the gospel ministry by Ms mother from Ms birth, and also by a father who was only hindered by years of poor health from entering the same profession. On his father's side he is descended from a member of Cromwell's Ironsides, whom he settled in Ireland, with a strong infusion of Welsh Presbyterian blood on both sides. He received his early education at Union Academy, Appomattox County, Va., under the instruction of distinguished educators, and was made assistant instructor of Latin in the academy at the age of sixteen. When seventeen years old he entered the junior class at Hampdon Sidney College, and graduated with honor at nineteen under the presidency of the late Lewis W. Green, D. D. The next three years were spent in prosecuting the academic courses at the University of Virginia, where he received the Master's degree in 1854 at the age of twenty-two. He was then married to Miss Lizzie Gessner, of Prince Edward County, Va., the sole surviving child of Johan Gessner, who came to America with three motherless daughters from Manheim on the Rhine. He spent the year 1854-55 at Gordonsville, Va., as principal of Kemper's High School, and then entered Union Theological Seminary, where he spent three years till 1858. From 1851 to 1858 every leisure hour was spent in private teaching, colportage, and later on in professional work, so that he was able to pay his own way without burdening others or incurring debt. He was ordained a minister of the gospel in 1858 by the Presbytery of Orange, N. C. and installed pastor at Chapel Hill, the seat of the University of North Carolina, where he remained till 1862. The war broke up the university, and he then moved to Black Walnut, Halifax Co., Va., where he took charge of Spring Hill and Mount Carmel Churches and taught a private school. In 1866 he founded the Cluster Springs High School, and remained teaching and preaching till 1870. On the invitation of the trustees of Stewart College, Clarksville, he moved to Tennessee as president of the college about to be reopened Here he has lived for sixteen years, and he will probably here spend the remainder of his days in labor to build up the Southwestern Presbyterian University, in the founding of which he has spent his best days. The crowning glory of Dr. Shearer's life is his Bible teachings. He has placed the study of the English Bible in the rank of the severe studies in the university, making it a three years' course, co-ordinate with languages and sciences—a course required of every student in the institution. He has published an outline of his course under the title of "Bible Course Syllabus" in three small volumes for the use of his classes and for others who may desire such a course. Much of interest might be given concerning Dr. Shearer's personal traits as a teacher, a preacher, a citizen, a business man and a friend and ready helper in every good work, but space will not allow. Besides it is not well to portray one's life-work till that life-work has been finished and tested. He is at present engaged in teaching the English Scriptures to the entire university, and besides is teaching Hebrew and New Testament Greek to the divinity class recently organized there.

Isaac H. Shelby, tobacco dealer, was born on the Cumberland River July 14, 1823, and was reared in Montgomery County, Tenn. His parents, Harvey and Rachel (Allen) Shelby, were of Swiss-Irish descent, born in North Carolina in 1788 and 1798, respectively. The Shelby family came from Switzerland to the United States prior to the Revolutionary war, and were early settlers of Tennessee. The father of our subject died in 1831, and the mother in 1885. At the age of fifteen years our subject went to Charlotte, Tenn., where he remained twelve years, and then came to Palmyra, this county. He enlisted in Company B, Fourteenth Tennessee, Confederate States Army, and served two years. Since the war he has resided in Clarksville, where he has been engaged in the warehouse business twenty years, commencing in November, 1865, with A. B. Harrison, doing business in the old Clarksville Warehouse until 1872, when they moved to the Grracey House. Since the death of Mr. Harrison the firm name has changed several times, Mr. Shelby continuing to be senior member of the firm. Later he built the Bailey House, and he and Mr. Rudolph became partners. Mr. Shelby is an experienced business man, and no finer judge of tobacco exists. He lost $5,000 by the fire of 1878, but has made life a financial as well as social success. He was formerly a Whig in politics, but is now Independent. He became a member of the Masonic fraternity in 1844

John F. Shelton, president of the Clarksville Street Railway, was born in Pittsylvania County, Va., May 13, 1824. He is next to the youngest in a family of eight children, and is of English lineage. His parents were natives of Halifax County, Va. The father, Thomas Shelton, was born in 1784, and Ms mother, Sarah Birch, in the same year. The family came to Kentucky in 1831, and purchased land in Harte County, where the parents passed the remainder of their days. Our subject was educated in the common schools, and came to Tennessee in 1839, locating near Springfield, in Robertson County. In 1841 he moved to Clarksville, and in 1852 went to Nashville and engaged in the livery business for four years. He then returned to Clarksville and followed the same occupation, continuing until the breaking out of the war. He then went to Nashville and started the St. Cecelia Omnibus Line, carrying on that business until 1868. Since that time he has resided in Clarksville. From 1869 to 1885 he was a business partner with S. A. Caldwell. At the latter date he organized a company to build the Clarksville Street Railway, and he is president of the company. December 16, 1885, the cars began running. He was married to Susan M. Thompson in 1855. She was born near Nashville in 1839. They have four children: William Rodolphus, Sim Noel, Tennie Noel and Robert B. Lee. Mr. Shelton is a Democrat and a member of the K. of H. He is a member of the Methodist Church, and his wife belongs to the Baptist Church, and he is a leading citizen of the city. He owns 258 acres of land on the Cumberland River.

Hon. Charles G. Smith, attorney at law, is a native of West Tennessee; born in Haywood County January 7, 1834; son of William and Nancy (Bradbury) Smith, and is of German and English descent. Both parents were born in Tennessee, the father in 1804 and the mother ten years later. She died in 1873, but the father yet resides in Haywood County. Our subject received the education and rearing of the average farmer's boy, and remained on the home farm until 1853, when he came to Clarksville and immediately began the study of law under the direction of Gen. J. G. Harnberger. In 1854 he was licensed to practice, and has followed that occupation without intermission to the present time. He has for many years been one of the best and most successful lawyers in this part of Tennessee. In 1869 he was elected chancellor of what was then the Seventh Chancery Division of Tennessee, composed of Stewart, Montgomery, Robertson, Sumner, Smith, Macon and Jackson Counties, and was re-elected to the same office after the adoption of the new State constitution in 1870 with an overwhelming majority. In 1875 he resigned his position and formed a law partnership with Col. J. E. Bailey. In 1876 he was elected to the lower house of the Tennessee General Assembly, and two years later formed a partnership in law with Judge Horace H. Lurton, and yet continues in this capacity. He is president of the Crab-tree Coal Mining Company, which was organized in 1882. Mr. Smith was united in marriage to Mattie Johnson in September, 1859. She was a native of the county, born in 1838, and became the mother of eight children, four of whom are living: Charles G. Jr.; Wiley J.; Laura and Earl. Mr. Smith is an earnest Democrat, and a member of the K. of P., and be and wife belong to the Methodist Episcopal Church.

James H. Smith, commission merchant, is a native of Logan County, Ky.; born January 28, 1851; son of A. L. and M. L. (Long) Smith, born in Kentucky and Tennessee in 1820 and 1825, respectively. The mother died in 1879, but the father still resides in his native county. Our subject was educated in the common schools and at the Bethel College, of Russellville, Ky., which institution he entered at fourteen years of age. When about nineteen he came to Clarksville and entered the employ of Turnley Ely & Co., remaining with them two years. He then became an employe of Harrison & Shelby, with whom he remained one year. He was two years with Grinter, Young & Co., and then purchased an interest in the business. In 1881 he became a partner of Smith, Anderson & Bell, and was senior member of the firm. The firm is now Smith & Anderson, and they are doing an extensive and paying business. In 1874 he was married to Lizzie A. Polk, a native of Robertson County, Tenn., born in 1853. They have three children: Thomas Polk, George Charlton and James H. Jr. Mr. Smith is a Democrat, and in 1886 was elected mayor of the city over his opponent, T. H. Hyman. He and wife are members of the Methodist Episcopal Church, and he is a man of fine business qualities, and is a representative man of this section of Tennessee. When the Farmers and Merchants National Bank was established he was elected vice-president, and has since retained that position.

John M. Smith, born in this county and State July 24, 1820, is the seventh of eight children born to Levi and Hannah (Goode) Smith. His parents are natives of North Carolina, and were born about the years 1778 and 1782, respectively. Our subject's father kept hotel for many years where the Franklin House now stands in Clarksville, and died there in 1823. Our subject was wedded to Miss Levina Martin, the sec-

248 | GOODSPEED'S HISTORIES

ond of two children born to William and Jane Martin. Her parents are natives of North Carolina and Virginia and both were born in 1800. Mr. John M. Smith had the misfortune to lose his wife, which occurred January 30, 1875. He is a molder by trade, but for the last thirty years has been engaged in farming, and is quite wealthy. He is an excellent man and a good citizen.

Dr. Alexander Smith is of English descent and a son of John Smith, born in Maryland in 1788. The father removed to North Carolina in 1804, where he married Peggy Rudolph, by whom he had ten children. He was a soldier in the Creek and Seminole war. About 1810 he came to Tennessee, where he died April 15, 1856, and the mother December 5, 1862. Dr. Alexander Smith was born January 3, 1809, in North Carolina and educated in the common schools of Montgomery County, Tenn. In 1834 he moved to Arkansas, where he remained until 1840, clerking part of the time in a store in Carrolton, and acting also as constable and deputy sheriff. In 1840 he moved to Texas, where he resided until 1842, when he returned to his old home in Montgomery County, Tenn. He followed school teaching and various occupations, and attended the medical colleges at Nashville and Philadelphia, Penn. He began practicing his profession in 1854 in Montgomery County, Tenn., near where his father first located. He also superintended a large farm, but of late years has retired from active business life. In 1857 he wedded Paralee E. Rudolph, who was born and reared on the farm where they now reside. They are the parents of these children, John W., born in 1858; James P., in 1862; Alexander T., in 1869. All are living on their father's farm. Dr. Smith is a Democrat and a member of the Fredonia Lodge of F. & A. M. He and family belong to the Methodist Episcopal Church.

John R. Steele, a native of this county and State, was born in the year 1845. He is the seventh of twelve children born to Moses and Louisa (Hunter) Steele, born in the years 1803 and 1812, respectively. Our subject was united in marriage in 1870 to Miss Henrietta James, to whom one child was born, viz.: Eliza L. His wife departed this life January 11, 1871. He married the second time, January 15, 1880, Miss Ida Ussery, who was born in Tennessee and is the first of a family of ten children born to John R. and America Ussery. Our subject is one of those free and independent farmers, who think and act for themselves; he has an excellent farm lying on the Louisville & Nashville Railroad, the principal products of which are corn and tobacco. In 1882 he was elected justice of the peace in his district, which office he has discharged in an able and honorable manner. It is not necessary to add, perhaps, that he is a stanch Democrat.

Bryce Stewart, a retired tobacco merchant and shipper, is a native of Scotland and son of Bryce and Marian (Kerr) Stewart, who were of pure Scotch lineage. The father was a merchant, and he and wife lived and died on their "native heath." Our subject here mentioned is one of three brothers who came to America and settled at Richmond, Va. Here he remained for some time and then removed to New Orleans, La., where he resided two years. In 1834 he came to Clarksville, Tenn., and this has since been his place of residence. On coming to the city he engaged in the tobacco business which he carried on extensively for years, also having large interests in Missouri, and continuing the business until the breaking out of the war. Since that time he has lived in retirement He took for his life companion, Eliza McClure, daughter of Alexander McClure, and by her became the father of three sons and one daughter, all of whom are dead except the youngest, Bryce Stewart, Jr., who is now in India. The daughter, Marian, the eldest child, married Hume A. Banker, of Louisville, Ky., and died in that city, leaving one son. Mrs. Stewart died in 1865, and in 1873 Mr. Stewart wedded Miss Sallie West Cobb, youngest daughter of Dr. Joshua Cobb. They have one son: Norman. Both husband and wife are members of the Presbyterian Church. Mr. Stewart was formerly a Whig but is now a Democrat.

Leonard P. Stewart was born in Cheatham County, Tenn., February 8, 1845. He is a son of James S. Stewart Jr., and grandson of James S. Stewart, Sr. They were all natives of Tennessee. The grandfather was a soldier in the Creek war, a farmer and blacksmith and died in 1855. His great-grandfather was Andrew Stewart. The father, James S. Stewart, was born in 1820. He married Mary J. Weakley, who was born in 1823, and bore eleven children. Our subject, Leonard P., was the third of the family and was educated in the common schools of Cheatham County. He learned wagon-making and blacksmithing and followed these occupations in his native county until 1864, when he came to Montgomery County, Tenn., and located where he is at present residing. In 1870 he married Martha A. Pace, born in Montgomery County, in 1847, and they became the parents of the following children: Clarence, born in (deceased); Madlean, born in 1872; Lulaula, born in 1875; Samuel, born in 1876; Robert, born in 1878 (deceased); Lovel, born in 1879 and Henrietta, born in 1881 (deceased). Mr. Stewart is a Democrat and is postmaster at Grantville. He and wife are members of the Baptist Church.

Maurice A. Stratton was born in Rockbridge County, Va., November 23, 1852, son of Richard H. and Eliza (Brown) Stratton, born in Virginia in 1814 and 1812. The grandfather, James Stratton, died in Virginia in 1862. Our subject's early days were spent in Albemarle County, Va., in attending school. From 1868 to 1870 he "tilled the soil" in Nelson County, Va., and in March, 1871, came to Clarksville, Tenn., and was salesman three years in the dry goods house of B. E Coulter. He then went West, but returned in 1875 and continued with Mr. Coulter until 1877. He then, in partnership with W. F. and J. B. Coulter, engaged in the dry goods business in this city. In December, 1882, he sold his interest and the month following opened a boot and shoe store. He has the best arranged house in the city, and one of the most complete line of goods in this part of Tennessee. January 15, 1879, he was married to Rachel Tucker, a Kentuckian, born June 15, 1856, daughter of John and Martha

Tucker. Their daughter Mary was born in 1879 and died in 1880. Mr. Stratton is a Democrat and a member of the K. of H. He and wife belong to the Christian Church. He has made his own way in the world, and is a careful and successful business man and a prominent citizen of the county.

Dr. James H. Sullivan, a native of the State and county where he now resides, is a son of Samuel and Mary (Henry) Sullivan, both of whom were natives of this State, their respective births occurring in 1805 and 1808. They both died in 1882. Dr. Sullivan passed his youth in much the same manner as the average boy of his day, securing a fair education. In 1865 Miss Georgia A. Lathann, who was born in this State October 27, 1845, became his wife, and to their union eleven children have been born: Jessie, Oscar, Mary, John P., Daniel H., Jennie, James, Anna, Samuel, Clay and William. When twenty years of age our subject began the study of medicine at Charlotte under Dr. Moody, and in 1855 he entered the Medical University at Nashville, which graduated him in 1858. After this Dr. Sullivan located on the farm where he now resides, and farming and the practice of medicine have since been his profession. During the late war he served in Company A, Fiftieth Tennessee Regiment. He was a participant in the battle of Ft. Donelson, after which he was taken to Camp Douglas and there remained until being exchanged in February, 1863. From that time until 1864 he served on the medical department, after which, by reason of ill health, he returned home. Dr. Sullivan is one of the most energetic and enterprising citizens of the county.

James T. Swift was born in Montgomery County, Tenn., June 26, 1833. He is the son of Evan T. and Margaret D. (McCauley) Swift, natives of Tennessee and born in the years 1810 and 1811, respectively. Our subject's mother died June 27, 1837, and his father was married the second time to Miss Matilda Welker, a native of Tennessee, born in 1819. In the year 1837 the subject of this sketch was united in marriage to Miss Martha E. Dickson, daughter of James and Mary Dickson, natives of Tennessee, the father born in 1802 and the mother in 1813. To Mr. Swift and wife were born five children: Luda, Samuel E., Mary D., Virginia E. and Emma. In 1861 Mr. Swift enlisted in Company A, Fiftieth Tennessee Regiment, under Capt. Thomas Beaumont He continued in the Confederate service until 1862, when he was taken sick and sent to the hospital at Clarksville, where he remained about four weeks and recovered sufficiently to venture about, but he never returned to the army. He was engaged in milling on Barton's Creek, and this mill was run for the benefit of the Southern soldiers. At the close of the war he returned home and began working at the carpenter's trade. He also manages his fine farm.

Dr. D. P. Sypert was born June 22, 1846, in Lebanon County, Tenn., and is of Scotch lineage. His father, H. S. Sypert, was a native of Wilson County, Tenn., born November, 1801, and about the year 1823 he married Miss Nancy Rogers, a native of Virginia, born in the early part of the century, and to them were born nine children, of whom our subject is the eighth. About 1883 Mr. H. S. Sypert died, and in 1885 Mrs. Sypert also died. Our subject received his education in the common schools of Christian County, Ky., and also at Center College at Danville in that State, from which latter school he graduated in the year 1861. He received his medical education in the University of Nashville, from which he graduated in 1867. He then located at Cherry Station, Montgomery County, and commenced the practice of his profession, and by his perseverance and thorough knowledge as a physician and surgeon he has gained an extensive practice, which he still maintains. He also has a large and productive farm near Cherry Station, and a handsome residence situated on an eminence from which a good view of the surrounding country is obtained. On February 27, 1868, he was married to Miss Amanda Warfield, a native of this county and State, and a daughter of George H. and Elizabeth Warfield. To this union one child—George

Warfield—has been born. Mrs. Dr. Sypert is one of the leading spirits in the Woman's Christian Temperance Union of Tennessee, and has served as treasurer of said union, and is president of a local union at the present time. In politics our subject is a Democrat and an active Prohibitionist. He and wife are members of the Christian Church.

J. A. Tate was born in Todd County, Ky., September 18, 1837. His father was a Virginian of French extraction, and his mother was the fourth daughter of Col. Anthony New, for some years a member of Congress from the Eighth Congressional District of Kentucky. The subject of this biography was educated principally at Elkton, Ky., but later attended a boarding school in Montgomery County, Tenn., and finished his course at Bethel College of Kentucky. He taught school for several years, and finally bought the school property where he had attended as a pupil, and there conducted a select boarding school. His health becoming delicate, he purchased the mineral springs of Montgomery County, Tenn., known as "Idaho Springs," and, finding this beneficial to his health, still makes that place his home. A description of these remarkable waters will be found elsewhere in this work. He was married, December 3, 1874, to Miss Ambie White, daughter of Rev. John F. White, of Triggs County, Ky. To this union three children have been born, two of whom are still living.

W. D. Taylor is the son of W. H. and Lucinda (Duncan) Taylor, and was born April 19, 1835, in Kentucky. W. H. Taylor was a native of Kentucky, and in early life was united in marriage to Miss Lucinda Duncan, also of Kentucky. To them were born nine children, five of whom are living, viz.: Nancy M., John, W. D., Josephine and Lou. W. H. Taylor, the father of our subject, died in Missouri while starting to cross the plains. Mrs. Taylor also died in Missouri in the year 1862. She was a member of the Methodist Episcopal Church. Our subject was reared on the farm, and received his education in the country schools. In 1865 he married Miss Jennie Mallory, of this State, daughter of Bev. S. S. Mallory, and their lives were rendered happy by the advent of four children, one of whom died in 1873. The living ones are John, Mary and Annie. During the late civil war he enlisted in the Thirty-fourth Missouri Regiment, where he remained twelve months; then into an infantry regiment under Col. Clark, and was with this regiment until 1863, his failing health preventing him from remaining in the war. He then came to Kentucky where he went to farming until 1865, when he came to this State and married his present wife. He was in the battles of Carthage, Springfield, Lexington, Prairie Grove and Elkhorn. In a skirmish while he was retreating out of Missouri he was maimed in the leg, and remained in the hospital for some time. He still carries the ball and is affected by it somewhat. He has been wounded four times. In 1870 he was elected constable in the Fourth District, which office he held for two years. He was also deputy sheriff for two years. He is a Democrat, casting his first vote for Stephen A. Douglas. He and family are members of the Baptist Church, and have a fine farm in the Fourth District. He is a member of the F. & A. M. and K. of P., and is a good man.

S. D. Tinsley, farmer, was born in Montgomery County, Tenn. January 5, 1851. His father, Oliver Tinsley, is a native of Virginia, and was born in 1820 and died in 1885. His mother, Eliza A. (Harper) Tinsley, is a native of Tennessee and was born in 1821. In the year 1872 our subject was united in marriage to Miss Ella W. Hunter, a native of Tennessee, born October 3, 1847, and a daughter of Drew and Ann (Dean) Hunter, both natives of this State and born in the early part of the present century. Our subject is a life-long farmer. In 1884 he moved to the farm on which he now lives; it lies on both sides of Barren Fork Creek and contains some very good land. The principal products are corn, tobacco, wheat and oats. He has a neat little residence situated near the public road. He has already been an extensive tobacco grower, thereby becoming thoroughly used to handling it, and has now begun buying and receiving it at his farm. Mr. Tinsley is a wide-awake man, thorough and energetic in all he undertakes.

Mrs. E. A. Tinsley is the widow of Oliver Tinsley who was born in Virginia in 1820, and came to Tennessee with his father when but three years of age. His parents are Linsley and Louisa (Sanders) Tinsley, natives of Virginia, born in the year 1780, and died in the years 1846 and 1836, respectively. Our subject, Miss Eliza Harper, was born March 16, 1821, and is the third of twelve children born to David and Ailsey Harper. In 1837 she was united in marriage to Oliver Tinsley, by whom she had seven children, viz.: William N., Burrell W., David L., David D., Louisa A., Ailsey E. and Stuart D. In 1854 Mr. Tinsley moved to the farm known as the Lafayette Furnace Farm, it lies on Barren Fork Creek, and contains fine land. Mr. Tinsley was manager of the old Tennessee Furnace for a number of years, but after moving to his farm he confined himself to raising corn, tobacco and stock until his death, which occurred April 9, 1885. His widow occupies one room in the old homestead, having had her son-in-law, T. L. Fain, move in and take charge of the farm.

William P. Titus, proprietor of the Clarksville Weekly Chronicle, was born in Buffalo, N. Y., May 16, 1852, son of Orin B. and Susan M. (Pierce) Titus, both natives of the Empire State, and of English lineage. The father was born in 1816 and the mother in 1824. Her death took place in Brooklyn, N. V., whither she had gone on a visit. Her remains were brought to Clarksville, and now repose in Greenwood Cemetery. The subject of this memoir came to Clarksville in 1876, and for a time was employed as a job printer by Messrs. Neblett & Grant, and in 1877 he bought Mr. Grant's interest in the paper. In September, 1885, he purchased Mr. Neblett's interest and became sole proprietor. He built up the job printing business in Clarksville, and is a man of enterprise and push. He introduced the only book-bindery in Clarksville, and his work testifies to his skill and ability. He is a Democrat and a K. of P., and was married October 14, 1878, to Miss Addie E. Griffey. They have three children: Herndon, Harry S. and J. Crusman.

Hannibal H. Tharpe, retired farmer, is a son of William A. Tharpe, who was born in North Carolina in 1793, and came with his parents to Tennessee about 1820. He died in 1870 and the mother in 1837. Our subject was born in Henry County, Tenn., December 1, 1835, and was educated in the Paris (Tennessee) schools, and the college at Jackson, Tenn. He began farming in 1857, continuing until 1871, when he removed to Stewart County. In 1873 he, in connection with farming, engaged in general merchandising at a place now known as Tharpe, Tenn. In March, 1883 he abandoned merchandising and resumed farming, and two years later came to Clarksville. He was one of the directors of the Clarksville street railway. He was united in marriage to M. C. Williams, December 27, 1862. She is a daughter of William Williams, and was born in 1843. Previous to the war Mr. Tharpe was a Whig in politics, but since that time he has been a Democrat. He joined the Masons in 1861, and he and wife are worthy members of the Methodist Episcopal Church.

Benjamin H. Thomas, M. D., was born in this State November 29, 1832. He is the second of eight children born to Robert W. and Arminta C. (Hardon) Thomas, both of whom were natives of Virginia, born in 1809 and 1813, respectively. His father died in 1877. Our subject was reared on a farm, and was educated in the best schools of the county. He was united in marriage to Miss Lucy M. West, who was born September 13, 1848. By her he had six children, viz.: Robert W., Drury P., Lucy H., Mildred L., Fannie M. and Arminta. In 1854 our subject entered the University of Pennsylvania at Philadelphia, and graduated in 1859. He then returned home and began the practice of his profession, which he continued in this county until the fall of Fort Donelson in 1862, when he took charge of the sick and wounded at that place. From there he went to Nashville, where he remained but a short time on account of the enemy's approach, leaving this place and locating at Lauderdale Springs, Miss. He remained in charge of the hospital for eighteen months. He then took charge of the hospital at Port Hudson and remained there a short time; he remained, also, a short time at the hospital at Clinton, La. He then went to Shelby Springs, Ala., and took charge of the hospital there for about one year. He then went to Macon, Ga., and was captured by Gen. Wilson, and was held prisoner till about the time of Lee's surrender. He at once returned home and resumed the practice of his profession.

J. W. Trahern is the son of William and L. J. (Thomas) Trahern, and was born March 20, 1832, in this county. His father, William Trahern, was born in Virginia in the year 1809, and emigrated to this State in early life, settling at Piney Fork, in this county. He was a farmer by occupation, and before the war owned several slaves. April 13, 1831, he was married to Miss L. J. Thomas, of Virginia, and to them were born four children, viz.: J. W., L. J., E. C. and A. A. He died in 1875, and was a Democrat, adhering strictly to that party. J. W. Trahern, our subject, was educated in the country schools of the day, and in 1865 was married to Miss Bell Baynham, of this county. To them were born seven children: W. J., W. E., O. L., J. T., E. M., E. M. and Charlie. Mr. Trahern was first a clerk in a dry goods firm at Knox, Ky., where he remained two years; a year or so after he went to Hopkins County, Ky., where he was engaged in the grocery business for one year, then coming to New Providence, Tenn., he entered the stock cattle and tobacco business. Here he remained until the year 1859 when he engaged in farming. In the year 1870 he bought a tract of land in Montgomery County, where he now has an extensive farming interest. He is also a dealer in leaf tobacco and handles about 150 hogsheads of this article annually. In politics he is a Democrat and cast his first vote for James Buchanan. While at Providence he was engaged in running a barrel manufactory, which was destroyed by fire in 1858, and in 1862 had his house and barns burnt by the soldiers of the Federal Army. Mr. and Mrs. Trahern are members of the Christian Church and make friends wherever they go.

Presley O. Travis, farmer, was born October 5, 1834, in Montgomery County, Tenn., and is of English descent. His father, John Travis, a native of North Carolina, was born in the latter part of the last century. He immigrated to Tennessee, and here, in 1808, he was married to Miss Demaries Pollock, a native of Clarksville, and to this union eight children were born, our subject being the youngest. The father and mother of our subject after their marriage lived and died in this county, the former died the same year that our subject was born, and the latter died in 1870. Presley O. Travis was educated in the country schools, and during his minority worked on his mother's farm until reaching his majority, when he continued the business on his own account, and cared for his mother until her death. About the year 1850 he and his mother moved upon the farm, where he has ever since resided. The farm consists of 275 acres and is well adapted to the raising of tobacco, corn and wheat. Our subject has no family, never having married. He served as magistrate for his civil district from 1856 to 1876. In May, 1861, he enlisted in the Fourteenth Regiment Tennessee Confederate Infantry, and served with his regiment, participating in all the battles and skirmishes in which it was engaged until the fall of 1862, when he was honorably discharged on account of being over legal age. Mr. Travis is a member of F. & A. M. and an elder in the Cumberland Presbyterian Church.

Andrew M. Trawick, M. D., was born in Carroll County, Tenn., October 8, 1844, son of John and Diana (Cook) Trawick, and of Scotch-Irish lineage. The Trawick family is traced to the great-grandparents of our subject, who came to America from Belfast, Ireland, in 1765. The great-grandfather was one of nine brothers who were all said to be soldiers in the Revolutionary war. The grandfather was Robert Trawick, a native of North Carolina. Our subject's father was also a North Carolinian and was born in 1792. His mother was born in 1808. The father died in Tennessee in 1848 and the mother in 1860. Andrew M. Trawick was the youngest of nine children and was reared on a farm. In 1860 he went to Arkansas and there, contrary to the wishes of an elder brother, attended school, having a thirst for knowledge. In 1861 he enlisted in Company F, Sixteenth Arkansas Volunteer Infantry as private and was afterward promoted to second lieutenant. He was in the battle of Eikhorn, in 1862, Corinth and Port Hudson, where he was made a prisoner of war. He was taken to Johnson's Island, Ohio, where he remained until the close of the war. During his imprisonment he made good use of his time and continued his studies. In 1865 he returned to his home in Tennessee, and a year later began the study of medicine in the office of Dr. A. J. Weldon, who was a benefactor to him. He attended lectures at the University of Louisville and subsequently located near Davis, Tenn., and there continued the practice fourteen years. He was appointed president of the Stewart County Medical Society in 1878, and in 1881 he attended the Vanderbilt University, and in March of that year graduated from the institution. In May, 1881, he came to Clarksville where he since continued, doing an extensive business. He was married, in 1867, to Mattie B. McSwain, a native of Henry County, Term., born in 1849. Of their eleven children ten survive: Archibald, Arcadius M., Ada, John D., Cora M., Lulu B., George C., Clara B., Mary E. and Thorpe B. Our subject is an ardent Prohibitionist, a Mason and K. of H. In 1863 while in prison he joined the Methodist Episcopal Church South, and he and wife and five children are earnest members of that denomination. He is a prominent and self-made man and excellent citizen.

Hon. John D. Tyler came to Montgomery County, Tenn., from Virginia in 1818. He was born and reared in the State of Virginia. At the age of five years he began attending an old Scotchman's school, and from him received a thorough classical education. Before he was fourteen he had completed the Latin and Greek course, and at the age of fifteen was offered and accepted the position of Latin tutor at the Academy of Warrenton, North Carolina. In the war of 1812 a company of cavalry was raised in his county and he was elected captain, though at that time barely eighteen years of age. At the age of nineteen he was married and came to Montgomery County, Tenn., and followed the occupation of school teaching. He followed no set rules or plans, but was very original in his mode of educating, and trustees were not allowed to visit his school. He purchased a farm near Clarksville soon after coming to the State, and there lived and conducted his school for nearly forty years. He won such a reputation as an educator and disciplinarian that parents from all parts of the South brought their boys to him to be educated, not seeing them again for years. He was an accomplished classical scholar, and many of his evenings were spent in reading aloud Homer and other Greek poets, translating in clear and attractive English. Shakespeare was his favorite English author and he was so fond of books that he was always glad to have others share their contents with him. Mr. Tyler was a firm Whig and objected to see soldiers occupy high civil offices, consequently he opposed Gen. Jackson in his race for the presidency. He was never a politician, but was twice sent to the Legislature and once to the State Senate, and in 1844 was one of the electors for Henry Clay. He died May 20, 1860, after leading a useful and happy life. Never was a man more worthy the confidence of his friends, and his hospitality was unbounded. Like Thomas Jefferson he was a famous fiddler in his day, and his evenings were spent in reading aloud and playing the violin. When the news of his death reached Clarksville (ten miles away), the court, which was then in session, adjourned, the business houses were closed, and the citizens held a meeting in honor of his memory. He was singularly pure and blameless in his private life and his death was mourned by all who knew him.

John R. Ussery was born in Montgomery County, Tenn., July 3, 1826, and is the second of seven children born to John W. and Rebecca (Niblett) Ussery. Our subject was united in marriage to Miss America Smith in the year 1853. To this union were born ten children, viz.: Ida, George, William, Sarah E., Maud H., Robert L., Edwin M., Eugene E., Frank and Norman. Mr. Ussery is an industrious and enterprising farmer, which occupation he has long followed. He has a fine farm located on the Louisville & Nashville Railroad and is one of the leading citizens of the county and a member of the Methodist Episcopal Church. He is respected by every one, and is of one of the first families of the county. For many years he has been Sabbath-school superintendent of the Antioch school.

R. H. Walker, tobacco commission merchant, is a native of Robertson County, Tenn., born March 9, 1840, son of John A. and Elizabeth (Bellamy) Walker, and is of Scotch-English descent. The family came to Tennessee in pioneer times and both parents died in Robertson County. Our subject was reared and educated in said county and when fifteen years of age began learning the cooper's trade and has always worked at that business. He enlisted in Capt. Bidwell's Company, Thirtieth Tennessee, C. S. A., and served about one year. He was taken prisoner at Fort Donelson and was held at Camp Butler, but after forty days captivity escaped and returned home. In 1863 he came to this county and settled in New Providence and continued the cooper's business until 1874, when he began dealing in tobacco. He was married in 1868 to Caroline Watts, and by her is the father of five children: Herschel, Alfonso, Tracy, Prince and Hattie. In his political views Mr. Walker is a Democrat. He belongs to the Masonic fraternity and he and wife are members of the Methodist Episcopal Church.

John W. Waller was born January 13, 1841, in Montgomery County, Tenn. He is the eldest of three children born to Alfred and Rebecca

(Parham) Waller, the former a native of Virginia, and the latter of Kentucky. They were married in the blue-grass State and soon after came to Tennessee. The father was a school-teacher and both parents died when our subject was a small boy, after which he and his brother and sister were taken to their Grandmother Parham in Kentucky. When eleven years old he returned to Montgomery County, Tenn., and in 1861 took for his companion through life Fredonia W. Neblett, a native of the county. To this union the following children have been born: Charles T. and Eddie E. Mr. Waller owns a large and fertile farm in District No. 1, about eleven miles from Clarksville. He has always been a farmer and his staple crops are tobacco, wheat, corn and oats. He was educated in the common schools of the county and is now a prosperous and well respected farmer.

George H. Warfield, a native of Maryland, was born May 9, 1804. His father, James H. Warfield was born in the year 1750, and was a native of Maryland, as was his wife, Miss Ann Gassaway. James H. Warfield died October 18, 1812, and after his death his widow immigrated to Tennessee, where she died June 10, 1849. Our subject received a plain English education in the schools of Maryland and on reaching his majority he entered into mercantile business, having charge of a number of vessels on the Chesapeake Bay belonging to a wealthy relative. At the age of twenty-three he married Miss Susan Waters, a native of Maryland, born March 23, 1802, and to this union the following children were born: James H., deceased; Ann Elizabeth; Milton, deceased; Susan Virginia; Charles H., deceased; Margaret, deceased, and George W. About the year 1835 our subject emigrated with his family to Montgomery County, and there his wife, Susan (Waters) Warfield, died October 28, 1844. In 1848 our subject married Miss Elizabeth Johnson, a native of Tennessee, born March 14, 1821, and daughter of Joseph and Nancy Johnson, of this county. To this union the following children were born: Amanda M.; Charles P.; Joseph G., deceased; Nannie M., deceased; Pattie

H.; Samuel J.; Laban L.; Hanson, deceased, and Alexander G. After reaching this county our subject bought a large tract of land, which he cleared and improved. He was for many years a stockholder and director in the Planters Bank at Clarksville, and at one time was president of the Montgomery County Agricultural and Mechanical Association. By economy and industry he amassed a large fortune. He was a member of the Methodist Episcopal Church and a very prominent citizen of the county. His death occurred December 9, 1870. In politics he was a Democrat.

George W. Warfield, farmer, is the eldest of the Warfield family now residing in the county, and was born December 21, 1843, son of George H. and Susan (Waters) Warfield, whose sketch appears in this work. Of their seven children our subject is the youngest. He grew to manhood on the farm, and was educated in the country schools and at Stewart College in Clarksville. In 1861, when he was but seventeen years of age, he enlisted in Company E, Fiftieth Tennessee Volunteers, C. S. A., and was captured at Fort Donelson and taken a prisoner to Camp Douglas, Chicago, where he was retained for seven months. He was wounded at Chickamauga, and at the time of the surrender at Appomattox Court House he was on patrol duty at Petersburg, Va. After his return home he engaged in agricultural pursuits, and is now one of the most extensive and prosperous farmers in Montgomery County. He owns 545 acres of land, and in Septembur, 1885, removed to Clarksville. He was married, October 20, 1869, to Dora Pollard, born April 30, 1850, daughter of B. F. and Susan A. Pollard. Mr. and Mrs. Warfield have six children: Walter Wilson, born July 30, 1870; Lula Belle, born January 27, 1873; Susie Lizzie, born January 17, 1876; Harrison Pollard, born February 10, 1878; Dora Pollard, born January 7, 1881, and Mary Rice, the baby, born March 7, 1886. Mr. Warfield is a Democrat and a member of the Methodist Episcopal Church. His wife is a Baptist.

Thomas J. Watson was born January 1, 1818, near Richmond, Va. His father, Josiah Watson, was born near the close of the last century, in Virginia, and was of Scotch-Irish extraction. He was a soldier in the war of 1812, and was in the famous battle of New Orleans. In 1814 he married Miss Martha McCormac, a native also of Virginia, and of Irish descent. To this union twelve children were born, of whom our subject is the second. When Thomas J. Watson was a small boy his parents moved to Montgomery County, Tenn., and in a short time moved from there to Marion County, Ill., leaving our subject and a brother and sister here. The father of our subject died just before the close of the late war, and his mother is still living, at the advanced age of ninety-one years. Her eyesight is so good that she does not use spectacles, and she now has her third set of teeth. Our subject was educated in country schools, and before becoming of age he learned the cooper's trade, which business he followed for some time; he then purchased the farm where he has ever since resided. In 1845 he married Miss Elizabeth A. Rudolph, a native of this county, and daughter of Jacob and Martha Rudolph. To Thomas Watson and wife were born the following children: Gustavus E., Thaddeus N., Ella W., Benjamin T. William B., John M., Margaret W. and Wallace W. Mr. Watson owns a very good farm, from which he raises the staple crops common to this county, and until recently he had an interest in the Cumberland Flouring Mills. Our subject is a Democrat and a member of Fredonia Lodge of F. & A. M. He and family are members of the Cumberland Presbyterian Church and one son is a minister of the gospel.

John J. West, attorney at law, was born in Todd County, Ky., December 30, 1853, son of Dr. J. B. and Mary (Jarrad) West, natives of Alabama and Virginia, born about 1825 and 1830, respectively. The father was a prominent teacher, and from 1866 to 1872 he had charge of the Clarksville Female Academy. For more than thirty years he has been a leading minister of the Methodist Episcopal Church, and at present has charge of the Tulip Street Church in Nashville. Our subject secured his rudimentary education in the common schools, and in 1868 entered what was then Stewart College, at Clarksville, from which he graduated in 1872. He immediately began the study of law under Hon. John F. House. During 1875 he was deputy circuit clerk of this county, and in the same year was licensed to practice law, and since that time has given his attention to his profession. In 1878 he was elected public administrator, and has since held that office. In 1882 he was elected city attorney for Clarksville, and has been re-elected each year since. He is a good lawyer, and has always been a hard student, and is now one of the best posted men of his age in Tennessee. October 3, 1878, he married Georgie Beaumont, born in this county in 1858. They have three children: Laura B., Mary and John. Mr. West is a Democrat and a member of the K. of P. and K. of H. He and wife are members of the Methodist Episcopal Church South.

Dr. H. M. Whitaker was born in Kentucky, July 17, 1819. He is the son of G. W. and Harriet Whitaker, the former born in Montgomery County, Md., 1781, and the latter in Amherst County, Va., 1791. When quite a lad G. W. Whitaker went to Baltimore, Md., and was engaged as clerk with the McDonald and Ridley wholesale dry goods firm. In 1800 he removed to Kentucky, where he was married in 1810. He then was engaged as cashier in the Commonwealth Bank where he owned upward of fifty shares. He was a good man and a member of the Presbyterian Church, and was respected by all who knew him. His wife died August 8, 1836, after which he moved to Illinois and lived with his son, George Whitaker, until 1854. He then moved again to Montgomery County, Tenn., and lived with his son, Dr. H. M. Whitaker, until he died, March, 1873. The subject of our sketch commenced the study of medicine at Meriville, Todd Co., Ky., until 1843. He then moved to Russellville and practiced his profession until 1846. He again moved to Montgomery County, Tenn., and in the fall of 1852 he built his present residence, where he had purchased 115 acres of land, which he still owns. January 20, 1853, he was married to Sarah E. Williams, daughter of Josiah Williams, near Nashville, Tenn. Their wedded life was blessed by eight children. Their eldest, Dr. H. W. Whitaker, is a surgeon in the United States Navy. The next, Fannie D., Ada H., Milbrey E., Andrew; Hallie, deceased; Mary and Louie, also deceased. Dr. Whitaker has been a practicing physician since 1842, and is regarded by his patrons as one of the oldest, most practical and successful physicians in the county. In politics he is a Democrat. Himself and family are members of the Oakland Christian Church.

Joseph W. Whitfield came from a line of ancestors who came from North Carolina to Tennessee in 1793. He was a descendant of George Whitfield, the preacher, and is consequently of Welsh-English descent. They were hardy, industrious and law-abiding, and were ever ready to protect the weak in those times of lawlessness and savage warfare. His father, Louis, and his uncles, Needham and Bryan Whitfield, were of a family of twenty-eight children, and their descendants are found in nearly all the Southern States. The three brothers settled in Montgomery County, Tenn., Louis on land now owned by Watton Barker and C. N. Meriwether, which land (now worth $500,000) he traded for a negro woman and eight children. His eldest son, Joseph W., our subject, was born August 23, 1806, and was married in 1833 to his cousin, Mariam (Whitfield) Fox, daughter of Needham Whitfield and widow of J. D. Fort. To their union were born Joseph N., Constantine, Needham L., Robert C., Sallie C., Mary L., James W. and Henry C. Joseph N. graduated from the medical department of the Louisville (Ky.) University in 1854, and practiced his profession in Clarksville, Tenn., until his death, in 1859. Constantine received a common school education, was married to Laura Waller in 1860, and became the father of five children: Martha, Mary, Constantine, Joseph and Jennie. Needham L., at the age of eight years, was placed under the tutelage of Prof. Q. M. Tyler and acquired the rudiments of a good classical and English education. He then attended the Oakland Institute and was there fitted for college. He entered the Bethel College at Russellville, Ky., in 1855, graduating in 1858, and received the degree of A. M. in 1860. He was twice married. His first wife, Anna E. Mart, lived four years and bore him two children, both of whom died in infancy. His present wife, Lou E. Bourne, has borne him three children: Herbert, Nannie and Edward. Before entering college Mr. Whitfield had selected civil engineering as his avocation, but owing to ill health was compelled to abandon his cherished project. He then began teaching, and in 1873 was elected superintendent of schools in Montgomery County. At the end of four years he began teaching at New Providence, continuing two years, and after a term of fifteen months at Ringgold was tendered the presidency of the graded school at St. Bethlehem, where he is at present teaching. Robert C. was educated at Bethel College, Ky., in 1858, and then graduated in the law department of the Cumberland University, at Nashville, and was admitted to the bar in 1861. He was among the first to enlist in the regular service in 1861, and was in the First Tennessee Regiment and transferred to the Fourteenth Tennessee. He was a gallant soldier, but unfortunately was killed at the battle of Fredericksburg, Va., December 13, 1862. He was much beloved by all who knew him, and his death was greatly lamented. He was a member of the F. and A. M. Sarah C. Whitfield was married to N. C. Lovelace in 1869 and has four children. Mr. Lovelace is a farmer. Mary L. was married to George R. Taylor in 1870. He was at one time local editor of the Liverpool (England) Mercury and is now a prominent minister of the Primitive Baptist Church. He came to America in 1862. He and wife have five children. James W. was educated at Russellville, Ky., and graduated in 1872. He wedded Margaret M. Carney in 1873. She bore him two children. He was afterward divorced and is now residing on the old homestead with his mother. Joseph W. Whitfield and family were the organizers of the old Baptist Spring Creek Church. They, in conjunction with the Killebrews, Johnsons, Forts, Metcalfs, Redfords, and other branches of the family, hold a family reunion each year. Marion Whitfield, the mother, has a fine recollection, and her mental activity and strength are wonderful All the family are Democrats.

Hervey Whitfield is a native of Tennessee, where he was born July 3, 1847. He is a son of Needham and Hannah (Wilcox) Whitfield (elsewhere written). To them were born nine children, our subject being the second. The father died in 1858, and the mother still resides on the farm she and her husband settled on coming to this county. Hervey was educated in the country schools of his native county, and when only sixteen years of age enlisted in the Fourteenth Kentucky Cavalry, a portion of Gen. Forrest's command, in which he served one year, and then until the close of the war. After reaching his majority he took charge of his mother's farm for eight years, and in October, 1875, was married to Ella Trigg, daughter of Thomas S. and Elizabeth Trigg, and to them were born these children: Arthur G., born in 1876; Roy, born in 1878; and Thomas B., born in 1882. After his marriage Mr. Whitfield moved to Arkansas, where he remained until 1882, when he returned and purchased the farm where he now lives. He raises the staple crops common to this county. In politics he is a Democrat, and he and wife are members of the Baptist Church. He has been a Good Templar about thirteen years, is an active worker in the cause of temperance and believes in prohibition.

T. H. Whitfield was born December 17, 1839, and is the son of M. Whitfield and Agnes (Boan) Whitfield. The father of our subject was born in the year 1811, and his mother in the early part of the present century. They were both natives of this State. Our subject is a miller by profession, and has followed this trade from early boyhood. In 1866 he began milling at the Ringgold Mills, of this county, and has been regularly employed there ever since. He is an extra fine miller, and to him the people of Montgomery County are indebted for the extra quality of flour they receive from that mill. He is an honest, upright man, as all say who have had any dealings with him. His flour competes with the best made in the county.

Samuel M. Wilkerson was born September 12, 1846, in this county and State. His father, John W. Wilkerson, was born in this State in the early part of this century, and is of Irish descent. He married Miss Martitia C. Hope, a native of Tennessee, and to this union six children were born, of whom our subject is the second. About 1845 the parents of our subject moved to Montgomery County, Tenn., where they still live. Our subject was educated in the country schools and lived with his parents on the farm until he was twenty-nine years of age, when he married Miss Myra T. Bagwell, also a native of this county and daughter of Pleasant and Nancy Bagwell. To this union the following children have been born: Minnie L. and Nannie H., both living. Soon after his marriage our subject purchased and moved upon the farm where he now resides, which is comparatively a new farm, a great portion of it having been cleared and the building having been erected by Mr. Wilkerson. In politics he is a Democrat, and he and wife are members of the Methodist Episcopal Church.

D. Walker Williams of the firm of Parish, Buckner & Co., is a descendant of an old Virginia family and was born near Ringgold, Montgomery Co., Tenn., in April, 1845. He received a good common school education, and in 1862 joined the Otey Battery at Richmond, Va., and served until the close of the war; for ten years subsequent to the close of the war he was engaged in sugar refining in Philadelphia, but is now connected with Parish & Buckner in the tobacco business in Clarksville. He is a Democrat and a highly respected and well known citizen of Montgomery County. He now resides at Ringgold; his parents, Fielding L. and Lucy E. (Ward) Williams were both born in Virginia and immigrated to Tennessee in 1835 and became residents of Montgomery County. Here the father died in 1845.

Joseph B. Williams is of Welsh descent and was born August 25,
1841, in Montgomery County, Tenn. His father, Joseph B. Williams, Sr.
is a native of the county, born in 1808; he wedded Adaline T. Bridge and
they became the parents of seven children, our subject the second of the
family. The father died in 1885; the grandfather, Septimus Williams was
born in Virginia; he came to Tennessee in 1795, being the first of the
family to settle in this State; he died in 1844. Our subject secured a fair
education in the schools of his native county, and at the breaking out of
the great civil war enlisted in the Fourteenth Tennessee Infantry, C. S.
A., and participated in the principal battles in which his regiment was
engaged. At the close of the war he returned home and began tilling his
father's farm. In 1870 he led to Hymen's altar, M. J. Davis, a native of
this county, born in 1841; they have two children: Neva and Jessie R.
Mr. Williams' home is about seven miles from Clarksville; he is a prosperous farmer, and politically is a Democrat, and is at present magistrate
of his district, a position he has held four years. He and wife are members of the Baptist Church.

Thomas W. Williams, a native of this county and State, was born
June 10, 1842; he is the second of the children born to William and Julia
A. (Rochell) Williams. His father was a native of Mississippi, and was
born in 1812; his mother was born in Tennessee in the year 1813. Our
subject was united in marriage to Miss Lucretia Jaiman, a native of Tennessee, born December 19, 1849; she is the third of twelve children born
to Josiah and Nancy Jaiman. Her father was born in North Carolina in
the year 1813, and her mother in Kentucky in the year 1817. To our
subject and wife were born nine children, viz.: James P., Agnes C., Nancy, Julia, Dora C., William E., Thomas D., Bulia M. and Emery W. In
1861 he enlisted in Company B. Fourteenth Tennessee Regiment C. S.
A.; was engaged in all the principal battles fought in Virginia, and never
received a wound; he surrendered with Lee in 1865; he then came home

and went to farming and merchandising which occupation he has followed ever since.

Henry B. Willson, dealer in boots, shoes and gents' furnishing goods, was born in Pulaski County, Ky., February 4, 1852, son of James M. and Elizabeth M. (Porch) Willson, who were born in Kentucky in 1828 and 1819, respectively. The grandfather, William Willson, was born in North Carolina. The family moved to Kentucky in early days and our subject was educated in the schools of Somerset, Ky. In 1869 he entered the A. & M. College of the Kentucky University at Lexington, where he remained four years. Subsequently he took a course of lectures in the Kentucky School of Medicine and the Louisville Medical College. In 1876 he went to Philadelphia and was for some time engaged in the boot and shoe business, having abandoned the medical profession. In the latter part of 1876 he came to Hopkinsville, Ky., and until 1879 was in the boot and shoe business in that city in the interest of Stribley & Co. In 1879 he came to Clarksville and in partnership with James M. Bowling engaged in his present business. They are now one of the leading firms of the city, and one of the leading shoe houses in this part of Tennessee. February 21, 1882, he wedded Susie Dorch, born in Clarksville in 1859, daughter of G. C. and Eliza Dorch. They have two children, Henry J. and Eliza M. Mr. Willson is a Democrat, a Mason, Knight Templar, an Odd Fellow and Knight of Pythias. He belongs to the Christian and his wife to the Presbyterian Church.

Robert A. Wilson, farmer, was born in Pennsylvania May 9, 1836. His father, John Wilson, was born in this State in 1805, and in 1830 was married to Mary T. (Jones) Flemming, a native of North Carolina, born in 1801. The fruits of this union were four children, our subject being the youngest. John Wilson died February 16, 1880. In 1860 our subject was united in marriage to Miss A. E. Barbee, a native of this State, born in 1843, and the daughter of Solomon G. Barbee and Nancy Trice natives of North Carolina and Kentucky, respectively. The fruits of the union of Robert A. Wilson and Miss A. E. Barbee were six children: Annie M., Nannie G., John H., Susie, Myra and Emma. Our subject was a farmer boy. In 1855 he began clerking in New Providence, where he remained for three years. Then he and his brother entered into partnership in the general merchandise business at this place, where they remained until the breaking out of the war. He then enlisted in Company A, Forty-ninth Tennessee Regiment, and was elected second-lieutenant. At the fall of Fort Donelson he was taken prisoner, but after four months was exchanged, and the company reorganized at Vicksburg, when our subject was made first lieutenant, and was in several of the principal battles fought in Mississippi. He was in the Atlanta campaign and also in Hood's retreat from Tennessee. At Selma, Ala., he was captured, but effected his escape from the enemy and came home. In 1866 he was elected constable and appointed deputy sheriff. In making an arrest at one time our subject had his right eye seriously injured. He then began merchandising in New Providence and was in this business for two years, when he sold out and began farming. In 1880 he moved to the farm on which he now lives. He is a member of the Masonic order and a Democrat.

Samuel E. Wilson was born in the village of Fredonia, Tenn., August 19, 1860. His father, Samuel Wilson, was born in 1813, and was of Scotch-Irish descent. He was an extensive land owner, and in 1843 was united in matrimony to Eliza W. Hunt, who was born in 1821, and a daughter of John Hunt, of North Carolina. Our subject's father died in 1871. He and wife were the parents of two children: Mary E. S. (deceased) and Samuel E., our subject, who was educated in the district schools and in Stewart College. Since attaining his majority he has farmed on his father's estate, which he now owns. He owns about 3,500 acres of land in one body, on the Cumberland River, and about 300 acres at Fredonia, the old homestead of his parents. From 1877 to 1883 he lived in Clarksville, but attended to farming all the time. March 7, 1883, he took for his life companion Flora De Graffenried, born in Williams County, Tenn., October 26, 1861, daughter of Mathew De Graffenried, a Virginian by birth, and of German and French descent. He died in Tennessee in 1868. Mr. and Mrs. Wilson became the parents of one child—Eliza, born December 3, 1883. Mr. Wilson is a Democrat and a member of the Methodist Episcopal Church. His wife belongs to the Episcopal Church.

Alexander S. Wood, wholesale and retail grocer, was born in Tennessee, near Franklin, December 24, 1830, and is a son of John and Mildred (Standfield) Wood. The father was born in Maryland, and came to Tennessee in 1837 and resided near Franklin about four years. In 1831 he and family moved to Kentucky, and in 1838 he died at Hopkinsville. The mother was born in Tennessee, and after the death of her husband she, with her family of seven children, returned to Montgomery County, Tenn. Here she died in 1839. Our subject is the sixth of the family, and on account of the early death of his parents he was thrown upon his own resources early in life. All the schooling he received was in the country schools of Montgomery County. In 1848 he began general merchandising at Woodlawn, and in 1860 engaged in the tobacco business. Excepting three years during the war, he continued his business at Woodlawn. In 1876 he came to Clarksville, and for two years dealt extensively in tobacco. The latter part of 1879 dates his engagement in the grocery business. He is a partner of Florence F. Abbott, and has been quite prosperous. He has been married three times: first, in 1857, to Jennie Frederick, who died in 1863; second, in 1866, to Bettie J. Brown, who died in 1871, and third, in 1873, to Edna B. Brown, a sister of his second wife. Mr. Wood was formerly a Whig, but is now a Democrat. He became a member of the Masonic fraternity in 1862, and also belongs to the K. of H.

Jonathan Franklin Wood was born in Meigs County, Tenn., September 11, 1851, son of J. and L. E. (Brittain) Wood, and of Irish extraction. Both parents were born in this State, and the father was a prominent business man of the city. He was born in 1802 and died in Clarksville in 1877. The mother was born in 1817. Our subject was reared on a farm, and in 1868 removed with his parents to Chattanooga, and there he was educated. Later he clerked in the hardware store of Wood & Coulter, remaining until January, 1872, when he came to Clarksville and became a member of the firm of Kincannon, Wood & Co. At the death of his father he inherited his father's interest in the above-named firm, and until 1882 was an equal partner in the business. He then opened his present hardware, glass, queensware, tin and stove store, and is one of the most substantial business men of the city. He was married, in 1875, to Bettie M. McReynolds, of this city. They have two children: Clara M. and Anna L. Mr. Wood is a Democrat, and belongs to the I. O. O. F., Masons, K. T. and K. of P. fraternities, and he and wife are members of the Methodist Episcopal Church.

J. N. Woodson is a native Virginian, born October 15, 1843, and of English descent His father, Jacob C. Woodson, married Susan Woodard, both born in the same State as our subject. To this union ten children were born, our subject being the ninth. The family came to Montgomery County, Tenn., in 1847, and located near Clarksville, where they resided until 1874, when they removed to Kentucky, and there the father still lives. The mother died in Tennessee in 1854. Until attaining his majority our subject spent his time in farming his father's land and attending school. At that time he married Sarah J. Smith, daughter of James and Mary Smith, and purchased the farm where he now resides, and began tilling the soil on his own responsibility, his principal crop being tobacco. To him and wife were born these children: George T., William N., Allen B., James A., Margaret J. and Josie E. Mr. Woodson is a Democrat in his political views, and he and wife are members of the

Cumberland Presbyterian Church. In 1861 he enlisted in the Fourteenth Regiment Tennessee Confederate Infantry, and served with his command in all the battles in which it was engaged, including Cedar Run, Seven Pines, Petersburg, Richmond and Manassas. On account of his minority he was discharged in 1862. He was captured at his home by Federal troops, and was held as prisoner of war in the following places: Nashville, Louisville, Baltimore, Fortress Monroe, and lastly at Petersburg, where he was exchanged in 1863 and returned home.

Francis M. Yarbrough was born in this county and State November 5, 1832. He is the fourth of ten children born to John and Mary (Vaughn) Yarbrough. His parents were natives of Virginia and Tennessee, and died in 1856 and 1857, respectively. Our subject was united in marriage to Miss C. Davis, May 1, 1856. She was a native of Tennessee, born February 13, 1838. She is the youngest of fourteen children born to Joseph and Elizabeth (Martin) Davis, who were natives of this county and State. Mrs. Yarbrough died in 1882. To our subject and wife were born eight children: David L., Josiah, John E., William H., Bailey, Louisa, Milton M. and Ada. Bailey died in 1869, Josiah died in 1882. Mr. Yarbrough is of English descent, and was educated in the common schools of the county. He is a member of the Cumberland Presbyterian Church, and a stanch Democrat. His boys manage the home farm, while he is principally engaged in working at his trade, blacksmithing and wagon-making. He is also a prominent contractor on the Louisville & Nashville Railroad.

Col. William F. Young, an ex-Confederate soldier, is a native of Kentucky, born near Bowling Green March 26, 1830. He is the youngest of five children, and of English descent. His father, Elliott Young, was born in Dinwiddie County, Va., in 1791. He was a soldier in the war of 1812, and a son of Tinsley Young, who served more than four years in the Revolutionary war. He was a man of much worth, and was distinguished for his patriotism. He died in 1828. Our subject's mother was Martha (Kidd) Young, born in Amelia County, Va., in 1792. In the latter part of 1828 the family came to Kentucky, where they resided until 1832, and then came to Tennessee, and settled northeast of Clarksville, where they lived until 1840. The father then sold out and purchased another farm in District No. 8, and here they lived and educated their children at the Mount Pleasant school. Here it was that William F. Young received an education that laid the foundation for his future usefulness, and that decisive character, firm integrity, unswerving devotion to all that is good and true which so plainly marked his pathway. At the age of twenty-two he purchased a farm, and his father and mother made their home with him until their deaths, July 5, 1865, and January 23, 1873, respectively. They lie at rest in the cemetery at Mount Pleasant. At the breaking out of the war William F. raised a company in his neighborhood known as Company G, Forty-ninth Tennessee. He enlisted as a private but was afterward chosen captain. In 1863 he was commissioned colonel, and filled this position very creditably until the close of the war. He was in the battles of Fort Donelson, Port Hudson, New Hope Church, Missionary Ridge, and in 1864 was in all the battles between Sherman and Johnson and Hood. At the third battle of Atlanta, on the 28th of July, 1864, Col. Young lost his right arm. He was taken to the hospital at Macon, Ga., and there remained for some time. In November following he joined his command at the battle of Franklin, though, on account of his misfortune at Atlanta, he did not assume command. The December following he came home on a ninety days' furlough. On reaching the Cumberland River, December 7, 1864, it was found to be badly swollen, and he hired a negro boy to take him across. When about half-way over the boat began to sink. The negro boy jumped into the water, and in doing so capsized the boat, throwing the Colonel into the water. He is indebted to James Oliphant, the negro boy, for saving his life. After a four days' rest at home Col. Young rejoined his regiment. He surrendered with his regiment at Columbus May 18, 1865. After his return home he taught school five years, and in 1870 began auctioneering, and has since been engaged as tobacco and real estate auctioneer. In 1873 he purchased property in Clarksville, where he has since resided. He was married, December 1, 1853, to Mary P. Shelby, by whom he had two children: Harvery C. and Mary Z. Mrs. Young died in May, 1858, and on December 20, 1859, Col. Young wedded Miss C. A. Caudle, a native of Virginia, born February 5, 1836. They have two children: Willie B. and Linnie Ada. Formerly the Colonel was a Whig in politics, but is now a Democrat and is a member of the K. of H. He and wife are members of the Cumberland Presbyterian Church, and there is no man in this part of Tennessee who is more highly respected than our subject.

H. C. Young, a merchant of Sky View, Tenn., is a son of Col. W. F. Young, who was born near Bowling Green, Ky., in 1830, and came to this State when but three years of age. Arriving at maturity he first bought a farm of 300 acres in the Eighth District, where he lived as a farmer until the beginning of the war. He was married to Miss Mary Shelby, and by her became the father of two children, one of which died in infancy, and the other is our subject. Mrs. Mary Young died in May, 1858. After her death Mr. Young married Miss Catharine Candle, by whom he had two children: W. B. and L. A. At the breaking out of the war Col. Young enlisted and was made captain of Company G. He was soon promoted to colonel. In the battle of Atlanta, Ga., he had the misfortune of losing an arm. Our subject, H. C. Young, was born December 30, 1854, in Montgomery County, and received his education at the county schools until 1873, when he went to Central Point Academy. Miss Eunice Pruitt became his wife in 1877, and by this union have been born three children, viz.: Lena, Gordie and Claud. In the year 1880 Mr. Young went into the mercantile business in Tennessee. After two years he went to Dotsonville, and from there to Caskey, Ky., where he staid twelve months; he then came back to Montgomery County and went into the dry goods and grocery business at Sky View, Tenn. He is a Democrat and a member of the Cumberland Presbyterian Church.